# Toward World Peace

Secretary-General U Thant, at his desk in United Nations Headquarters

# Toward World Peace

Addresses and Public Statements
1957-1963

By U Thant

Selected by Jacob Baal-Teshuva

Foreword by Adlai E. Stevenson

New York · THOMAS YOSELOFF · London

Thomas Yoseloff, Publisher
South Brunswick, New Jersey

Thomas Yoseloff Ltd
18 Charing Cross Road
London, W C 2, England

6179
Printed in the United States of America

# Publisher's Note

Early last autumn, Mr. Jacob Baal-Teshuva, in the course of a conversation in my office, pointed out to me that there was not available in any convenient form the major addresses and policy statements of the Secretary-General of the United Nations. We agreed that it seemed a lack that ought to be remedied, and the present volume is the result.

When the advice and consent of the Secretary-General was solicited, he suggested that it might not be desirable to combine in a single volume his utterances as Permanent Representative of Burma to the United Nations and as Secretary-General. In the first instance, he pointed out, he was speaking as the representative of a single government, presenting its special point of view, and as Secretary-General he speaks for the entire world, trying to maintain a balance between often sharply divergent views.

However, this volume is an attempt to assess not only the words of a Secretary-General in his official capacity, but the mind of a man who stands in a position of great power and great influence in this most critical period of the world's history. This I felt could not fairly be done by excluding those statements he had made in his relatively freer capacity as the Permanent Representative of Burma, when it was not necessary for him to be concerned with the reactions of governments whose official views differed from his own.

The format of the present volume is, therefore, the result of the effort to place the Secretary-General's statements in their proper context. The first portion of the book is devoted to statements made as Permanent Representative of Burma to the United Nations, and the second part presents statements made as Secretary-General. This offers a special sort of illumination to the reader seeking a key to the mind of U Thant, for a comparison of specific utterances in the two sections will prove most rewarding.

There emerges from this book the figure of a man who is passionately and uncompromisingly devoted to the twin causes of world peace and the rights of all men. In his present capacity, he must walk unerringly the narrow line that separates the opposing factions in a world struggle, but the discerning reader will find ample evidence that the man behind the words is a man of courage, that his grasp of world problems is heartening and that his understanding of the issues that divide the world today is profound.

Thomas Yoseloff

New York
June, 1964

# Foreword*

Only last week we celebrated the sixteenth anniversary of the United Nations.

It is fitting and reassuring that we should begin the seventeenth year by putting our house in order with the election of our distinguished colleague, U Thant, to the high office of Secretary-General.

There is much to be thankful for here today:

First of all, we may rejoice that there was available to us a diplomat of such character, ability, and experience that he could command the unanimous esteem and confidence of this world organization. That augurs well for the future.

The regard in which he is held has been earned by a lifetime of public service, both at home and abroad. We at the United Nations know at first hand the many contributions he has made to this institution.

We have worked with him in his capacity as Permanent Representative of Burma. We know of his notable contribution to the work of the Congo Advisory Committee. We know of the great esteem in which he was held by the late Secretary-General, Mr. Hammarskjold. And we are also aware of his stature as educator, scholar and author.

Some of you may not know that almost thirty years ago, when our colleague was a young man of twenty-three, he wrote a book about the League of Nations. Even then he understood this century's profound need for a world organization to help keep the peace. And this understanding has grown with the years.

* Statement by Ambassador Adlai E. Stevenson, United States Representative to the United Nations, before the General Assembly, November 3, 1961.

I confess that I have sometimes been discouraged during the long weeks of discussion that preceded today's election. But, as we say, all is well that ends well. And this prolonged ordeal has ended brilliantly. Moreover, during these weeks we have often been impressed anew by Ambassador U Thant's independence of mind and spirit, his high intelligence, energy and idealism, and that becoming modesty which is characteristic of his countrymen and co-religionists.

He has not, for instance, hesitated in recent weeks to make known his views on the character of the office of the Secretary-General. That is how it should be. I myself was struck by his statement that "whoever occupies the office of the Secretary-General must be impartial, but not necessarily neutral."

In this connection, I agree fully with his statement a few days ago that an important reason for according Dag Hammarskjold the high place which he shall always hold, was "because of his qualities of initiative."

As I have said, we have much to be thankful for today. Not only because of the individual who has just been appointed, but equally because of the propitious circumstances in which the General Assembly has appointed him.

The sole objective of the United States Delegation, which has carried much of the burden of negotiation, has been to protect the integrity of the Charter and the office of the Secretary-General. That has been the purpose of many others who want to see this Organization grow in strength and influence. And that has been accomplished.

There will be no veto in the Secretariat and no weakening of the office of the Secretary-General. The principles contained in Article 100 and 101 of the Charter have been fully preserved. He will have the full powers and responsibilities of that office. He will appoint his own staff and consult them entirely as he alone decides, in a manner consistent with the Charter.

May I say, in passing, that I think there is a valuable lesson in the events that led up to today's action. The path of quiet diplomacy often requires endless patience and perseverance, especially when it encounters seemingly unsurmountable obstacles. I am frank to say that there have been some discouraging moments since Dag Hammarskjold died. But there have been other such moments in the history of the United Nations. And they have been overcome. My own belief is that we should always act in the belief that, for those who are truly faithful in their ideals, the darkest hour is the time to light the brightest light.

Recently I saw a news item about a scientist who was on the brink of an important breakthrough. When he described his experiments to a gathering of fellow specialists, "a wave of *guarded enthusiasm* swept through the audience."

In the light of everything I think we delegates might be permitted a wave of unguarded enthusiasm.

I am happy to report to you that the President of the United States is one of those who shares our hopes here today. I have just received a telegram from President Kennedy which he has asked me to read to you. I am happy to do so. The President says:

"The election of U Thant is a splendid achievement in which the whole world can rejoice.

"Please express the congratulations of the United States Government to the United Nations membership for their action in electing so distinguished a diplomat to succeed the late Dag Hammarskjold.

"In preserving the integrity of the office of the United Nations Secretary-General, they have reaffirmed their dedication to the United Nations Charter.

"To Ambassador U Thant, please express my personal congratulations, and assure him on behalf of the people of the United States that as he begins one of the world's most difficult jobs, he has our confidence and our prayers."

In my own capacity as the American Representative to the United Nations, I should like to add that all of us at the United States Mission feel we owe a great debt to those delegates who have worked so hard and patiently to solve the problems created by the death of Mr. Hammarskjold.

And to my dear friend and colleague, U Thant, I would like to say just one more thing:

It is written in the Bible that "To whom much is given, of him also much shall be required."

There is little doubt, Sir, that enormous things will be required of you, and there is even less doubt that you will fulfill them. God bless you.

—Adlai E. Stevenson

# Contents

# CONTENTS

# Illustrations

Secretary-General U Thant at his desk in United Nations Headquarters (frontispiece)

*(The following photographs appear as a group following page 124)*

U Thant, as Acting Secretary-General of the United Nations
U Thant taking the Oath of Office as Acting Secretary-General
U Thant's family at United Nations Headquarters
The Acting Secretary-General at the tomb of Dag Hammarskjold
Appointment as Secretary-General by the General Assembly
The Secretary-General discusses the Congo situation with Dr. Ralph J. Bunche
U Thant with the first Secretary-General, Trygve Lie
Conferring with U. N. colleagues on the Cuban crisis
U Thant returns from his mission to Cuba
Addressing the assembly of students at Charles University, Prague
President Kennedy at United Nations Headquarters
President Kennedy addressing the General Assembly
The signing of the Nuclear Test Ban Treaty in Moscow
U Thant addressing signatories to the Nuclear Test Ban Treaty
U Thant with Prime Minister Harold Macmillan in London
Meeting with representatives of the Big Three Powers

*(The following photographs appear as a group following page 188*

At United Nations Headquarters with President Johnson
President Johnson addressing the General Assembly
U Thant addressing the Students Association in Copenhagen, Denmark
The Secretary-General visits Florence, Italy
Inspecting a Guard of Honor in Jamaica
U Thant with President Adolf Scharf of Austria
U Thant with President Urho Kekkonen of Finland

He who is afraid knows no peace.

Unity comes before peace.

Whenever there is love, there is peace.

(*Three Burmese proverbs quoted by U Thant*)

# I

## As Permanent Representative of
## Burma to the United Nations

# 1

# A Burmese View of the World

A BURMESE VIEW OF WORLD TENSIONS*

I am indeed very grateful to The American Academy of Political and Social Science for the honor of the invitation extended to me to address this 62nd Annual Meeting, and I feel highly privileged to be able to present my views to so distinguished an audience.

In many ways it would have been better for an address of this kind to be delivered by a person sufficiently detached from day to day preoccupation with political affairs dealt with by the United Nations. A diplomat assigned to that World Organization must necessarily be discreet and correct, and candor is not always regarded as a desirable trait. However, I feel rather strongly that one ought to be candid if one is to be helpful towards the creation of better understanding, and if my observations are considered to be more outspoken than they should be, then I hope the motives will be properly understood.

It is a commonplace that we are witnessing tensions all over the world. There are, what is generally known as East-

* Address delivered at the 62nd Annual Meeting of the American Academy of Political and Social Science, at Philadelphia, April 11, 1958.

West tensions, tensions between the Haves and Have-nots, tensions between the Rulers and the Ruled, between Whites and non-Whites and so on. Dictionaries define the term "tension" as "a strained condition of relations." It would be historically inaccurate to say that tensions are a present day phenomenon. There had been tensions all through the ages, but now they have assumed new characteristics.

One of the most fascinating sidelights on the history of mankind is the gulf which persisted between urban societies and rural societies. All ancient civilizations and forms of society bear testimony to this truth. The countryside was earthbound, and it shared very little the intellectual excitement and social comforts of the urban dwellers. Between the two there has always been hostility. The country was exploited by the town and could not share in what the town could give it. The labor of the country dweller fertilized the life of the town, but he was shut out from its excitements. Country labor was too hard for leisure, and without leisure the mind remained torpid. The neglect of the countryside has always been a feature of human societies and it has constituted a perennial social tension. This neglect entailed ever-widening social and economic disparity between peoples, and we see some countries endeavoring to remedy this defect by the introduction of planned economic systems. One of these systems is known as socialism.

It is not my intention to dwell at any length on a discussion of the concept of socialism, but in so far as it relates to the relaxation of social and economic tensions, a brief reference to its characteristics may be pertinent.

Burma is committed to a system of parliamentary democracy; Burma believes in democratic ideals and the dignity of man. Burma is thoroughly averse to the idea of dictatorship in any shape or form. This dedication to parliamentary democracy and aversion to totalitarianism has been the consistent theme of utterances and actions of the Burmese leaders. They feel rather strongly that the rebuilding of their country will be meaningless if the democratic ideals are discarded. The type of society they are trying to evolve is not patterned after maxims mechanically lifted out of textbooks. They see to it that its roots are in the Burmese soil, Burmese history and Burmese background. The experiences of the past decade, since independence, have helped in moulding a new type of society which, for the sake of convenience, is generally known as democratic socialism.

Those of you who have not gone through the same experiences, and shared the same background, will not easily understand either the real significance of the term "democratic socialism," or the need for laying stress on this ideology which to most of us in Burma is not just a school of thought, but a new culture, a new civilization. The aims of a democratic socialist movement in Burma are the creation of a society of free and equal peoples, with equal opportunities for all, a society based on certain values of human and social life. In a country like Burma, this movement is the only sensible movement which can and will remove the age-old social and economic tensions.

Perhaps a brief amplification may be necessary. Democratic socialists believe that the society in which we live is divided into classes. The very nature of its economic system has produced a clash of interests which has generated class struggle and class consciousness. In doing away with this clash of interests Burma adheres strictly to democratic methods. Burma is convinced that in the circumstances prevailing there, the democratic method is the only right method to work for socialism. There is thus no ambiguity in Burma's policy on this score.

These observations may seem irrelevant to the general

theme of this address, but they are in fact relevant. We see around us social and economic tensions of varying degrees. The safety and survival of free political institutions depends upon resolving these tensions before they become intolerable. Many of the political tensions come from this source. In tackling this basic problem opinions differ regarding the respective roles of the public and private sector. Where the frontier between the public and private sector should be fixed, is a question that will be answered differently in different countries, according to their traditions and stage of historical development. In countries with a primitive economic development, where revolutions have occurred, it is natural that industries will grow up in the public domain. It is now evident in many countries of Asia and Africa, as it was the case in Russia and China, although of course methods widely differ. In the Western world the extension of the principles of public ownership will be influenced by the extent to which large aggregations of private capital have formed into monopolies in which profit becomes a burdensome tax on the community and no longer a reward for investment and speculation. This, I venture to think, reflects the views of many Asians who are interested in finding solutions to the most pressing problems facing their countries.

However, political tensions, and not social tensions, are receiving prior attention of most of us because of their urgency and their explosive character. Let me, therefore, deal with political tensions as a Burman sees them.

One of the difficulties of international relations is that it is hardly possible to express critical views about the policy and action of a nation to which one does not belong, without exposing oneself to the charge of being anti that nation. This unfortunate reaction is fed by various influential mass media such as newspapers, radio and television, and of course by those whose policies and actions are criti-

cized. Now if there is one thing which I find very objec-
tionable it is generalizing about whole peoples. There are
no doubt good or bad, brave or timid, cultured or wild
individuals but when we apply such adjectives to nations
and groups of nations, what we are in fact doing is describing our own emotional reactions to things and peoples
which meet with our approval or disapproval.

Before I proceed, let me make one point absolutely
clear. Within three months of Burma's attainment of independence, the Communists in our country went underground and started a widespread insurrection. A couple or
so of other dissident factions followed suit and at once the
whole country was in a veritable state of anarchy. While
the young Burmese Government is suppressing the Communist and other rebellions in Burma, our relations with
all countries, Communist and non-Communist, continue
to be friendly. Our dedication to democratic ideals do not
preclude us from viewing the world around us with a
proper perspective. It is true that many countries have
chosen systems of government very different from our own.
It is, however, not our business to pass judgment on the
internal affairs of other countries. The recognition of this
basic fact enables us to subscribe to the principles of peaceful co-existence.

Our attitude towards political systems prevailing in
other countries is governed solely by considerations of
peace. We are convinced that it is not the path of wisdom
to form military blocs, to enter into a hectic armament
race and to rant hysterically at each other. They certainly
do not make for peace; they only increase tensions. If the
world's great religions like Islam and Christianity, after a
prolonged and bloody war for centuries, flourish side by
side in peace and amity, why should not Communist and
non-Communist systems be permitted to co-exist peacefully? This is Burma's approach to international problems.

We are convinced of one thing: man must learn to live with himself. Regardless of his beliefs, traditions, ideologies, and the economic, social and political systems to which he subscribes, he must learn to live with his neighbors. This calls for a new out-look, a new approach, and even for a new philosophy. Past history, dealing with a completely different kind of era and circumstances, will no longer stand him in good stead. He must rise to the challenge of the thermo-nuclear age. More than ever, he needs to exercise courage, patience, tolerance and imagination. Fear and suspicion which for so long have characterized international relations must no longer feature in this hydrogen age. In this new situation, how are the nations of the world to be guided in their relations with one another? I believe that the answer is to be found in the most sensible art of living together in peace.

Let me be candid. When American foreign policy did concern itself with what was happening in the rest of the world, it did so out of fear and suspicion—fear of Communism and suspicion of Communist motives. Fear and suspicion are very undesirable states of mind. They breed hatred, and hatred in turn breeds cruelty and intolerance. Fear of Soviet Communism has led the United States, and those who follow her lead, to take a distorted view of the world situation, and of the forces that are at work in modern society. I do not wish to be misunderstood. I look upon free institutions as not only the most desirable of political systems, but also as those most congenial to the flowering of human genius. But these institutions are threatened not only by political dictatorships. The resistance to social and economic change *inside* our own societies, undermining the faith of the masses in their own power, can be equally deadly.

When I say that American foreign policy is unduly dom-

inated by fear and suspicion of of Communism, I think I
reflect the views of most thinking Asians. The weapons of
the Soviet are in the first instance economic, social and
ideological: only secondarily military. If she relied primarily upon military action why has she not resorted to it
before now? The Western Powers have assured the Soviet
of their present weakness and of their future strength.
Why has Russia waited for the strength of the Western
Powers to grow? Why should Russia wait for a time most
unfavorable to her? These questions really must be faced.

This brooding sense of fear and suspicion also breeds a
tendency to escape from reality. There is at the moment a
very considerable uneasiness in this country regarding
"poor" American propaganda, in contrast with "good"
Russian propaganda. For instance, when the Indian Prime
Minister Jawaharlal Nehru warmly welcomed the Soviet
Union's announcement of the suspension of nuclear tests,
the reaction of this country was that Russian propaganda
works better than American propaganda. In this connection I think I cannot do better than quote Mr. Walter
Lippmann who observed,

This theory rests on the notion that our many reverses and the
decline of our influence are due not to defects in our policies
but to the superior advantages of the Soviet Union in propaganda. That is to say, when our products do not sell, the
trouble lies not with the engineering in the quality of the product but in the packaging and the advertising. . . . . . American
propaganda is in trouble not because the Russians are able to
lie with impunity but because in so many critical areas
American propaganda is trying to sell policies which for one
reason or another are obsolete, are fictions, are profoundly un-
popular.

There is the central fiction in the Far East that Formosa is
China and that the actual government of China on the mainland ought to disappear. No propaganda can make a policy

based on that fiction credible, much less convincing and inspiring. . . . . . . . In the Middle East there is the fiction that the Arab States will remain with the West if only we can prevent the Soviet forces from invading them.

And in Europe, there is the fiction that Adenauer's Germany will absorb East Germany and that in some unknown way the Red Army will roll itself back out of Eastern Europe. The fact of the matter is that the mass of the people do not like these fictions and the informed leaders of opinion know that they are fictions and do not believe in them. That is why our propaganda works badly.*

Mr. Lippmann's reference to this country's China policy, it seems to me, needs some elaboration, as it is directly related to the existence of tensions in the Far East. I think that this is the appropriate occasion to put across the views of a citizen of an uncommitted nation like Burma to the leaders of American life. Let me endorse Mr. Lippmann's contention that the United States' policy towards China is unreal. It needs a thorough re-examination and reappraisal. The State Department holds the view that the Government in Peking should not occupy the Chinese seat in the United Nations. The Security Council is invested by the Charter of the United Nations with permanent executive authority. It is the body invested with authority to pronounce judgment in any dispute which is of international concern. The composition of such a body is therefore a matter of the utmost importance. The legal title of each of its Members is beyond question. Under Article 23 of the Charter the "Republic of China" is allotted a permanent seat on the Security Council. But this Article has been violated by the presence of a Chinese member who no longer represents, in any sense, the Government of his country. The nature of the problem is much more profound and much more significant than most of us are apt

* Today and Tomorrow, New York *Herald Tribune*, April 3, 1958.

to think, since it is a fact that if only the United States decided to reverse her attitude towards China, more than fifty nations of the world would follow suit overnight. The reason behind the United States' attitude towards China is the contention that Communist China is bent on world domination. It is an aggressor and morally and politically unfit to be a Member of the United Nations. Normally one would expect to be at war with a country of which one spoke in such terms; and the United States is in fact at war with Communist China in every respect except the one usually associated with a state of war—it is not fighting China by force of arms. The only logical sequence of such a policy is the inevitability of conflict, a doctrine which the United States attributes to the Communist camp. I find it difficult to understand this attitude when military force is neither in use nor immediately in prospect. However, the United States has very rightly avoided this attitude in her dealings with the Soviet Union.

The significant fact is that many of the closest colleagues of the United States have recognized Peking. The United Kingdom and many others claim that recognition implies neither approval nor disapproval, but is merely a practical arrangement suitable for maintaining contact with any government, whether friendly or unfriendly.

The refusal of the United States to support the admission of China to the United Nations is based on two assumptions: that the Peking Government's grip on China may be broken at any moment. No one, however, believes this. The second assumption is that the Chinese Government's behavior unfits it for membership in the World Organization. Many instances are cited in support of this view.

In this connection, it is important to remember that the

United Nations's main job is to settle disputes without wars. The more the countries disapprove of one another, the more important it is that their accusations and counter-accusations should take place within the Organization. Otherwise they may settle their disputes only on the battle-field. The United Nations exists precisely to prevent this from happening. By excluding the Peking Government, one damages not Peking but the United Nations, which is thereby ruled out as an effective instrument of interna-tional conciliation. I believe this is not the intention of the United States' policy, but it is its unhappy consequence.

If the above argument holds good, them it is true that the trade embargo to China has no justification. Britain's breakaway from the United States' embargo has considera-bly damaged Angol-American solidarity. Moreover, the re-cent breach in the economic blockade of China has now ended whatever effectiveness United States' policy might previously have claimed. Trade is beginning to flow be-tween China on the one hand and countries such as Canada and Japan on the other.

One may very well ask what can now be gained by a change in the United States' policy. No one of course be-lieves that the diplomatic recognition of China by the United States, the admission of China to the United Na-tions and opening up of trade relations with that country would transform Peking overnight into a cooperative regime. The question, therefore, is not helpful. The only helpful question would be to ask what dangers and disad-vantages might be avoided by the diplomatic recognition of China and the general normalization of relations. The answer is plain to all who care to think objectively. The United States, everybody knows, has sufficient power and resources to be able to buy the friendship of a few Asian States who need its military protection, but it is generally true to say that no one in Asia, except two or three leaders, comes anywhere near to sharing the American attitude to Peking.

Let me now turn to a few other factors which are responsible for the existence of tensions. The West argue that Communism is basically international in character, that the Soviet Union has been an aggressor and disturber of peace, in as much as Poland, Rumania, Bulgaria, Czechoslovakia, etc., were compelled to set up pro-Soviet governments, if not as a result of military invasion at least by means of political pressure. This argument raises a maze of complex issues from which it will be difficult to draw correct conclusions. The Communist reply, as we all know, is that in all these countries pro-Soviet regimes were established by the will of the majority of the inhabitants. But even if we reject this plea as false and insist that Soviet pressure was the decisive factor, we have to recognize that at the termination of the second World War, two clear-cut groups—Communist and Western—emerged in Europe. The West was suspicious of Communist intentions, and the Communists were likewise suspicious of Western intentions. The Soviet Union, rightly or wrongly, considered the situation to be such that it must establish a cordon of friendly States around itself. It may be likened to the United States' anxiety to make Latin American countries "safe for Democracy." Britain and France, together with other West European countries, moved closely together and established close association with the United States. To ask which party started this process is as unprofitable as to ask who fired the first shot in a war between two countries. The relevant consideration in this context is that, unlike Nazi Germany, the Soviet Union did not compel by actual military invasion any of its neighbors to become satellites. Eastern Germany and Austria are exceptions, but Soviet troops established in those territories were, like Western forces, legitimate armies of occupation.

It can be argued, however, that though the Soviet Union has not as yet attempted to impose its will on any State outside the Communist cordon, the Soviet has had and still has the intention to do so whenever the circumstances are favorable. But it is very difficult to arrive at any objective appraisal of such suppositions. Suspicions are not proof, and it is doubtful whether any proof has been established to sustain this charge. The usual Western explanation of why Russia has not resorted to openly aggressive measures is that she has been deterred from doing so by Western armed strength. Let us do a little plain thinking. If the Soviet Union in the immediate years after the war desisted from launching a military offensive because of Western armed strength, Western strength must have been sufficient to preserve peace even at that period. But, the contention of the advocates of Western rearmament has always been that the Soviet forces were relatively so much stronger than those of the West that rearmament was essential. If that were so, and if the Soviet intentions were to attack the West, why did not Soviet Russia launch the attack while the West was so comparatively weak? Why wait until the West had grown strong?

The plain fact is that Soviet Russia does not want to launch a shooting war against the West, in the same way as the West does not want to launch one against the Soviet Union. Everybody knows that a third world war will be a hydrogen war and that the consequences of such a war will be catastrophic both for victor and vanquished. In the event of a war between the Soviet Union and the West, many Western European countries could be virtually annihilated and the United States seriously injured. The Soviet Union would suffer the same fate. The leaders of the Kremlin know full well that a third war, even if the

Soviet forces were nominally victorious, would put back Soviet progress many decades. That is a price they are not prepared to pay.

Then why do they persist in Cold War tactics? The answer is that they distrust the West, that they detest the Capitalist System just as fully as the West distrust and detest Communism. In the same way as the West believe that Communism, by its inherent defects such as the suppression of fundamental human rights, is doomed eventually to oblivion, the Communists are convinced that the Capitalist System is doomed eventually to decay. This mutual dislike need not make war inevitable. Indeed, the more Communists believe that Western civilization will eventually collapse, the less inclined should they be to pay the price of going to war merely to hasten the process. That is why the Communists are now clamoring for a peaceful and competitive co-existence. If the West is really convinced of the superiority of its own system, it should welcome it with open arms.

The possibility and desirability of peaceful co-existence in the plane of diplomacy and international relations does not of course mean that co-existence is possible and desirable on the plane of ideas. I for one regard the fundamental freedoms as of paramount importance in human societies. In the context of the twentieth century, freedom of expression, freedom of association and the dignity of man are the essence of culture. I hold it a great truth that humanity cannot be half slave and half free. But these beliefs and convictions do not shut me off from the knowledge that there are others who believe differently. To put it plainly there can be no co-existence between the culture of democracy and the culture of communism.

This brings me back to my previous contention that if the world's great religions such as Islam and Christianity, after a prolonged and bloody war for centruies, flourish side by side in peace and amity, why should not Communist and non-Communist systems be permitted to co-exist peacefully? Wars of Crusades were fought hundreds of years ago between the adherents of these two religions, each determined to eliminate the other. The European Christians then thought that the followers of Islam were a menace to the Christian faith and therefore they must be put to the sword. The Moslem Saracens regarded the Christian Crusaders as evil heretics and thus a long war of attrition ensued. When tempers calmed down and common sense prevailed it was discovered by both sides that hostilities were a folly and that the two great religions could exist side by side peacefully, without any side surrendering any of its beliefs. This, I consider to be an apt instance to serve as a beacon light both to the Western Democracies and the Communist countries.

But there is one significant difference between the two episodes. Both Christianity and Islam are no longer *competing* for supremacy; they just flourish side by side in amity. By the very nature of their concepts, however, Democracies and Totalitarian systems must compete for supremacy, though by peaceful means. Victory will come to the side which understands and takes into account the most important phenomenon of the twentieth century—nationalism. The problem is in essence the problem of equality of opportunity. Let me touch briefly on this.

There are millions of people in the world who do not have enough to eat and enough to cover themselves with, and whose children cannot go even to the primary schools. It seems comic to talk to them about the virtues of democratic ideals and the dignity of man. During the last war there was a great deal of talk of the imperative need for Democracy to triumph over Fascism. Mr. Churchill had then invited the Burmese people to take part in that "war for Democracy." Young Burmese nationalists had said then that Burma would not fight for democracy when she herself was enchained in slavery. And for that answer "Democracy" did not hesitate to shut up a number of young Burmese leaders in prison.

Is the situation different today? Take Africa for instance. Over a hundred million people are being ruled today by the free nations of the world. What does the fight against totalitarianism mean to these millions of people? When France, for instance, proudly proclaims to the world that her soldiers are killing four thousand Algerians every month, is the cause of Democracies enhanced? The white settlers of South Africa, who treat the colored people as worse than lepers are greater enemies of Democracy than the Communists. They are generating tensions much more ruthlessly than the Cold War tactics allegedly employed by the Communists.

Let us not delude ourselves with the over-simplification of the world issue. The issue today is not only that of Communism versus Democracy. The more essential issue is the division of the world into the weak and the strong, the prosperous and the abject poor, the ruler and the ruled, the master race and the sub-human. Therefore, if the war for democracy has any meaning, it is necessary that we all sit together and create here and now the conditions that will guarantee freedom, justice, well-being and equality to all.

## ON TENSION IN THE MIDDLE EAST*

I take the floor with a good deal of trepidation, since any expression of opinion, however sincere, on the present crisis in the Middle East, is bound to be interpreted as taking

* Statement before the Special Session of the General Assembly of the United Nations, August 19, 1958.

sides one way or the other. Perhaps, a passage here or a paragraph there may be torn out of context and presented as reinforcing any such interpretation. However, as the record of our delegation's activities in this world organization in the last ten years will show, our approach to problems is solely governed by considerations of what seems to us to be right or wrong. There is unfortunately a very pronounced school of thought which still believes that a nation that does not choose sides and join irrevocably with one or the other camp in the heavily armed uneasy truce that exists in the world today lacks courage and conviction. And very often the inference which seems to be drawn is "if you are not with us, then you are against us." Let me take this opportunity of reiterating once again, Mr. President, that Burma, while not irrevocably attached to any armed camp, is also not against any. This somewhat detached position enables us, I believe, to view the problems around us with a considerable measure of objectivity.

It is the view of my delegation that the immediate problem of the Middle East is more political in nature than economic, and therfore any attempt to solve it speedily must necessarily be focussed on the political character of the crisis. Fortunately, the general debate in this world organization in the last few days has cleared the foul air of recriminations and accusations, and the positions of the two contending blocs are within negotiating distance of really effective and imaginative proposals. There is no doubt a consensus of opinion that, given the background to the present situation in the Middle East and particularly the complex forces at play in that area, the entry of foreign troops could only create more problems than it could solve. There also seems to be a general agreement among the nations that these problems will become more complex and difficult as the stay of the foreign troops in the area is prolonged. Therefore, the only logical step for the United Nations to take is to find some suitable ways and means whereby the foreign troops may be speedily withdrawn from Lebanon and Jordan and stability restored to the area.

There also appears to be a general agreement that some kind of United Nations presence in these two countries is necessary to ensure the speedy withdrawal of foreign troops. Only the nature of this "presence" is in dispute. Some Member States favor the strengthening of the United Nations Observation Group in Lebanon in accordance with the plan presented by the United Nations Observation Group in its second report, and to send a fresh United Nations Observation Group to Jordan to perform similar functions. The advocates of this action insist that the enlargement of the functions of the Observation Group is not warranted by the prevailing circumstances.

The other school of thought, however, prefers to enlarge the functions of the United Nations force. It advocates some kind of an international constabulary with police, if not strictly military, functions. The functions of this constabulary, recruited from among the small nations, if my interpretation is correct, would fall short of the normal functions of a fighting force. It would be authorized to shoot but carry only small arms.

On the basis of all available information in the Middle East, my delegation cannot agree to the substitution of the Observation Group with limited functions by an international police force that would be expected to enforce its authority by force of arms. In the uneasy political climate prevailing in the Middle East, the presence of such a force will certainly pose additional problems. Apart from the increased financial obligations to be imposed on all Member States, various intricate issues will emerge. What will be the criteria in selecting the countries from which the projected constabulary is to be drawn? By what authority would the force act? What would be its code of conduct? What steps need to be taken to ensure that it would not be dragged into local conflicts and civil wars? Would the supply of such an international force be able to cope with the demands which are likely to increase if a precedent is once set?

I do not want to be misunderstood. Perhaps it is worthwhile exploring the possibilities of building up a stand-by United Nations constabulary, defining its specific functions, with a view to its utilization in future contingencies, when the cold war atmosphere no longer exists. But in the existing circumstances when fear and suspicion still dominate the political scene, the formation of an international semi-military forces is bound to aggravate the situation rather than to ease it. And there is the added danger of this world organization inadvertently stemming the rising tide of national and progressive forces rampant everywhere against the forces of outmoded and obsolete legacies of the past.

As an Asian, let me confess that a major weakness of Asia is religion employed as a weapon for political ends, and the existence of politics of community or language, or a combination of all. These undesirable forces corrode within, and foul the relations existing between nations. Asia has to overcome these forces in order that the potential strength of the masses for a more peaceful and good neighborly feeling may be fully developed. The most effective weapon to fight this malady is the development and encouragement of democratic institutions and legitimate national aspirations, and to combat prejudice and ignorance. The United Nations, in the view of my delegation, has a significant role to play in this fight.

Coming to the economic aspect of the Middle East crisis, one feature emerges clearly: Middle Eastern dependence upon revenues from oil and the Western dependence upon this oil. The simple recognition of this fact can lead to the right solution. The first task of statesmanship in the immediate future is the substitution of a purely commercial relationship between the West and the Middle East for an imperial or military relationship which has proved to be not only outmoded but definitely dangerous. The continued presence of foreign troops in the area will not facilitate the success of this task. On the contrary it will make it much harder. The sooner the troops leave, the sooner will a more favorable climate of opinion be created among the Arab States. The problem is how to do it without too much heaping the blame on past actions and without leaving chaos and anarchy behind. From all accounts, it will be comparatively easy in Lebanon, but immensely difficult in the case of Jordan whose spokesman in this world organization has peremptorily closed the door to any contemplated United Nations move in his country. Perhaps the Secretary-General, whose sincerity and ability no one doubts, will be in the best position to bring about a reversal of that attitude. His Majesty King Hussein has given every evidence of personal courage, and in the view of my delegation, he would not be found wanting in giving evidence of nobility also, if the right approach were made, by showing his personal interest in the welfare of his people by responding to their legitimate needs and aspirations.

Mr. President, what the Middle East requires is to be left alone, converted neither into a battleground nor a recruiting field for the contending great powers. Any program or plan designed for this area will not work if it is not acceptable to the countries concerned. Similarly, any attempt by any of the Middle East countries to alter their frontiers by armed force will be catastrophic. Once stability is restored in the area, peaceful progress should be the sole concern of all peoples of the area.

In this second half of the twentieth century, man must learn to live with himself. Regardless of his beliefs, traditions, ideologies, and the economic, social and political systems to which he subscribes, he must learn to live with his neighbors. This calls for a new outlook, a new approach, even for a new philosophy. Past history, dealing with a completely different kind of ear and circumstances, will no longer stand him in good stead. He must rise to the challenge of the thermo-nuclear age. More than ever, he needs to exercise courage, patience, tolerance and imagination. Fear and suspicion which for so long have characterized international relations must no longer feature in this hydrogen age. In this new situation, how are the nations of the world to be guided in their relations with one another? I believe that the answer is to be found in the most sensible art of living together in peace. Let me express the hope of my delegation, Mr. President, that the deliberations in this Assembly will not only lead to the formulation of a sound, sensible and just solution to the immediate problems of the Middle East, but also lay firm foundations for an enduring peace in the area.

### A BURMESE VIEW OF ASIAN-AMERICAN RELATIONS *

First of all let me say how grateful I am to the United States National Commission for UNESCO for the honor of the invitation extended to me to address the Sixth National Conference. I sincerely appreciate the opportunity

---

* Address delivered at the sixth National Conference of the United States National Commission for UNESCO at San Francisco on November 8, 1957.

of speaking to so many distinguished leaders of American
life who are interested in the furtherance of Asian-American relations.

Let me confess at the outset that my views may not necessarily reflect the views of the average Burman, in the
same way as the views expressed by a certain American
individual do not necessarily reflect the views of the average American. Then it will certainly be too far-fetched to
assume that the views of an average Burman necessarily
reflect the views of an average Asian. In the circumstances,
it will be only proper to assess my judgment as that of a
Burman who is a student of Asian-American relations and
who has at heart the improvement of such relations.

Before I deal with the question of Asian-American relations I think it will be pertinent to touch on the basic
characteristics of an Asian country—Burma. With the attainment of independence in 1948, Burma, like other
countries, was attracted to the United Nations by the lofty
idealism of the Charter. Burma subscribed whole-heartedly
to the purposes and principles of the Charter, and looked
forward to a new era of peace, progress and prosperity for
mankind. Burma, like many other Member Nations, will
endeavor her utmost to strengthen this world Organization
and to make it the really effective organization which had
been planned by its founders, and Burma believes that the
first step in the direction of strengthening the United Nations is to rid the Member Nations of fear and suspicion.
Burma believes that the political atmosphere is too much
contaminated with these twin evils.

I think it will be relevant to reiterate our well known
policy of consistently throwing our weight on the side of
peace, and against the forces of war or tensions. Burma has
consistently supported any move, made at any time and
from any quarter, which in her view is genuinely designed

to prevent war and to promote the cause of peace. This stand has been made unmistakably clear by our Prime Minister at the historic Asian-African Conference, popularly known as the Bandung Conference, in April 1955. The decisions of the Bandung Conference have served, and will continue to serve as our guiding principles in the formulation of our foreign policy and in our approach to world problems.

Burma is firmly and irrevocably committed to a system of parliamentary democracy. Burma believes in democratic ideals and the dignity of men. Burma is thoroughly averse to the idea of dictatorship in any shape or form. The Burmese people are determined never to exchange their way of life for any other way of life. But this firm conviction and dedication do not preclude us from viewing the world around us with a proper perspective. We understand why some countries have chosen systems of government very different from our own. We consider it not our business to pass judgment on the internal affairs of other countries. The recognition of this basic fact enables us to subscribe to the principles of peaceful co-existence.

As I have stated earlier, Burma cannot be regarded as representative of Asia, in the same way as no country in Europe can be regarded as representative of that continent. But certain unmistakable forces are at work in the whole continent of Asia towards a synthesis. A reborn nationalism of formerly dependent areas has risen in revolt against the domination of the world by the West and is now defying the latter's leadership. This post-war phenomenon is not properly understood in many countries, including America, and this lack of understanding is at the root of occasional frictions in Asian-American relationship. The newly resurgent nationalism of Asia is sometimes misconstrued in America as pro-Communist and anti-Ameri-

can. But the plain fact is that all the countries of Asia, with
the exception of China, North Korea and North Vietnam,
are not Communist and are not likely to turn Communist
so long as their economic and political stability is maintained and promoted. In this great task of maintaining
and promoting stability in Asia, the United States of
America can play a significant role. There is no fundamental incompatibility between American outlook and
the nationalism of newly awakened Nations of Asia, and
the closest cooperation between them is essential to a
greater future for both of them.

The vitality of the American people is reflected in the
extraordinary pace of your everyday life, the vehemence of
your reactions and your feeling and the fantastic growth of
your economic enterprises. This vitality, this vigor and this
exuberance of your national character have been in the
past both an asset and a liability in your relations with
Asia which is emotionally calm, contemplative and proud.
On the credit side the United States of America has been a
pillar of a dynamic form of democracy and your contributions to the methods of mass democracy have been impressive. You have also given proof of vigor and inventiveness
in the realm of foreign policy. This is especially true since
the 1930's when you began to give up isolationism and
entered the arena of world politics.

A large number of intelligent Asians think of the
Americans as a great people because of your vigor, your
history, your traditions and your devotion to the principles
of freedom and democracy. These ideas and characteristics
have been the inspiration and hope of Asia for more than
half a century. They had a tremendous impact on Asia
where there was no recognition of the equality of man;
where there was little recognition of the fundamental
rights of man; where governments were generally imposed

from above, and has as their primary objective the exploitation of the people. It is true to say that these ideas played a leading part in inspiring Asia's fight for freedom from colonial bondage.

This is not the only reason why Asians think highly of the American people. Your glorious record in the two world wars in which you undoubtedly saved the world from tyranny and dictatorship, at great sacrifice and expense; cannot be ignored or made light of even by your most severe critics. Finally, your post-World War II record, in which you have contributed so much towards the relief and rehabilitation of the war-devastated countries, is entirely without precedent in the annals of history.

Yet, in spite of this most impressive record behind you, you have not won as many friends and influenced as many people as you should in Asia. The explanation, I think, is your extraordinary vigor, the vehemence of your reactions and your feelings and your failure to see the Asian mind. The incompatibility, though not fundamental, is emotional. In several respects this incompatibility is due to other factors than mere emotion. Your historical association with the West, your sympathy for Western institutions and attitudes and your close identity with Western policy have been a hindrance in Asian-American relations. The equivocal attitude which you seem to have taken in recent years on colonial issues has been regarded as surprisingly reactionary by the progressive Asians. To an Asia which had come to regard America as the symbol of freedom, the spearhead of the attack against colonialism, and the champion of the underdog, this has indeed been a disappointment. Some hard-thinking Asians have begun to wonder whether you had abandoned your precious heritage and your honorable tradition. Explanations which have been given, to the effect that colonialism is dying, and that a new and even greater danger has emerged, have left nearly all of Asia unconvinced. On many occasions, we Asians feel that leaders of American life and thought—administrators, legislators, journalists and educators—fail to make a distinction between nationalism and communism. Many under-developed countries of Asia, the moment they regained their independence from the colonial powers, chalked out their own policies and built their own future. Many believe that the launching of agrarian reforms, the operation of State enterprises and the adoption of "neutral" policies in respect of foreign relations are in the best interest of their own countries. Burma, for instance, has chosen a democratic, parliamentary and non-totalitarian type of socialism. In America, I understand that the term "socialism" is anathema. You find it difficult to think of "socialism" in terms of democracy and individual freedom, but in our socialist Burma, we enjoy the fruits of parliamentary democracy and fundamental human freedom. We enjoy freedom of speech, freedom of expression, freedom of association and freedom of belief as you do here. But the newly resurgent nationalism and this sudden adoption of so-called "socialism" put you into confusion. You are apt to think that a certain Asian nation has gone to the other camp when that nation refuses to toe your line. With your traditional vigor and the extraordinary vehemence of your reactions you then alienate many of your most sincere admirers. I think that your attitude towards colonialism and your failure to distinguish between nationalism and communism are mainly responsible for the present lack of warmth in Asian-American relations, although of course they are generally friendly. Perhaps your attitude is born out of youthful dynamism not yet restrained by experience and tradition.

This dynamic quality and vigorous application of policies are responsible for your all-out support to certain regimes simply because they subscribe to all your views without questioning. It is a fact that you are pouring your precious millions into the coffers of regimes which by no stretch of the imagination can be regarded as "governments of the people, for the people, by the people." You are vigorously supporting certain of those regimes in spite of the fact that they are undemocratic, corrupt and discredited. The effect of this on some Asian minds has been to build up the impression that America is against change and that it wishes to preserve the *status quo*. Let me hasten to add that this is a view not *generally* held, but that it *is* held cannot be doubted.

Another source of misunderstanding between America and Asia stems from the activities and statements of some of your leaders, and a section of your press. These are the people who are responsible for building the impression abroad that America is bellicose, subjective in her views and fond of distortion. If some of your leaders and a section of your press try to understand "the other fellow's point of view" then there is sure to be greater understanding and better relations between America and Asia. No doubt it is a two-way traffic. Some of the Asian leaders and a section of our press are equally guilty of this shortcoming. It is up to both Asia and America to make the necessary psychological adjustments, to become themselves once again, to live up to their respective heritage and to the great moral principles which each of them spawned.

As a well-wisher of better Asian-American relations, let me say that American leadership tends to limit itself to grants of material aid to the needy. It is far from my intention to underestimate its importance. The Marshall Plan aid to Europe and the Economic Cooperation Assistance to Asia have been an indispensible help in restoring the two continents' economy after the war. To raise the living standards of the millions who still exist in the barest poverty and squalor is one of the main challenges to American wealth and American generosity. But this humanitarian act alone is not sufficient to create better understanding and closer friendship between America and Asia. No self-respecting nation will accept another's guidance and appreciate another's motives merely because the other is wealthier and prepared to share some of his wealth with him. On the contrary, the sad truth is that between nations, as between individuals, this seems to make for resentment rather than for gratitude. The battle for the minds of the millions will not be won by just holding out to them better drinks and faster cars, particularly in countries of Asia where spiritual values are always paramount. America and the West possess two spiritual values which can be put across with immense benefit to Asia: religious devotion and democracy. The whole Asian continent is thirsting for a religious renaissance, the rebirth of cultural values and the improvement of moral standards. America can certainly help fill the need.

My observations on Asian-American relations will not be complete without a reference to the United States' policy towards China—what is commonly called here as Communist China. I think that the occasion is appropriate to put across the views of a citizen of an uncommitted nation like Burma to the leaders of American life. It is not my intention to inject politics or political remarks into these discussions which are essentially non-political. But complete silence on this aspect of Asian-American relations will certainly render our discussions not only incomplete but futile. I am afraid I shall have to say something which is not likely to be palatable to most of the distinguished ladies and gentlemen assembled here today,

but what is to be said must be said. Let me say straight-
away that the United States' policy towards China needs
a thorough re-examination and reappraisal.

The official policy of your Government is too well
known to be reiterated. You hold the view that the Government in Peking should not be diplomatically recognized. You also hold the view that the Government in
Peking should not occupy the Chinese seat in the United
Nations. You still hold the view that there should be no
trade and cultural relations between Communist China
and the United States.

Let us face the facts. If the United States decided to
reverse her attitude towards China, more than fifty nations
of the world will follow suit overnight. Therefore the nature of the problem is much more profound and much
more significant than most of us are apt to think. What
then are the reasons behind the present United States attitude towards China? Communist China, it is argued, is
bent on world domination. It is an aggressor and morally
and politically unfit to be a member of the United Nations. Normally one would expect to be at war with a
country of which one spoke in such terms; and the United
States is, in effect, at war with Communist China in every
respect except the one usually associated with a state of
war—it is not fighting China by force of arms. The only
logical sequence of such a policy is the inevitability of
conflict, a doctrine which the United States attributes to
the Communist camp. The Chinese are, however, clamoring for an understanding with America, for trade with
America and for cultural exchanges with America. To us,
uncommitted countries, it is difficult to understand your
attitude of cutting diplomatic relations and forbidding
your citizens to communicate or trade with China, at a
time when military force is neither in use nor immediately

in prospect. You have very rightly avoided this attitude in your dealings with the Soviet Union.

Many of your closest colleagues have recognized Peking. The United Kingdom and many others claim that recognition implies neither approval nor disapproval, but is merely a practical arrangement suitable for maintaining contact with any government, whether friendly or unfriendly. Here, one sees the difference between the British approach to foreign affairs and your approach. The British view has grown out of generations of living alongside unfriendly neighbors and experiencing ups and downs in her overseas adventures. Against such a background, toleration of the enemy seems mere common sense.

The American view, on the contrary, has its roots in the isolationism of the nineteenth century. A country which aimed at having nothing to do with foreign countries, could afford to treat as non-existent any government of which it strongly disapproved. Your national vigor and the vehemence of your reactions and feelings are mainly responsible for this rigid attitude. Such an attitude, however, makes no sense for the deeply involved United States in the middle of the twentieth century.

Closely linked with diplomatic recognition is the question of China's representation in the United Nations. China is, under the Charter, a member of the World Organization and a permanent member of the Security Council. The refusal of the United States to support the admission of China to the United Nations is based on two assumptions: that the Peking Government's grip on China may be broken at any minute. No one, however, believes this. The second assumption is that the Chinese government's behavior unfits it for membership in the World Organization. Many charges are made in support of this view.

In this connection, it is important to remember that the United Nations' main job is to settle disputes without war. The more the countries disapprove of each other, the more important it is that their accusations and counter-accusations should take place within the Organization. Otherwise they may settle their dispute only on the battlefield. The United Nations exists precisely to prevent this from happening. By excluding the Peking Government, one damages not Peking but the United Nations, which is thereby ruled out as an effective instrument of international conciliation. I believe this is not the intention of United States policy, but it is its unhappy consequence.

If the above argument holds good, then it is true that the trade embargo to China has no justification. Britain's break-away from the United States embargo has damaged your solidarity more than it has held up Chinese development. Moreover, the recent breach in the economic blockade of China has now ended whatever effectiveness United States policy might previously have claimed.

You may very well pose the question: What can now be gained by a change in the United States policy? No one believes that the diplomatic recognition of China by the United States, admission of China to the United Nations and opening up of trade relations with that country would transform Peking overnight into a cooperative regime. So, the question is wrongly posed. The right question to pose would be to ask what dangers and disadvantages might be avoided by the diplomatic recognition of China and the general normalization of relations. It will perhaps need another paper to go into this aspect and therefore, let me say only this. The United States has, of course, sufficient power to be able to buy the friendship of a few Asian States who need its military protection, but it is generally true to say that no one in Asia except two or three leaders comes anywhere near to sharing the American attitude to Peking.

Ladies and Gentlemen, let me conclude this speech with a fervent appeal to the conscience of the American people. Please frame your Asian policies upon the basis of an honest appraisal of events, current trends and the actual working of the Asian mind, and not upon the basis of prejudices deriving from your own domestic situation and your isolationist past. To base your policy upon make-believe will be not only unreal but will inevitably deceive your well-wishers and admirers. It will lead to the striking of fine attitudes followed by last minute withdrawals. Please take these words as coming from one who has the highest admiration and profoundest respect for American ideals and institutions. I hope this small cry from a far corner of Asia will receive the necessary attention in this great country. May the United States of America be a potent force for peace and progress of mankind.

### ISRAEL IN THE WORLD FAMILY OF NATIONS[*]

First of all I want to express my profound sense of grati-tude to the Springfield Community Committee to Cele-brate Israel's Tenth Anniversary for the opportunity afforded to me to associate myself with the celebrations commemorating the tenth anniversary of the Founding of Israel, and I certainly feel it a great privilege to address such a distinguished gathering.

Before I deal with the subject of "Israel in the World Family of Nations," let me repeat what our Prime Minis-ter said on September 27, 1957, in the course of his address

[*] Address delivered at the Jewish Community Center of Springfield, Mass., celebrating the 10th Anniversary of Israel's Independence, May 28, 1958.

delivered in the Chamber of Deputies. In his reference to Israeli-Arab relations, our Prime Minister observed:

It is our earnest hope that a lasting solution can be worked out between Israel and the Arab States. Perpetual hostility can only bring harm to both sides. Therefore we would urge both sides to abandon all claims to belligerent rights. We recognized Israel because it is a living reality. As long as our Arab friends refuse to accept the fact of Israel, there can be no real progress towards a solution. But once this fact is accepted, we feel that the principal psychological barrier to a settlement will be removed, and the way opened to the ending of the present deadlock. We hope that our Arab friends will not take amiss this expression of views which is made with the highest of motives. Indeed we are quite confident that they will not, considering that both in and out of the United Nations we have given our support to all legitimate Arab causes. For example, we gave our full support to the struggle of the Moroccan and Tunisian peoples for freedom, and today stand behind the Algerian people in their fight for the right of self-determination. We supported Egypt when she nationalized the Suez Canal Company, and condemned Britain and France when they tried to regain control over the canal by recourse to arms. Thus we cannot be accused of being anti-Arab. At the same time, we urge our Israeli friends to be patient, and to scrupulously refrain from any action which will add to the difficulties of the Arab States.

As a citizen of a country which has consistently maintained the friendliest of relations with Israel, I wish to venture on an analysis of common factors between our two countries. Despite all disparities of history, geography and climate, Israel and Burma are endeavoring to revive their respective ancient cultures against the background of modern civilization. They are both facing the most formidable and fascinating tasks of national, social and economic reconstruction and they are both upholding democratic ideals, the dignity of man and systems of parliamentary democracy. Both Israel and Burma are averse to the idea of dictatorship in any shape or form. Although our two countries are dedicated to the principles of democratic socialism, we are not patterned after maxims mechanically lifted out of text books. Both Israel and Burma have one aim in common: the creation of a society of free and equal peoples, with equal opportunities for all, a society based on certain values of human and social life. Both countries were reborn just a decade ago, and since then both have slowly and painfully been working out their basic ideals and methodology. This process is not complete yet, but a fairly clear-cut body of thought has emerged out of the painful experiences usually associated with the pangs of birth.

I had the good fortune to accompany our Prime Minister U Nu when he visited Israel in May/June, 1955, and I saw with my own eyes a new nation imbued with an extraordinary intensity of purpose and an abundant hope for its future. I had the privilege of touring various parts of the country with our Prime Minister and viewing a comparatively full picture of the country's life and aspirations. I had the opportunity to speak to the settlers in the hills of Galilee and in the valleys of Jordan and Yezreel which are very important agricultural centres. In the arid south, U Nu could see the implementation of Israel's bold plans for the conquest of the desert which he had earlier seen graphically at the exhibition of the same name in Jerusalem. The Prime Minister's party visited collective settlements, a unique feature of Israel's agricultural and social experiment. Visiting a number of industrial enterprises, we could see the contribution made by skill, ingenuity and perseverance to the nation's economy. We also saw various activities comprising measures for the integration of new immigrants, the promotion of social and cultural progress and the teaching of skills. We saw the efforts of Israeli scientists to harness science into the service of their country. Chance encounters with settlers, townspeople, workers and school children revealed to us a glimpse of Israel's soul. Our Prime Minister, who is a very devout Buddhist, had the opportunity to evaluate the place of religion in this young, dynamic, hard-working and imaginative country.

During the nine-day visit to Israel I had the opportunity to meet many of the country's leading personalities: politicians, soldiers, artists, scientists, industrialists, trade unionists, administrators and educationists, and they all impressed me with their devotion to their tasks, their dedication to their country, and their determination to achieve their cherished ideals. Prime Minister U Nu summed up his impressions of Israel and her people as follows, in the course of a farewell reception given in his honor in Tel Aviv:

In fact I have been impressed not only with the friendliness of the people of Israel, but with their keenness for work. I have admiration and respect for the people who work hard, as I have the lowest opinion of those who don't. The leaders and the people of Israel have achieved a very creditable measure of success in their march towards their goal, against heavy odds. In the last few years the very face of Israel has been changed and a new dynamic spirit has been infused in the minds of the people. Hope springs eternal in the human breast, and in you, the people of Israel, I see unmistakable evidence of this wise adage. You are spurred on to greater efforts in the building of your new land: with hope and determination success is inevitable. I must admit that what I have seen here exceeded my expectations.

One of the things that strikes me most is the development of new forms of rural life, expressing themselves in entirely new types of rural society—the Kibbutz and the Moshav. The people of Israel are building a new way of life and the results so far achieved have been most encouraging. The people, young and old, are moulding a completely new society based on the noble principles of common weal and common progress, and healthy bodies and happy faces I saw everywhere are a standing testimony to the success of this grave and far-sighted experiment. I have a feeling that the spirit of the Kibbutz will extend beyond the frontiers of Israel and contribute towards the building of a peaceful and progressive society.

This conception of the Kibbutz, I am glad to see, conforms to the tenets of Buddhism which I profess. Ego has no place in Buddhism which tells us that *sakkara ditti*—belief in Ego— must be got rid of. Attachment to property leads to a chain of undesirable consequences, and I find that the idea of the Kibbutz is primarily directed against the selfish attachment. It will be my pleasant task to study more about this unique experiment with a view to adapting the way of life encouraged in the Kibbutz in certain parts of Burma.

Israel and Burma gained independence about the same time but due to a number of circumstances, Burma has not been able to achieve the same pace of industrial progress as Israel has. Burma is rich in natural resources, and Israel is rich in skilled technicians. But natural resources by themselves do not carry a country to progress and prosperity; it is the human factor that counts. It will be in the interest of our two countries if we join hands together and work for closer economic relationship. Let us therefore work concertedly for a new era in which our economic ties will be still further strengthened.

Since U Nu's return to Burma, the bonds of friendship between Israel and Burma were strengthened still further, and this close relationship is illustrated by the fact that thirty-four experts from Israel are at present working in Burma in the fields of agricultural planning, mechanization, vocational training, irrigation, economic planning, public engineering, medical services, industry, etc. A number of officials and official missions have also visited Israel for study and observation in the above and other fields. This in brief describes the nature of relations between Israel and Burma as a Burman sees it. Now let me deal with the wider aspects of Israel's position in the World Family of Nations.

Israel's geographical situation and her long historic contacts with both East and West has placed her in the position of a bridge connecting the two. Israel belongs to an area which is not only very ancient, but which has witnessed many wars and many conflicts. It is also a part of the world which has given to humanity three great religions which have spread to all parts of the world. Today, as in the far distant past, Israel is situated on an international crossroads of supreme importance. The Mediterranean Sea connects it with Western Europe and beyond. West Africa and Eastern Europe are also easily accessible, while Eilat is now the new gateway to East Africa, Asia and the Far East.

The facts of history reinforce those of geography. The Jewish nation was originally formed in its homeland in Western Asia. Together with the two old historical stalwarts—Greece and Rome—it has made a basic contribution to Western civilization. Jewish wanderings and dispersal have enriched the life of various societies and the Jews everywhere contributed materially to the promotion of discipline, religious devotion and dedication to certain cherished ideals.

The second return to Zion is also characterized by various factors, one of which is the variegated composition of Israel's population. The vast majority of the people of new Israel were born in a wide variety of Western and Oriental countries with different traditions and historical development. Thus Israel acquires new characteristics of dynamism and "melting pot" atmosphere which impress all discerning observers. This cosmopolitan character of the Israelis also makes Israel destined to play more and more the role of a bridge, or a mediator, between various contemporaneous civilizations, linking the geographical areas in which these cultural groupings have arisen. This peculiar nature of her position and historical background makes Israel increasingly aware of the political, economic, cultural and ideological implications and possibilities. This is shown by Israel's increasingly successful efforts to develop intensive all-round relations with various countries in Asia and Africa, while reinforcing at the same time her ties with Europe and the Americas.

The representatives of Israel attended the first Pan-Asian Conference in New Delhi in 1946. Valuable contacts were then established between the representatives of Palestinian Jewry and their Asian counterparts. For once, these contacts served to show the great community of interest that existed between various countries in Asia and Jewish Palestine. This community was based not merely on the negative aspect of a common struggle against Colonialism at the time but carried the seeds of positive cooperation in the future especially in the field of peaceful reconstruction.

The future leaders of Israel were then very much aware, as indeed were the leaders of most countries of Asia, that the real test of independence for the young States of Asia would come in combating the results of centuries of neglect of the soil and the effects of disease, poverty and ignorance. Already in 1946 and even more so in 1958 Israelis have felt that this struggle can best be waged on a basis of mutual help and have demonstrated their willingness to share the burden by sending experts in sanitation, salt production, irrigation, sand-dune fixation, tropical medi-

cine, forestry, community development, etc. have gone out
to Burma and other countries of Asia. Government officials
and educators from many Asian countries have also come
to Israel to study her achievements and to share in her
experience. It is significant to note that wherever Israeli
experts go they set out not only determined to teach as
much of their skill is possible, but also to learn from the
lives of the peoples of Asia amongst whom they work. Such
has been my experience of Israelis at work in Burma.

Encouraged as they were by the contacts made during
the Pan-Asian Conference in New Delhi in 1946, Israel's
political leaders were looking forward to the setting up of
even closer relations after the establishment of the State.
Unfortunately, however, the effects of pressure from certain quarters on a number of Asian states began to tell,
and as a result of it Israel was not invited to the historic
Asian-African Conference in Bandung. Though a number
of her friends, and especially Burma, endeavored for the
inclusion of Israel in the Conference, it was nevertheless a
set-back to all those in Israel who strove for a closer integration of their country into the Asian family of nations.
After the first wave of disappointment resulting from the
decisions taken regarding the Bandung Conference had
subsided, Israel's leaders continued in their efforts to establish closer ties with States especially in East Asia, who
were, so to speak, uncommitted in the Israel-Arab dispute.
Israel had already recognized the People's Republic of
China, and I understand that within the last two years
Israel and Japan have considerably strengthened their economic ties. Excellent relations exist between Israel and the
Philippines, and a Minister Resident in Rangoon was ac-
credited also to Manila. Recently, the Israel Legation in
Rangoon was raised to the status of an Embassy. Friendly
relations also exist between Israel on the one hand and
Thailand and Ceylon on the other.

In the economic field too, Israel has been a model of systematic development to all under-developed countries. In the brief space of ten years Israel has achieved results unparalleled in the history of young nations. Its population has almost tripled during that period; industry has increased sevenfold; exports have also tripled; the area of cultivation has more than doubled and agricultural production has almost tripled. In the field of education too, tremendous strides have been made. Elementary school attendance has almost quadrupled, and it is particularly significant to note that Arab school attendance has risen from 6,780 in 1948 to 36,550 in 1957. In the sphere of public health too, the results achieved have been most impressive. To cite an instance the number of hospitals has almost doubled in the past ten years, with a triple increase in the number of hospital beds.

To us, however, interested in the trade union movement, Israel's *Histadrut* stands as a symbol of perfect trade union organization, worthy of emulation by all newly-independent countries. In fact *Histadrut* is not simply a trade union in the Western sense; it is a fully-integrated workers' economy embracing everything from ordinary trade unions to the control of outright ownership of communal and cooperative villages, banks, insurance companies, etc. The structure and activities of the *Histadrut* should be studied with profit by all peoples who are interested in the future of the trade union movement which is playing and will continue to play a very significant role in the economic life of the countries.

One feature of Israeli society which deserves close study is her attitude towards the people of differing religious denominations. The official attitude towards the minority Druse community is exemplary. In spite of religious differences the Druse are not subject to any kind of discrimination at the hands of the majority. Upon the establishment of the State of Israel in 1948, the Israel Druses, then 15,000 in number, were poor, inadequately educated and lacking in communal autonomy. Today their number has increased to 20,000, and they enjoy the benefits of economic progress. Compulsory education introduced by the Israeli Government has greatly assisted the cultural advancement of the Druses, and modern methods of instruction has imbued their youth with the spirit of freedom and democracy. A first group of Druses have already completed their secondary and university studies. This manifestation of religious tolerance and the promotion of democratic principles are some of the most encouraging features of new Israel, and she will no doubt stand as a beacon to those countries which are unfortunately still steeped in the medieval darkness of intolerance, ignorance and feudalism. This is the message of Israel to the less enlightened nations in the middle of the twentieth century.

If a survey were to be made of Israel's relations with Asian States in the first ten years of its independence, it is becoming abundantly clear that no one can in the long run prevent the acceptance of Israel as an equal member in the Asian family of nations. When tempers calm down it will be revealed that the nature of the Jewish State is essentially peaceful and constructive. It is in the fitness of things that Israel is conscious of the importance of cultural and scientific exchange programmes with several Asian States.

Much more, however, should follow. Especially important in this connexion are the scholarship schemes in Israel for students from Asia and vice-versa. A fuller understanding of each other's problems can begin only when Israelis and Asians stop looking at each other through alien specta-

cles. I understand that many Israelis who come into contact with Asians have often felt that the peculiar and
unique history of the Jewish people has never been properly understood in Asia because it was learned from history
textbooks written by those who do not understand the
mind of Israelis. The same applies to Israel's understanding of Asian problems as most popular books on Asia are
written by those who do not understand the Asian mind.
Too much of what Israelis know of the history of Asian
countries has come to them through the media of Western
observers. In the years to come much of Israel's relations
with Asian states will depend on the extent to which the
younger generation of Asians and Israelis will get to know
each other's way of life untrammeled by prejudice and
historical misconceptions.

I believe that Israel's sympathy for the struggle for independence of the African states has been especially acute
because of the feeling of kinship that an Israeli invariably
feels with victims of racial discrimination. This sympathy
found a practical expression when the young State of
Ghana came into existence. A joint Ghana-Israel shipping
line was established, and I understand that suitable provisions have been made for the training of African seamen in
Israel's maritime schools. A close relationship has also been
developed between the National Federations of Labor of
the two countries.

With Ethiopia and with Liberia too, Israel has within
the period of the last five years developed strong bonds of
friendship and growing commercial and economic ties.

Israel's Foreign Minister, Mrs. Golda Meir, has recently
come back from an extended visit to Ghana, Liberia,
Nigeria and French West Africa. Her speeches and statements reveal that her journey was not intended as a mere
official visit but represented an attempt by the Minister

responsible for Israel's foreign relations to learn first hand
the problems and needs both of sovereign African states
and those who are standing on the threshold of independence. Mrs. Meir, therefore, made special efforts to go from
village to village to see for herself how best Israel experts
could be employed to help Africans to combat some of the
urgent problems that beset so many of the under-developed countries. In promising technical assistance to Africa,
Mrs. Meir made it clear that there were "no strings" attached to Israel's preparedness to help. I have no doubt
that many Africans and Asians alike realize the advantages
inherent in the help coming from a small country like
Israel, which by the natural limitations of its size and population cannot harbor any ulterior motives other than the
building up of good will for itself.

There are perhaps two other reasons for the popularity
of Israel experts in Asia and Africa. One is, that having
learned to solve problems at home often on a "shoe string"
basis, Israel experts are not likely to propose expensive
schemes that are far beyond the possibilities of under-
developed countries. Secondly, Israelis going to Asia or
Africa don't set themselves up as a separate class of highly
paid experts but live the ordinary life of the people they
work with.

It is gratifying to note that Israel is ever anxious to establish normal relations with her immediate neighbors so
that she will be able to export her skill also to countries
nearer home. It is only a matter of time that she will play
her due part in contributing to the common weal. From
that great region of immense historical significance will
rise again the forces of peace, progress and prosperity for
humanity.

SOME REFLECTIONS ON BURMA'S FOREIGN POLICY*

Before I reflect on Burma's foreign policy I think I might start off with a brief outline of certain significant aspects of that policy.

It will be recalled that in the first ten years of Burma's independence, the predominant political party in Burma was the Anti-Fascist Peoples' Freedom League. The AFPFL at its inception was not a party based on ideological foundations. Before independence it was essentially a nationalist organization. Capitalists, socialists, communists and even a sprinkling of feudalists gathered under its banner to fight for national independence. Under the inspiring leadership of General Aung San it was a political front and U Nu's leadership since 1947 has not basically altered its composition. Even before the Communist Party was expelled from this organization and after the Communists went underground after independence, the AFPFL stressed at its annual gatherings the need for a socialistic pattern of planning.

The Right-wingers, mostly out of personal loyalty for U Nu, supported his policies. They still do and this perhaps explains why Burma's policies—both domestic and foreign —are a blend of democratic socialism and meticulous application of Buddhist tenets.

It has long been assumed in the West that the danger to Burmese democracy is from the communists. It was no doubt true at one time, but the situation has altered considerably in the last few years due to a variety of factors chief among which are the rejection of un-Buddhist philosophy of Communism by Burmese Buddhists, dedication of our armed forces under General Ne Win to the princi-

* Address delivered at the South East Asia Seminar at Yale University on April 13, 1961.

ples of parliamentary democracy and Prime Minister U Nu's image of a great Buddhist leader with high moral principles in the minds of the vast majority of the people of Burma.

As soon as Burma regained her independence in January, 1948, she applied for membership of the United Nations, and she was elected the fifty-eighth member on April 19, 1948, without opposition by any member state. Since then Burma showed very keen interest in the activities of the United Nations and associated herself with almost all the decisions arrived at by this world organization. When the United Nations was faced with the greatest crisis of its life in the form of the Korean War, Burma supported the Security Council's action of June 27, 1950. For obvious reasons including her preoccupation with internal disorder, Burma could not render any military assistance to the United Nations contingent in Korea, but she sent four hundred tons of rice as a token gesture of participation in United Nations operations. Burma, along with most of the Asian nations, opposed the crossing of the thirty-eighth parallel and appealed for a cease-fire and a negotiated settlement with the Chinese. At that time it was common knowledge that the Chinese Government had warned the Indian Ambassador at Peking that if the United Nations forces crossed the thirty-eighth parallel, China would enter the war.

Disregarding the warning, the United Nations plunged north, and the Chinese army promptly crossed the Yalu. It will be recalled that three years later the United Nations finally decided to accept a truce at roughly the same thirty-eighth parallel. In the meantime 96,000 additional Americans and no one knows how many Chinese and Koreans had been killed or wounded.

When the Chinese crossed the Yalu the United Nations

General Assembly called for an embargo on the shipment
of war material to China, and Burma, though she ab-
stained from voting and despite her geography, announced
her intention to comply with the request. In this connection it should be remembered that Burma was the first non-
Communist nation to recognize the Peoples' Republic of
China, on December 17, 1949. The primary reason behind
this act was Burma's belief that recognition of a government carries with it no implied approval of the form of
government or of the means by which the government
came into power. Burma has been consistently advocating
for the seating of the representative of the Peoples' Republic of China in the United Nations, since we feel that this
is the only policy based on reality. Our consistent advocacy
of Chinese representation in the United Nations is in no
way based on political or ideological considerations, since
it is well-known that Burma and China have very different
political and ideological backgrounds. If the United Nations is to function as an effective instrument of international conciliation we feel that we can no longer afford to
close its doors to the nation of 650 million people.

Burma hit the headlines in the world's press in March,
1953, when she lodged a formal complaint with the United
Nations on Kuomintang aggression in Burma. It will not
be relevant with the purpose of this address to go into
the history of this aggression, but it will suffice to mention
that as a result of the United Nations action, the United
States and Thailand offered their good offices in repatriating to Formosa about seven thousand Chinese nationalists. In spite of this substantial repatriation, a very large
number of Chinese nationalists still remained in the deep
jungles of eastern Burma. Burmese military operations
against them culminated in the capture of their headquarters early this year and the shooting down of a Chinese

nationalist four-engine plane which was dropping supplies to the marauders in Burmese territory. After representations by the Burmese Government, the United States government cooperated with the Thai government in repatriating more nationalists to Formosa and I understand that evacuation operations are still going on.

Another highlight of Burma's international activity is her cosponsorship of the historic Bandung Conference of April, 1955. This conference was one of Burma's first attempts to practise positive neutralism or non-alignment, one of the basic principles of Burma's foreign policy. Sponsored by Burma, Ceylon, India, Indonesia and Pakistan this conference stands as the first serious and fruitful attempt to find some common ground among the Asian-African nations.

At Bandung, four key issues were thrashed out—colonialism, racism, economic development and peace. On all these issues the 29 participating countries came out with one voice. Premier Chou En-Lai of the Peoples' Republic of China made an immense personal impression at Bandung not only by his moderate approach but also by the skill with which he identified himself with the deepest aspirations of two-thirds of mankind represented there. Although it is not difficult to understand China's identification with the rest of Asia and Africa on issues involving colonialism, racism and economic development, one is apt to doubt China's identity of approach with other countries towards the problem of peace. Surprisingly enough, support for the United Nations was one of the first principles endorsed. Membership in the United Nations, the conference resolved unanimously, should be universal and representation of the Asian-African region on the Security Council was held to be inadequate. The conference even recognized "the right of each nation to defend itself, singly or collectively, in conformity with the Charter of the United Nations," but warned against letting such arrangements for collective defence "serve particular interest of any of the big Powers." The Chinese endorsement of the principle of collective defence pacts under the United Nations is, in my view, one of the most significant features of the Bandung Conference. Premier Chou even endorsed the United Nations Bill of Rights. He agreed to the resolution supporting outside economic aid and capital development. He did not press his claim to the seat held by Nationalist China in the United Nations, and his government was omitted from the list of those whose admission to the United Nations was advocated at Bandung. The keynote of the Bandung Conference was moderation and a surprising degree of unanimity was achieved in the declarations. Tensions were relaxed and representatives of highly divergent political ideologies went on record as favoring closer and friendlier relations.

Burma's activities in the United Nations are a standing testimony of her independent policies. When the question of Hungary came up for discussion Burma took a stand different from that of most of her neutral colleagues of Asia and Africa. Burma is convinced that what occurred in Hungary was essentially a spontaneous nationalist uprising, though there were undoubtedly other elements which made the most of the national struggle for self-determination to further their own ends. Burma also adheres to the view that this nationalist uprising was suppressed by the armed might of the Soviet Union and that a government not of their choice was imposed on the Hungarian people.

Regarding the question of Algerian independence, Burma feels that the crux of the whole problem is political and not military and that any attempt to tackle only the military problem is bound to fail. It is vital that the

Algerian problem should be handled with a view to political reconciliation between France and North African nationalism. Whatever the precise solution, recognition in some form of Algerian nationalism and the legitimacy of Algerian aspiration for independence seems an indispensible starting point for negotiations. The problem of Algeria continues to poison Franco-Moslem relations, to the distress of the Burmese people who want to see happy relations between the two.

On the problem of colonialism Burma stands by the Bandung Declaration. I had occasion to observe on a previous occasion a very true historical maxim: when independence is too long postponed, a mood of frustration and desperation occurs which breeds undesirable traits like bitterness and hatred. If a country has to win independence too late, then some extreme forces come to the surface and become dominant. This certainly does not help the cause of democracy to which most of us are deeply dedicated, nor the cause of friendship and amity between nations.

On the very topical question of the Congo, our Prime Minister told the Burmese Parliament on the 13th March that the United Nations offers the only hope of restoring stability and security to an independent Congo. The Government of the Union of Burma welcomes the Security Council resolution of 21st February authorizing the United Nations Congo command to use force, if necessary, to prevent the occurrence of civil war; calling for the immediate withdrawal from the Congo of all Belgian and other foreign military and para-military personnel and political advisers not under the United Nations' command and the convening of the now immobilized Congolese Parliament and the reorganization of the Congolese armed forces. Burma is also convinced of the imperative necessity of maintaining the territorial integrity and political independence of the Republic of the Congo.

These, in brief, are some of the significant aspects of Burma's foreign policy—or more correctly, Burma's approach to certain foreign problems and developments. Now, let me attempt an analysis of this policy and approach.

Almost all Burmese leaders are firmly convinced that the main obstacle to the settlement of international problems and the achievement of world peace is the persistence of the so-called "cold war," the chief feature of which is the sharp division of the world into two hostile ideological camps, the one suspicious and fearful of the other and both trying to enlist new recruits into their respective camps. Under such conditions, an alignment with either of these two power blocs would do a grievous disservice to the cause of peace. On the other hand, Burma believes that peace cannot be achieved through passive neutralism which would mean a withdrawal from the battle for peace. Hence, Burma has pursued, and continues to pursue, a policy of positive neutrality or complete independence in her approach to problems. The word "neutralism" is often misunderstood and misinterpreted in this country. When we say that Burma is "neutral" we do not mean to imply that Burma is neutral as far as political principles or ideologies are concerned. In the sphere of ideologies Burma is not neutral. Burma is committed to a system of parliamentary democracy; Burma believes in democratic ideals and the dignity of man. And Burma is thoroughly averse to the idea of dictatorship in any shape or form. The dedication to parliamentary democracy and aversion to totalitarianism has been the consistent theme of utterances and actions of the Burmese leaders. They feel rather strongly that the rebuilding of their war-ravaged country must be through democratic processes, that is, by the will and consent of the people. The type of society we are trying to evolve is not patterned after maxims mechanically lifted out of text books. We see to it that its roots are in the Burmese soil, Burmese history, and Burmese background.

In the formulation of our foreign policy too, Burmese geography, Burmese history, Burmese culture and Burmese religion—which is predominantly Buddhist—play a major role. We refuse to believe that totalitarian systems can be obliterated by show of strength or the accumulation of armaments or even by a hot war. Hot wars bring in their train death and destruction, desolation and disease, which have proved the best incentives to the growth of totalitarian regimes. Burma's foreign policy is, therefore, essentially based on the anti-war concept. In the Western world, a profound belief in Russia's potential aggression is the emotional basis of the nuclear deterrent which finds its expression in NATO. It is a belief which holds prisoner so many parlour generals. They cannot see the world of 1961 through the eyes of those who believe that the only alternative to co-existence is no existence. Their eyes are blurred by harsh memories of the past and by their own personal experience of bitter conflict with the communist party line in the political battle field in their own countries.

I believe that no sane nation, and no sane leaders of a nation, can, in today's circumstances of highly developed nuclear weapons seek to risk war by committing aggression. This seems to me particularly true of Russia which is achieving such a rate of scientific and technological progress that she is beginning to demonstrate the superiortiy of a planned and socialist economy. She is certainly not likely to risk her economic and scientific progress for any pros-

pect of territorial gains. She is understandably more occupied with improving the material standards of her people
than with anything else. She must also think, in the context of what seems to be a certain degree of liberalization
and freedom of thought achieved in recent years, of justifying her Marxist philosophy in material terms. For these
reasons, amongst others, there seems good ground for accepting the sincerity of Russian leaders' expression of their
desire for peace.

But there is another deeper factor involved in this basic
difference of attitude between those who believe in peaceful co-existence those who accept the political and international implications of their policy—and those who deeply
distrust Russian intentions. It is the difference between a
faith in the future of mankind—a profound sense of optimism springing, perhaps, from some instinct for living—
and what seems to be a disturbing, deeply-rooted pessimism. It is as though those who support the policy of absolute distrust and suspicion have plunged themselves into
a sea of despair from which there is no escape by drowning.
Those of us who believe in peaceful co-existence as enunciated at Bandung Conference are asserting our hope for
the future. And in doing so, we are demonstrating that
we are committed to our positive belief in humanity.

We believe that those of us who are advocating peaceful
co-existence—the philosophy of live and let live—care passionately about the world. Many of us are the same men
and women who are roused to furious protest against
South Africa for its rabid race policies, and against all explosions of atomic and hydrogen bombs. For it is all part of
the same compassion for humanity and the same commitment to a belief in the future of man which is the
essence of all great religions of the world. The philosophy
of peaceful co-existence is just a reaffirmation of what

Albert Schweitzer has described as "reverence for life." It is an affirmation of community, a mass declaration that human beings must learn to understand one another even if they cannot agree with one another or like one another. It is a challenge to the spiritual corruption of the present society—a society characterised by fear, suspicion, frustration and violence. And of course the nuclear bomb is the most grotesque symbol of violence in our violent society. That's why we protest against its insanity, and we feel we must also protest against the society which needs the bomb.

Both the United States of America and the Soviet Union already have weapons of complete annihilation. If ever they should turn the cold war into real shooting war, sooner or later, by design or by accident, someone will use the most dreadful weapons available. Such a war would mean the annihilation of all that the human race has built, besides the catastrophic end of millions of men, women and children. Such survivors as there might be would envy the dead.

Many leaders and political analysts maintain that a balance of terror will be sufficient to keep nations from using the most terrible weapons of destruction. A theory has been advanced that this sense of fear—fear of retaliation—will at least prevent the big powers from putting an end to human history on this little planet. But this so-called balance of terror can at best produce a very uneasy, precarious and expensive peace. No balance of terror can last indefinitely, since all through history men always have ultimately got what they prepared for. It is characteristic of tensions that sooner or later they break or explode. Therefore, the indefinite continuation of this highly-strung state of tension is bound to end up in disaster.

This leads me on to my next point: Burma's faith in and

reliance on the United Nations. We are in complete agreement with Mr. Dag Hammarskjold, Secretary-General of
the United Nations, when he said that it is the small uncommitted nations, rather than the great powers, which
need the protection the United Nations can give. Here,
then is common ground between the uncommitted nations and the Western powers, which by now can surely
agree that their interests are adequately served if the independence of states is assured on a basis of non-com-
mitment to any military bloc. If the West were to set about
strengthening United Nations authority upon the basis of
this widely shared common interest, the possibility of
effective United Nations intervention for the peaceful resolution of dangerous situations will be greatly increased.
Disarmament provides an additional reason why the West
should try to prepare the United Nations for a more positive role. Agreed disarmament, which all the major governments profess to want, requires as its inescapable condition the establishment of an international authority with
substantial powers. To do so, the first pre-requisite is confidence. The build-up of confidence can succeed only if the
United Nations is made to reflect adequately the interests
and aspirations of its new membership. In particular, it
must make room for proper Asian and African representation in the Security Council, the Economic and Social
Council and elsewhere, and this in turn involves a change
in Western policy over the seating of China.

A substantial section of Western opinion at present
shows unnecessary nervousness about the role which a
strong United Nations might play, now that African and
Asian votes are so numerous in the organization. In fact,
these new members largely share Western political ideas,
and are rarely attracted by the dogmas of the totalitarian
creeds except when they suspect the West of neo imperalist

designs. With some imagination the West could find in the building up of the United Nations authority a common platform with these newly emerging nations, for many of whom this would be the best guarantee of their independence. For the Western powers it would be the rational sequel in world politics to their renunciation of national control over their empires. It would, moreover, pave the way for new techniques of international control, which even the greatest powers are beginning to need in our age of nuclear destruction.

### WORLD TENSIONS AND INTERNATIONAL MISUNDERSTANDING*

I certainly deem it a great privilege to have this opportunity of addressing the 19th summer session of Elementary School Principals, National Association of Secondary School Principals and the University of Wisconsin. The theme of this session is "World Tensions and Education" and it has been suggested that I deal with the subject: "World Tensions and International Misunderstanding."

At the outset let me confess that a diplomat has very great limitations in dealing with such a subject. He is not very free to speak his mind like one who is not restricted by formal briefings by his government, as he is required to observe certain set rules of protocol. As you are no doubt aware, an ambassador is expected to be correct in what he says or does, and any infringement of this recognized principle is considered as a breach of diplomatic privilege. In these circumstances, whenever I was called upon to speak on international relations or tensions, it has always been my endeavour to confine my remarks within the four cor-

* Address delivered at the 19th Summer Conference of the Elementary and Secondary School Principals, NEA, at the University of Wisconsin, July, 6, 1961.

ners of my government's set policy and statements. In other words I have always attempted to reflect the views of my government in my approach to and analysis of the issues I am expected to deal with.

In the present case I feel more at ease. Being associated with the educational development of my country for a number of years before the war—as a principal of a high school and as a member of the Council of National Education—I feel quite at home whenever I find myself in the midst of teachers and educators, as I am here today. I feel rather strongly that teachers in any country have as important a role to play for their country as any other type of citizens including politicians and diplomats. My association with the service of education in Burma for about twenty years and my continued interest in the development of education both in my own country and elsewhere prompt me at all times to view things from the point of view of a teacher, and my concept of the role of a teacher may perhaps be of some interest to you.

In this second half of the twentieth century, I consider that the primary task of the educationist everywhere is to dispel certain age-old assumptions. I am bringing in this element because it is directly concerned with some aspects of international misunderstanding which is the topic of my address. It seems to be assumed that there is one civilization in the East and quite a different one in the West, resulting in seeds of tension or conflict between peoples of different geographical regions. I consider this concept to be a fallacy. The distinction of civilization into Eastern and Western seems to me almost meaningless. Moreover, I would seriously question whether tension or conflict between one people and another ever arises from any conflicting viewpoints in their respective cultures or civilizations. England and France or France and Germany may be said to share the same civilization and yet there have been frequent conflicts between them. The same can be said of many Asian countries who share the same civilization and profess the same religion and who have been at war off and on for centuries. I feel strongly that conflicts between nations or individuals generally arise, not out of viewpoints in their civilization, nor from reasons of their traditions and history, but from uncivilized elements in their character.

The term "civilization" is very hard to define, but men are civilized or uncivilized in respect of certain qualities of their heart. Civilization connotes some mental and spiritual excellence, just as health means a certain physical excellence. Health does not mean one thing for an American and another for a Burman. Similarly civilization should mean one and the same thing for all. The so-called difference civilizations mean either the different stages in our approximation to the ideal of civilization or else the different expressions which civilization has found for itself in different circumstances.

When we speak of the civilization of a country we are apt to suppose that all the people of the country are civilized more or less the same way, but really the different individuals of the same country are not civilized in the same way or to the same extent. A civilized Burman will not differ essentially from a civilized American, but they will differ widely from their relatively uncivilized compatriots in their own countries. By this I do not of course mean that our cultural standards are identical. When I first came to the United States I was rather shocked by the public embracing in city parks and the American habit—though not widespread—of treating a parked car as a bedroom. Such behavior would be inconceivable in Burma. Perhaps an American tourist in Burma would be equally shocked to know that there is no "dating" system among young men and women and that it is considered indecent for a woman to touch a man who is not her husband. These are concerned with cultural and sexual *mores* rather than with civilization, and the explanation is that the Burmese society is still Puritan although of course this society is in the process of throwing off its Puritanism. Sexual emotions, traditionally checked by Buddhist asceticism are now spilling over aimlessly, because of our increasing contacts with the West.

Another striking feature of our times is the amount and nature of sex in America—and for that matter Western literature—which is inconceivable in the Burmese world of letters. One would have thought that by now the twentieth century rediscovery of the physical aspect of the subject as a literary theme would have spent its force, but not at all. I have recently had to look through a few "best sellers" and I have emerged with the impression of having spent some time in a specialised hospital ward. It appears to me that there is a sort of high tide in sex which is not really connected with literary values. I notice that this epidemic is gradually catching on in Burma too both in the fields of literature and screen and this phenomenon is greatly resented by the traditionalists as alien invasion of Burmese culture.

I am bringing out these instances to illustrate certain areas of cultural conflict between East and West. In the East, traditionally we attach more importance to mind than to body and still more to spirit than to mind. In fact one man is considered better than another in attaching more importance to the higher parts of his nature. One of the most important tasks of the teacher, as I understand it, is to bring to clear consciousness the ideals for which men should live. Education cannot mean merely the development of our intellect or potentialities, because there are potentialities for good in us as well as for evil. Nor can it mean mere preparation for life, because life may be worth living or not. Our educators must realize as clearly as possible what kind of potentialities they are to develop in the students, what kind of life they are to educate the young people for. The ideals which constitute the essential elements of culture must first be clearly understood and appreciated. But all are not equally qualified to pursue the highest ideals. For many people, mere health or physical well-being is a good enough ideal; some aim at moral and intellectual excellence and still fewer can aspire after higher spirituality. In a well-ordered society, there should be room for people of different ideals.

Perhaps I have devoted too much time on the cultural aspects of education, but I feel that a deeper understanding of different cultural *mores* will contribute towards the elimination of international misunderstanding, and in this field teachers can play a significant role. Though the differences in cultural values do not actually constitute tensions, they are pertinent to our consideration of other areas of tension with which I will deal now.

Dictionaries define the term "tension" as "a strained condition of relations." It is a commonplace of observation that strained relations between different races is a distressing phenomenon not only of our times but of all times. They have generated tensions for times immemorial, but in the last few decades this relationship has assumed new characteristics for a variety of reasons. One of them is the phenomenal growth of knowledge and education among the less fortunate races and their yearning for justice and equality.

As our Prime Minister U Nu said on his visit to Independence Hall in Philadelphia six years ago, the ideas and ideals, the ringing words and slogans of the American Revolution, have a tremendous emotional importance to all men who struggle for liberty. U Nu said, "In all parts of the world where man lives under tyranny, or under foreign domination, or in feudal bondage, those who dream and plot and fight for freedom do so in the name of the eternal principles for which your revolution was fought. In those parts of the world the ideas of the American Revolution are today the most explosive of all forces ... that is why I was so very anxious to visit your city and this hall and to see this great symbol of human freedom—the Liberty Bell."

U Nu spoke for millions of other peoples when he said this. Among other things the United States of America symbolises human freedom and human equality, but this image has been greatly tarnished by reports of violent racial conflicts in the deep south. Understandably, these happenings have tremendous repercussions abroad, especially in non-white countries of Asia and Africa, and they create tensions which are in many ways more explosive than political or cold war tensions.

One may well argue that over the years race relations in the United States of America have been peaceful and harmonious, but this peace and harmony has been only the absence of overt tension rather than the presence of justice which your great country stands for. The "Freedom Riders" journeying to the south are looked upon in Asia and Africa as the champions for the American negroe's holy war for freedom. It is obvious that their struggle is not purely a racial one; it has profound political implications. The traditional battleground of fighters for civil rights in this country for many years has been the courts of law. But court victories are only limited victories, since Congress has consistently refused to endorse them by passing law-enforcement legislation. Therefore, to fight in the courts is considered ineffectual, and more important, it is also to limit the negroes' goal to the integration of specific institutions rather than to the political revolution that would transform the institutions.

The fighters for racial equality have, in the last three years, changed their strategy. In 1958, 30,000 young men and women marched on Washington; last year lunch-counter sit-in demostrations were organized and now we are witnessing "freedom rides." These developments are transitions from the old law court strategy to the new strategy of mass direct action. From available news reports, the next strategy will be mass sit-downs not at lunch counters or in bus waiting rooms but at the polling stations. I have a feeling that in no distant future the battle for enfranchisement will supersede the battle for integration. Most Western democracies have travelled the road to universal suffrage, often with considerable class warfare, in the nineteenth century, and the Southern States will walk the same road, I hope, without serious blemishes on the image of the United States.

Mr. Edward R. Murrow, head of the United States Information Agency, was quite right when he said last week that the violence against Freedom Riders in Alabama had had a harmful effect on the American image abroad. In his testimony before the House Committee on Education and Labour, Mr. Murrow said, "This agency's job of counteracting the detrimental effects of civil rights violations is not easy. We cannot make good news out of bad practice." He then went on, "I think it would be a mistake to base our action against discrimination mainly on the ground that our image abroad is being hurt. We should attack this problem because it is right that we do so. To do otherwise, whatever the overseas reaction might be, would violate the very essence of what our country stands for."

These are wise words in keeping with the highest ideals of the United States. They truly reflect the spirit of your Constitution which is clearly designed to secure equality and personal liberty to all your peoples and to ensure political, economic and social justice. As one who feels very close to the ideas and ideals cherished by your Constitution, and as one who is distressed to see your image tarnished, I would appeal to the great American people, especially the educators and leaders of thought, to help in the acceleration of the common objectives of justice and equality.

World tensions which have now assumed a very serious character are, however, not related to cultural conflicts or racial conflicts. They are born out of different political ideologies and are basically psychological and emotional. As I have made it clear earlier, Burma is dedicated to democratic ideals and a parliamentary system of government. We in Burma look upon free institutions as not only the most desirable of political systems but also as those most congenial to the flowering of human genius. We are deeply attached to the democratic way of life and fundamental freedom such as freedom of speech and expression, freedom of work, freedom of association and freedom of religion. But, this dedication and this attachment to the democratic way of life does not blind us to the fact that there are millions of others who believe otherwise. As we believe that the State exists to secure the conditions of a free and full life for the individual, others believe that the individual exists for the service of the State. We must also remember that in many countries democracy is not functioning well. In too many cases it is merely a mask, behind which organized class interests wield real power.

The truth is that democracy is a very difficult system to work, because it involves the harmonizing of many wills, whereas dictatorship is an easy system to work, since it involves the forcible subjection of all *wills* to one. Whatever its defects, the democratic system has two great compensating virtues. It substitutes reason and persuasion for force in the management of human affairs; and it makes possible a change of government without a violent upheaval.

When Burma regained her independence on the 4th January, 1948, she chose democracy for the reasons I have set out. But in choosing democracy our leaders realized that there was the need to change the economic pattern of society. Americans are conservative because they are wealthy and see no reason for change. Even if President Kennedy's programs of domestic reforms were accepted in full, it would hardly do more than drag the United States reluctantly into the position of where Britain was half a century ago. Social revolution is not an obsession with the Americans because an affluent society like theirs do not need, at least at present, a social revolution. But countries like Burma are in a totally different category. Burma is a land of great natural resources but her people are poor. The chief reason is that Burma was a colony for over a hundred years, and as in the case of all colonial systems, almost all the wealth extracted from the soil has gone into the pockets of the colonial investors. As you all know, the primary motive of all colonial powers in developing the natural resources of a colony has been their own commercial profit.

So, when Burma became independent the primary concern of our leaders was to rebuild the war-devastated country and to raise the living standards of the people. Our leaders felt that to accelerate these objectives, planned economic systems must be introduced, and we chose to adopt a type of democratic socialism which has even been embodied in our Constitution.

It is not my intention to weary you with a discourse on the character of Democratic Socialism, but a deeper understanding of this system by Americans will certainly help to dispel a great deal of misunderstanding in this country regarding social revolutions taking place elsewhere. It is a fact that the American tendency is to identify capitalism not only with democracy but with virtue itself and any form of socialism is seen as a threat to democracy.

Our leaders who have chosen Democratic Socialism as our guiding principle are convinced that pure unadulterated capitalism is not the remedy for Burma's ills. For one thing, so long as profit is the driving force in our economy, money available for investment will be invested in those undertakings which will give the greatest profit, not in those which our country needs most. Secondly, Burma cannot accept the theory that wealth should still give access to the best education, and to positions of influence and power. It has been our experience during the colonial days that those whose income is the least and whose education is the poorest, and who therefore need the most help from society are those who get the least. Thirdly, our leaders feel strongly that there is something wicked about a system of society in which a successful trader can make a fortune but a successful teacher has to strike before he gets an adequate reward. These are some of the basic considerations which have prompted the Burmese leaders to choose Democratic Socialism. Similar systems have been adopted in many other newly-independent underdeveloped countries, and it will certainly help in the promotion of international understanding if genuine efforts are made to appreciate these trends. I need hardly add that Burma is still a long way from her set goal of Democratic Socialism. For practical reasons, private sector still plays a very significant part in our economy although public utility services, transport and communication are now in the public sector. Foreign capital is still being invited to operate in Burma with specific guarantees against nationalization for a certain number of years.

Now, let me deal with the so-called "cold war" which is the most glaring manifestation of world tensions. It relates to East-West relations. It is a commonplace of observation that there is a deep and intense anti-communist feeling in the United States, as there was a deep and intense anti-Islam feeling in Christendom and deep and intense anti-Christian feeling in Asia Minor at the time of the Crusades many centuries ago. Communism is generally regarded here as an absolute evil as the Crusaders and the Saracens regarded one another. It is perhaps an expression of original American isolationism which saw in all foreign influence a threat to the new Republic. This tendency is fed by daily articles and cartoons in the American press, by radio and by television. Although this anti-communism cannot be called hysteria, it is a dogma deeply held and sincerely believed. Co-existence with such an absolute evil is hardly imaginable.

My feeling is that most Americans ignore the real nature of the enemy they claim to be fighting. Communism is not a disease like plague or cholera that can be stamped out by force. Most Americans seem to think that if only they can keep on supplying machine guns and tanks to the hungry people of Asia and Africa, communism will be "contained." The general feeling here is that communism can be crushed by arms. But the plain fact is that communism is an idea however we may detest it, and it is one of the most persuasive ideas for the poor and the underprivileged. Mr. Khrushchev, for instance, takes for granted, as the air he breathes, that the world is seized by a world-wide revolutionary movement, opposed by the West, encouraged by the Soviet Union, but so strong and inevitable that there is nothing one could do to arrest its progress.

It is a fact that there are millions of people in the world, especially in Asia, Africa and Latin America, who do not have enough to eat and enough to cover themselves with, and whose children cannot even go to the primary schools. It seems comic to talk to them about the virtues of democratic ideals and the dignity of man. What is urgently needed is to take vigorous steps by the wealthy West to raise the living standards of these sub-human two-thirds of the world's population. And it is fundamentally wrong to keep on sending machine guns and tanks to the countries of empty stomachs. During his recent tour of South East Asia, Vice-President Lyndon B. Johnson gave warning that America's Asian allies must cooperate with the United States to bring economic and social benefits to their own millions and not, as he has since added in Washington, to "dictators and aristocrats". His announced enemies were not Communism but poverty, disease and illiteracy. This attitude certainly reflects a major change of United States' traditional policy, and I for one welcome it.

At a news conference on 22nd June, Secretary of State Dean Rusk said that "the full amount of President Kennedy's $26 billion foreign aid program for the next five years was essential to the survival of this nation and the free world." He added that the United States and the free world must channel the growing world revolution into constructive economic programmes.

On the same day Under Secretary of State Mr. George W. Ball told the House Foreign Affairs Committee, "What has not been said often enough is that, if the ambitions and expectations of the newly emergent peoples are frustrated, if they find progress is a delusion, and decent life seems unattainable, then disappointment will lead to bitterness,

bitterness will breed chaos, and they will be swept inexorably into the Communist orbit."

These are certainly heartening trends in United States' Foreign policy. In this connection I want to make a passing reference to the gigantic expenditure proposed to be spent in "the race to the moon." It is understandable that President Kennedy should wish to maintain the morale and prestige of the American people by competing to reach the moon. It is certainly less dangerous that the United States should engage in a technological prestige race with Russia than in arms race pure and simple. But the two activities are dangerously near to each other, particularly in the hearts of the people. It is also wantonly costly in comparison with any tangible results it can be expected to achieve.

Many eminent scientists consider that the United States stands to lose in this new competition. The Russians invented this race because they thought they would win it. They have a head start, and many experts think that the gap cannot be closed in many years, however much is spent.

But even if America wins, what then? It will of course hearten the Americans, and millions of people in other lands, but its political effects are far more doubtful. No sensible person can believe that an American on the moon will make all hungry nations come flocking to the American flag. What is more, the race will have to go on, and its cost will go up by leaps and bounds. If these billions of precious dollars could be utilized for raising the living standards of the sub-humans, the United States would help in creating a more sane and sensible world. A well-planned, imaginative and properly executed economic aid programme alone can keep the under-developed countries safe for democracy and reduce existing tensions.

The most serious source of world tension today is the division of the world into rich nations and poor nations. This division of the world is more real, more lasting and ultimately more explosive even than that between Communists and non-Communists. In the cold war which is being waged relentlessly by East and West, both believe that they can still win it while avoiding nuclear war. Both have the strength given by faith and material resources. Premier Khrushchev believes in the "inevitability of Communism." President Kennedy believes that "democracy is the destiny of future humanity." President Kennedy will be right if the wealthy West which generally represents the forces of democracy can read the signs of the times.

## STATEMENT IN THE GENERAL ASSEMBLY*

Since this is my first intervention in the general debate, let me take this opportunity of extending through you, Sir, the very warm felicitations of my delegation to Mr. Boland on his election as President of the fifteenth regular session of the General Assembly. His election is a clear manifestation of the very high esteem in which the Members of the United Nations have placed him personally and the courageous and virile country of Ireland which he represents.

The proceedings in this Assembly are the focus of extraordinary attention all over the world, both for the extreme urgency of most of the problems listed on the agenda and for the participation in its work by a number of distinguished Heads of State or of Government.

This session is also highlighted by a feature of very great historical significance: the admission among us of seven-

---

* Statement before the Fifteenth Session of the General Assembly of the United Nations, New York, October 10, 1960.

teen new states—sixteen African states and Cyprus—all of which recently won their independence. On behalf of the people and the Government of the Union of Burma, I wholeheartedly welcome their admission and offer to them our very sincere congratulations on their newly won status. The emergence of these new states in Asia and Africa and their membership in the United Nations will certainly enhance the authority and effectiveness of this world Organization.

At the outset, let me reiterate Burma's firm conviction that the main obstacle to the settlement of international problems and the achievement of a genuine world peace is the unmitigated persistence of the so-called cold war, the chief feature of which is the sharp division of the world into two hostile ideological camps, the one suspicious and fearful of the other, and both scrambling to entice new recruits into their respective ranks. Under such conditions an alignment with either of these two power blocs would do a grievous disservice to the cause of peace. On the other hand, Burma believes that peace cannot be achieved through passive neutralism, which would mean a withdrawal from the battle for peace. Hence, Burma has consistently pursued, and continues to pursue, a policy of strict but active neutrality. However, Burma does not aim at setting up a new grouping of neutral or unaligned States, for, by the very nature of things, this would mean bloc policy, which in turn would result in a further splitting of an already divided world.

Once again, the fifteenth session of the General Assembly opens in an atmosphere of increased tension. We are now witnessing a general deterioration in international relations, especially among the great powers, and the protracted disarmament negotiations have yielded very little result. The Summit Conference, on which the entire world had placed such great hope, collapsed before it could get started. As all of us are aware, different reasons have been assigned for the collapse of the Summit Conference. The Soviet Union and its allies put the blame entirely on the flight of the United States U-2 aircraft over Soviet territory and to the United States Government's assumption of responsibility for it. The United States and its allies maintain that the U-2 flight was used only as an excuse, and that the Soviet Union had never any intention of letting the Summit Conference succeed. The Prime Minister of the Union of Burma, U Nu, in the course of his statement before our Chamber of Deputies on 22 September this year, observed:

As we understand it, the U-2 flight constitutes a violation of international law. The American justification for the flight is new, and to us unconvincing. Having said this, however, we are bound to add that the U-2 flight, in our view, did not justify calling off the Summit Conference. As a peace-loving country, we deeply regret these unhappy developments. All the patient and painstaking endeavours of years by eminent statesmen throughout the world—and among them I deliberately include Premier Khrushchev and President Eisenhower—to reduce to practical day to day terms the truism that there is no alternative to peaceful coexistence, were swept away when the Summit Conference collapsed. With it, the possibility of armed conflict has correspondingly increased.

The collapse of the Summit Conference, of course, disrupted negotiations on disarmament, which is the most pressing problem of our time. My delegation associates itself wholeheartedly with the resolution adopted by the Disarmament Commission calling on all those concerned to resume negotiations on general and complete disarmament. We believe it to be of paramount importance that effective contact should never be broken among those most directly concerned with this pressing problem.

Against the background of this gloomy situation, a silver

lining is discernible. It is a fact that a fair measure of agreement has been reached on matters of principle as well as of substance. Agreement has been reached on several aspects of the nuclear test control and every endeavor should be made to pursue this progress, both in and outside the United Nations. A willingness to accept the other side's good faith is as great a stride forward to peace as a signed treaty itself. A ban on testing, which will halt the arms race, is an essential preliminary to a disarmament agreement. Such a ban was at one time in sight, and we were heartened that the big powers had begun to speak the same language. There was hope in the air, but the collapse of the Summit Conference once again poisoned the atmosphere.

The disarmament problem changes its character with every day that passes. Once it could be framed in terms of the existing nuclear powers getting rid of their nuclear weapons. Now it is becoming a question of preventing potential nuclear powers from manufacturing nuclear weapons at all. The people's Republic of China is now the most important of these powers. Even without outside assistance, China is almost certain, in the absence of political agreements, to have its own bomb within a couple of years. In the light of these facts, the rejection by this General Assembly last Saturday, 8 October, of even the inscription on the agenda of an item on the representation of China at the United Nations is a demonstration of our inability to read the signs of the times and our refusal to face realities.

Modern diplomacy is in most cases a series of conditioned reflexes. Whatever proposals come from Moscow or Peking are sure to be denounced by the West as propaganda. And whenever the West comes up with a really worth-while proposal, it often gets the same treatment from its antagonists. This is regrettably true of the very

abrupt Western dismissal of Premier Chou En-lai's statement last July that China would be prepared to conclude a
peace pact that would clear Asia and the Pacific of nuclear
weapons. As the Latin Americans are very desirous of maintaining peace in their region, and as the Africans are very
anxious to keep their region free from big power rivalries,
most Asians also welcome any move from any quarter to
keep Asia free from military entanglements. In this
context, Premier Chou En-lai's statement that there must
be created in the Far East and in the whole Pacific area a
zone of peace, free from atomic weapons, deserves very
close attention. There is no need to go into the merits of
the proposal as such. A non-nuclear Pacific would be a
greater step towards a peaceful world than a nuclear Pacific, in view of the fact that China has very great poten-
tials for the manufacture of atomic weapons, and the
United States of America is already a leading nuclear
power.

One may very well question if China is sincere. It seems
to my delegation that it is a pointless question, since the
word "sincerity" has long been dropped from the vocabu-
lary of diplomacy. The only criterion that should be applied to Peking's proposal is the more reliable one of
whether it serves China's long-term interests. It is obvious
that China cannot afford, with her very ambitious industrial revolution and all the colossal cost it entails, to become a nuclear Power also. Development in the one field
implies some retardation in the other, in view of the vast
handicaps it has to go through. The best way for the West
to find out if Premier Chou En-lai was indulging in mere
propaganda or not would be to take his proposals at their
face value and initiate discussions on them.

Let me now deal with the situation in Algeria, which
continues to cause deep concern throughout the world.

Many representatives who preceded me have dealt with
the problem more or less comprehensively, and therefore I
will not attempt to narrate the events which took place
since the question came up before the fourteenth session of
the General Assembly. The hostilities continue unabated
with grievous suffering and loss of human life. Over a
million Algerians remain displaced and regrouped in
various parts of Algeria. Impartial observers have testified
to the hardship and distress of the Algerians detained in
internment camps and prisons. The situation indeed continues to embitter international relations and increase
international tensions, thereby constituting a threat to the
peace of the world. Therefore, on 20 July of this year,
twenty-five Asian-African nations, including Burma, requested the inscription of the question of Algeria on the
agenda of this session.

While dramatic changes have taken place in what was
once called French Africa, the problem of Algeria, to our
regret, still remains unsolved. It will be recalled that in
September 1958, eighteen French territories, not including
Algeria, were each given the offer of, first, full integration
with France as a "Department" of the French Republic,
second, retention of its present territorial status, with the
right to representation in the French Parliament as hitherto; or, third, membership in the new Community as a
fully autonomous unit. This offer was made on the condition that rejection of the Constitution by any territory
would mean its immediate secession and the cutting off of
all French assistance. Of the eighteen territories offered
this choice, Guinea rejected the Constitution, thereby
severing its connection with France completely. The
remaining seventeen all approved the Constitution, and of
them, twelve chose to become autonomous units within
the French community. The other five, consisting mainly

of small territories, decided to maintain the status quo. Of these, only one is in Africa, this being French Somaliland. The French Community, it will be noticed, fell short of the British Commonwealth, where it is possible for a completely independent State to remain a member of the British Commonwealth. Earlier this year, the Constitution was amended and the French Community of today is, in all essentials, similar to the British Commonwealth, all its members being independent and equal in status.

I recount these facts just to highlight the contrast between the French treatment of Algeria and other of its colonies. The smooth transition from the French Union to the French Community and the revision of the Constitution of the Community to meet the requirements of the present era reflect President de Gaulle's realistic and statesmanlike handling of the problem of its colonies. However, the President's handling of the Algerian problem is far from gratifying. While the President has not abandoned the principle of self-determination, which this world Organization has advocated, he has emptied the word "self-determination" of all its meaning.

It is certainly regrettable that the Government of France is now engaged in two wars, both equally far from glorious. In Algeria, it fights the Algerian nationalists. In France, it is fighting French editors, writers and intellectuals. And so far, it has won more victories on the second front. Since April of this year, several French newspapers and journals have been seized; several books and publications banned or confiscated and authors arrested. Its successes in defending its honour against unarmed writers, however, is poor compensation for its continued failure to defeat the Algerian nationalists in Algeria. After six years of pacification, the Algerian nationalist forces are stronger, better organized and better equipped than ever.

The great danger, of course, is that countries, not only adjacent ones to Algeria, but others, may be sucked into the Algerian war if it continues. Algeria, in fact, is no longer a French problem, nor even an Algerian problem; prolonged war has turned the country into an international powder keg. Either President de Gaulle offers proper negotiations on the necessary guarantees for self-determination to the Algerian nationalists, or the war will be intensified, and more and more of Africa will be drawn into the blood bath. No African government, however desirous of good relations with France, will be able to maintain even official neutrality much longer.

The indications are that the war will be resumed even more fiercely and bloodshed will increase. There is now a vast chasm between the President and the Algerian nationalists struggling for their birthright of independence. The President wants negotiations only on the issue of a ceasefire and envisages self-determination in the form of elections under the supervision of French armed forces. The Algerian nationalists understandably cannot accept these conditions. It is difficult to imagine that the Algerian nationalists, after six years of revolution against the French, would ever agree to exercise their vote under the sole control of the French army. The only way out of this impasse seems to be to seek to implement the principle of self-determination through the agency of some form of international action. However, my delegation still entertains the hope that the two parties concerned will enter into pourparlers, which has been the general consensus of opinion in this world Organization, before any internationally supervised referendum is envisaged. President de Gaulle, who is responsible for France's great achievements in other parts of Africa, can surely evolve a formula for Algeria, a formula based on the same principle of self-determination that has been applied to the other territories.

The developments in the Republic of the Congo have graver implications for the United Nations than anything that has gone before. It will be recalled that the original purpose of its intervention was to replace the Belgian troops and to hold the fort while order was being restored. The United Nations forces had neither the mandate nor the responsibility to cope with the next phase—the growing internecine strife among the Congolese, which from time to time assumed the character of civil war. This strife, at one time, threatened to become an international conflict. It is a matter for gratification that many leaders of independent African States, with full consciousness of the gathering war clouds over the heart of the African continent, which they rightly feel to be their own, rallied to the help of the United Nations and averted a major catastrophe.

Events in the Republic of the Congo will no doubt have their impact on the evolution of other African States, and the United Nations operations there are a test of how far this world Organization can contribute towards the restoration of law and order in the new Republic. The United Nations involvement in the Republic of the Congo must be viewed as a test case for this Organization. Its future is certainly at stake. My delegation wishes to see the United Nations making a perceptable advance towards the conception of a world order. If it fails to make any headway in its primary task of restoring law and order in the young Republic, then the Organization is likely to relapse into immobility and impotency, as experienced at one time by its predecessor, the League of Nations, before its total collapse. My delegation, therefore, considers it essential that the present enterprise should not be allowed to break down. We feel that the United Nations must, in some sense, assert its legitimate authority in the Republic of the Congo, or lapse into humiliating passivity.

In assessing the success or otherwise of the United Nations operations in the Congo, we must look at the results in the context of the tangled events of the past few weeks. It will be recalled that the breaking point in the situation was reached about the middle of August. By that time the United Nations Emergency Force had virtually secured the primary objective for which it had been sent there: the Belgian troops had left, although there are still indications that many of them have come back as technicians, and a United Nations contingent had established itself in Katanga. The terms given to the Secretary-General by the Security Council had been fulfilled, and my delegation has every confidence that the Secretary-General is sincerely and efficiently discharging his functions assigned by the United Nations. We have noted that each time any controversy arose about his Congo mandate, the Secretary-General referred the dispute back to the Security Council. We are satisfied that all his authority is solely based on the decisions of the Security Council.

In these circumstances, my delegation does not see any need at present to modify his office or his functions or to reorganize his Secretariat. Any such course is not only bound to retard the efficiency of the United Nations operations, but is sure to weaken the Organization itself.

The world has never so desperately needed an organization whose existence expresses not a Utopian fantasy but the biggest international reality of all. It symbolizes humanity's collective need for peace for the sake of survival, a need which overrides the national or ideological interests of any Member State.

The Congo affair has marked the start of a new phase in

the evolution of the United Nations. It is our fervent hope that it will emerge as the world's indispensable agency to pour oil on troubled waters. We must admit that the world is entering a period of acute crisis, with the cold war at its peak, but the most interesting and perhaps hopeful sign is that all significant campaigns involved in the cold war are being fought out in the United Nations. The gathering at this momentous session of the General Assembly of an unprecedented number of Heads of State or of Government itself is a tribute to the new importance of the United Nations forum in world affairs.

# II

## As Secretary-General of the United Nations

# 1

# Acceptance Speeches at the United Nations

AS ACTING SECRETARY-GENERAL*

Speaking for the first time in this Hall, not in my familiar role as the delegate from Burma, but in the role of Acting Secretary-General of the United Nations, my first thought is to thank my fellow delegates for the honor they have done me, and the confidence they have placed in me, in electing me to this high office. May I at the same time thank you, Sir, for your very gracious words of welcome, as also the President and the Members of the Security Council for unanimously recommending my name to the General Assembly for election as Acting Secretary-General.

Most of my colleagues present in this Hall know me personally. They know that I come from a relatively small country in Asia. They also know that my country has steadfastly pursued over the years a policy of nonalignment, and friendship for all other nations whatever their ideologies. In my new role, I shall continue to maintain this attitude of objectivity, and to pursue the ideal of universal friendship.

* Statement at the United Nations on November 3, 1961.

Having been the Permanent Representative of my country to the United Nations for the last four years and more, I am not unaware of the heavy responsibilities I am undertaking today. The debates in the General Assembly have already shown that the international climate can hardly be described as sunny. The Organization is also facing a serious financial problem. In the Congo operation, which is one of the major undertakings in the history of the Organization, we continue to encounter serious difficulties which clamor for an urgent solution.

If I am to discharge these responsibilities, surmount these difficulties, and resolve these problems, I shall need, in the first instance, the wholehearted support, friendly understanding, and unstinting cooperation of all my colleagues. I have enjoyed such friendly cooperation from you all for so long as a delegate that I would fain hope that in my new role I shall receive it in even greater measure. For my part, I shall endeavor to cooperate with you all in every possible way.

In addition to your cooperation, I shall also need the loyal support of my colleagues in the Secretariat. I know how hard the Secretariat has had to work during the last 16 months, especially in connection with the Congo operation. The Secretariat has shown itself capable of meeting all demands on it so far, and I count on the continued assistance and team-spirit of my colleagues in the Secretariat, especially in the difficult days ahead that we shall face together.

In particular, it is my intention to invite a limited number of persons who are at present Under-Secretaries, or to be appointed as Under-Secretaries, to act as my principal advisers on important questions pertaining to the performance of functions entrusted to the Secretary-General by the United Nations Charter.

In extending this invitation, I am fully conscious of the paramount consideration of securing the highest standards of efficiency, competence and integrity, and with due regard to the importance of as wide a geographical basis as possible, as laid down in Article 101 of the Charter. I intend to include among these advisers Dr. Ralph J. Bunche and Mr. Georgy Petrovitch Arkadev.

It is also my intention to work together with these colleagues in close collaboration and consultation in a spirit of mutual understanding. I am sure that they will seek to work with me in the same manner.

Of course this whole arrangement is without prejudice to such future organizational changes as experience may reveal to be necessary.

Mr. President, once again I thank you, my fellow delegates in this Hall, and the President and members of the Security Council for entrusting me with these heavy responsibilities. In discharging these responsibilities, I shall count on the support of all men and women of good will all over the world, whose overriding interest in the peace, security and progress of the world it will be my task to reflect and serve.

## AS SECRETARY-GENERAL*

Exactly fifty-six weeks ago today I assumed what was to me an unfamiliar role, as Acting Secretary-General of the United Nations. Today the General Assembly has done me the further honour of appointing me to serve out the normal term of five years as Secretary-General of the United Nations, beginning with my assumption of the office as Acting Secretary-General on 3 November 1961.

* Statement at the United Nations on November 30, 1962.

I am grateful to you, Mr. President, for your gracious words, to the President and Members of the Security Council for their unanimous recommendation, and to the General Assembly for my unanimous appointment as Secretary-General. I deeply appreciate and value this mark of your confidence in me, which I shall endeavour my utmost to justify and deserve.

On this occasion, I would recall the words of my distinguished predecessor on his re-election to a second term. He said, and I quote: "Nobody, I think, can accept the position of Secretary-General of the United Nations, knowing what it means, except from a sense of duty."

He had had over four years experience in that office when he made that statement. My experience has been shorter, but I believe that I do know what that office means, and I accept my extended mandate with humility and out of a sense of duty.

I also take this occasion to re-affirm my oath of office, and I solemnly swear to exercise in all loyalty, discretion and conscience the functions entrusted to me as Secretary-General of the United Nations, to discharge these functions and regulate my conduct with the interests of the United Nations only in view, and not to seek or accept instructions in regard to the performance of my duties from any government or other authority external to the Organization.

At the same time, I enter upon this fresh period of service to the international community with a due sense of responsibility. When I was questioned on this subject at a press conference just before the present session of the General Assembly began, I stated that my decision to accept the position of Secretary-General for a longer term would "be governed primarily by a few considerations, including an early settlement of the Congo problem, the prospect of stability of this world organisation as a potent force for peace, the prospect of my playing a humble part in bringing about a more favourable atmosphere for the easing of tensions, and if I may say so, the prospect of my ability to bridge somewhat the gulf between the two giants."

If I now accept this extended term, it is because I do believe that I may be able to play a role, however humble, in the easing of tensions and in bridging the gulf between the major powers. In this task, I shall count upon the assistance of my colleagues in the Secretariat, high and low, who have, as always, shown a truly admirable team spirit, marked by ungrudging effort, willing co-operation, unflagging devotion to duty and dedication to the high purposes of the Charter. Without their assistance I could not have achieved much during the last year, and I wish to take this opportunity to pay public tribute to them. I shall call on them for advice and assistance, as I have done in the past year, individually, collectively, or otherwise, as the occasion may demand.

I referred a moment ago to the problem of the Congo, a problem which has been with us now for over two years and to which I referred in my acceptance speech of last year. The problem remains unsolved in spite of the best efforts of all concerned. As a consequence, the financial problem of the Organization also remains unsolved. Both these problems must, however, be solved, and soon, if the usefulness of the Organization for the future is not to be seriously affected. And today I appeal anew to all Member Governments, who have come to value the usefulness of the Organization, to assist in solving these long-standing issues.

On the credit side, however, I may perhaps recall that the Organization was able to settle one source of tension in South and South East Asia, namely, the problem of West

New Guinea (West Irian). The implementation of the tripartite agreement between the Governments of the Netherlands and Indonesia and the United Nations, which was approved earlier in the current session by the General Assembly, has worked smoothly, and I am sure that we will be able to carry this unique operation to a successful conclusion, with the co-operation and scrupulous observance of the terms of the agreement by the Governments concerned. Again, in the Cuban crisis which seemed so serious some five weeks ago, I believe we are now over the most dangerous phase, even though complete agreement on all outstanding aspects has not yet been registered.

I now look at the years ahead. I would hope that these years would be marked by an improvement in the international climate, and by better understanding of the difficult problems which the world faces today. These problems can be solved only by good will and mutual understanding, and by a spirit of "give and take." When the future of mankind itself is at stake, no country or interest-group can afford to take a rigid stand, or claim that its position is the only right one, and that others must take it or leave it. No difficult problem can be solved to the complete satisfaction of all sides. We live in an imperfect world, and have to accept imperfect solutions, which become more acceptable as we learn to live with them and as time passes by. In solving these complex problems, I myself and the Secretariat, of which I am proud to be the chief administrative officer, are at the service not only of all Member Governments but of "the peoples of the United Nations."

# 2

# On His Predecessor

UNVEILING OF PLAQUE IN MEMORY OF DAG HAMMARSKJOLD*

We are gathered here this morning in a ceremony whose purpose it is to pay solemn tribute to cherished colleagues lost just one year ago in the train of duty. But this occasion serves also to enrich the present for each of us by recalling the strength, courage, wisdom, and devotion to the international ideal of those who were so abruptly taken from us. The great require no eulogy. It is thus with Dag Hammarskjold, whose inspired works in more than eight years of dedicated service to this Organization live after him and recall his imposing stature more eloquently than any words I might pronounce.

The other day I received a letter informing me that a year ago, at the time of the crash, some African students wrote some moving laments about the death of Mr. Hammarskjold. These were students from various parts of Africa who were attending the Africa Literacy and Writing School in Kitwe, Northern Rhodesia, which is about 40 miles west of the scene of the tragedy at Ndola. Since these expressions came straight from the hearts of young Afri-

* Address delivered at the United Nations on September 17, 1962.

cans, I take the liberty of reading one of them to you, which was written by David Rockson of Ghana:

> The world leader is dead, yet he speaks;
> He speaks to the world in accents soft and clear.
> What is he saying to Africa?
> Yes, what is he saying to the world?
> The message is: "peace on earth."
> The message is: "unity among the nations."
> Citizen, if thou art constrained to mourn
>      Dag Hammarskjold,
> Pray God to make you a peacemaker, too.

It is particularly appropriate, I think, that we meet on this occasion in the outer area of the United Nations Meditation Room. For that room was of deep and very special concern to Dag Hammarskjold. He devoted very much of time and thought and planning to its conception and to its arrangement. He wished it to be universal in its invitation —to appeal to all who come into this house to find in that room an atmosphere uniquely conducive to quiet reflection, to introspection, to an inward look away from the tumult and cynicism of the world around us. He wished that room to have a symbolism all its own, expressed in the massive solidity and strength of the center stone of Swedish ore and the reach toward eternity of Bo Beskow's impressive al fresco. You are invited to visit and make use of this room.

Dag Hammarskjold, with his profound knowledge and perception of man—of man's history and ways—would be the first to recognize that it is the way of fate to make the commonplace suddenly and dramatically momentous. It was in such a vagary of fate that my late predecessor and his companions lost their lives a year ago. For Dag Hammarskjold, Secretary-General of the United Nations, the trip of a year ago to the Congo and the incidental mission to Ndola were natural and unexceptional acts undertaken purely and without question in the line of duty. The September journey was not his first to the shattered Congo, where he had gone with the same spirit as previously to other troubled areas. As was well known to his close collaborators on the thirty-eighth floor of this building, Mr. Hammarskjold accepted the invitation of the Prime Minister of the Republic of the Congo last September to visit that country on the eve of the opening of the Sixteenth Session of the General Assembly primarily because he saw in it an opportunity to reduce if not remove the Congo as a critical and bitter issue before that Assembly. The main, though unpublicized objective sought was to induce Mr. Tshombe to go to Leopoldville, or elsewhere in the Congo, for talks with Prime Minister Adoula toward the ending of the Katanga secession through reconciliation of the differences between the Central Government and that Province. I have no doubt that, had Mr. Hammarskjold lived, he would have achieved that objective, which was, indeed, later twice achieved, although with disappointing results to date. The United Nations effort in the Congo persists, however, and will, in time, I am confident, fully succeed.

As to the fateful flight to Ndola, we know, from one of Mr. Hammarskjold's last messages, that it was only when he reached Accra, en route to Leopoldville, that he learned, from a "tendentious" press report, as he put it, that the latest United Nations effort to eliminate mercenaries in Katanga had encountered stubborn resistance and that serious fighting had broken out in Elisabethville between United Nations troops and mercenary-led elements of the Katangese gendarmerie. This unexpected news must certainly have come to him as a severe shock. In the light of these circumstances, it was then both natural and necessary for him, as Secretary-General, to do all that he could do to bring the fighting to an end and to stop any further blood-letting. This, clearly, was why Mr. Hammarskjold and his companions took the ill-fated trip to Ndola. When they embarked upon it, they had sound reason to anticipate that it would be successful in inducing Mr. Tshombe to enter into reconciliation talks, no less than achieving the cease-fire.

I am confident that Dag Hammarskjold saw no extraordinary risk in his journey to Ndola, which was, in fact, attended by much more than normal precautions. One may be even more positive that he would not have hesitated a moment had any such risk been apparent.

There are, to be sure, certain unavoidable risks in any United Nations field operation: the hazards of chartered flights to unfamiliar airfields, of vehicular accidents, of health in harsh climates, of sniper's bullets. United Nations personnel are often subject to such hazards in missions far and wide. If, however, the United Nations is to project its peace-keeping actions into the areas of active conflict, as it must if its peace-making function is to be really worthwhile, such risks to its personnel cannot be entirely voided.

It is fitting here, I believe, to commend highly those many—indeed, many thousands—of men and women, civilian and military, from within and without the United Nations Secretariat, who have served and now serve the Organization in its peace-keeping operations in various parts of the world, from the Congo to New Guinea, not infrequently at considerable personal sacrifice, under conditions of genuine hardship and at times of danger. The casualties suffered by United Nations personnel in the field have been substantial enough to establish that peace-making can be costly also in lives.

In the United Nations peace operations such as Palestine, Kashmir, Suez, and the Congo, there have been those who are, indeed, entitled to the accolade "hero of peace." Dag Hammarskjold was definitely one. By odd coincidence, another was his fellow country-man, Count Folke Bernadotte, who on this very date in 1948, gave his life in Jerusalem while serving the United Nations in the quest for peace in a war-ridden Palestine.

We honor also today Count Bernadotte's memory and his sacrifice, and the memory of all those others who have given their lives in the peace actions of this great Organization.

The Meditation Room, on whose outer wall the plaque rests, was poetically described by Dag Hammarskjold in these prophetic words: "This is a room devoted to peace and those who are giving their lives for peace. It is a room of quiet where only thoughts should speak."

The plaque about to be uncovered from now on will serve as a reminder for all those who pass by it, for all the generations of the future, of the deep gratitude, the sense of tragic loss, and the profound sorrow over colleagues prematurely gone, which we who live today carry in our hearts for those sixteen who are no longer with us.

Will you please join me in standing as the plaque is unveiled.

The inscription on the plaque, which is done in bronze, reads as follows: "In memory of Dag Hammarskjold, Secretary-General of the United Nations 1953 to 1961, and those who with him lost their lives at Ndola in September 1961 in quest of peace in the Congo."

May *they* rest in peace. May *we* secure it.

## DEDICATION OF THE DAG HAMMARSKJOLD LIBRARY*

The last time Dag Hammarskjold visited the old United Nations Headquarters Library he said to the staff in parting, "I hope that when we meet again I shall find you in more appropriate quarters."

Fate denied him that appointment, but today we are gathered to dedicate a splendid new library building which I am sure would satisfy him as "appropriate." That it should be named for Dag Hammarskjold is not in the circumstances an unusual action. Buildings often are named in memory of men who have contributed brilliantly and uniquely to the cause for which they labored, although the completion date of an appropriate building less commonly follows so closely the death of one in whose name it is dedicated. But how rarely is a building named for a man who by choice and temperament was wholly sympathetic with the purpose for which that building was constructed, and who himself had worked for its creation and overseen every detail of its planning.

That is the possibly unique distinction of this dedication, for Dag Hammarskjold was a man of learning and a poet of the breed for whom books and libraries are necessary delights. He was an intellectual whose training and daily work embraced history, economics and the law, and whose private pleasures included philosophy and poetry. He read Kierkegaard and Sartre and Buber, Eliot and Perse, as he listened to Bach and looked at Picasso; they delighted his mind and gave flight to his imagination.

For such a man, architecture's combination of precise physical and mathematical principles with the most subtle aesthetic harmonies was a most congenial combination. It

* Address delivered at the United Nations, New York, November 16, 1961.

is not surprising, therefore, that the late Secretary-General took a close personal interest in every detail of the Library's design, from its general outline to the texture of the fabric on a single chair. He looked at plans, drawings, models, samples of wood and marble and leather; he requested construction of model rooms to display alternate lighting fixtures and flooring materials; he expressed opinions and took final decisions on such questions as the curve of the roof, the color of the draperies, the dimensions and design of a mural. And he did these things with delight, as a relaxation from the daily responsibilities of his office, and with such good humor and evident taste that, far from annoying the professionals—the architects, designers, engineers, artists—he won their immediate respect and their admiring cooperation.

As the building neared completion, he began planning its dedication and gave to this, too, his earnest consideration. It was his intention, as it had been from the very beginning of the discussions with the Ford Foundation, that the Library should become a great center for the study of international affairs, and he wished in dedicating the building to emphasize its function as a library designed, equipped and staffed to contribute to the rule of law in the world. Accordingly, he proposed that the dedication be marked by a gathering of librarians from all over the world for the purpose of discussing their general professional concerns and the specific role of the United Nations Library as a member of the global family of libraries.

With the agreement of the Ford Foundation a portion of the building grant was set aside to make this possible, and in the summer of 1961 preliminary plans were made for a two-day library symposium to be held in connection with the library's dedication. To this symposium Mr. Hammarskjold invited the leading librarians of about 40 countries, a number of whom were further asked to prepare papers to be read at the symposium or to particiapte in panel discussions of library problems, the emphasis of their papers and their discussions to be upon the United Nations Library itself.

His hopes for this library and his plans for its dedication to the cause of peace in the world deserve our respect and our pledge of fulfillment. His plans have remained unchanged, and we have among our guests today those librarians whom he invited to share his hopes and to counsel him on this library's mission. They will meet together tomorrow and on Saturday, as he had planned, and I am sure that they and all of you will share with me the conviction that this dedication of a splendid building to the memory of an exceptional human being of rich talents and dedicated effort, is not only appropriate but is an expression of the faith we all must have in the ultimate triumph of truth —that flame which libraries help to keep alight.

It is in that spirit that we now dedicate this new library building as the "Dag Hammarskjold Library," not as a monument but as a center of research and learning inspired by his zest for knowledge and his earnest search for truth. It will serve delegates to the Assembly and to the other principal organs, the members of the Permanent Missions of member countries, the staff of the Secretariat, research scholars and others who are seriously concerned with the work of the Organization and the problems which it now confronts and which it will face in the years ahead. The rows upon rows of books, its facilities and quiet atmosphere for reflection and research provide an ordering of the experience of mankind as it has found expression in books, and an offering of that collective experience to all who seek it.

This building is a fulfillment of a librarian's dream and

a guarantee of a reader's delight. Its efficient and corre-
lated arrangement of processes and services natural to a
library, of acquisition, processing, cataloging and index-
ing; its well lighted and splendidly arranged stack areas; its
reference collection and services; its arrangement for official documents; its microfilm facilities; its map collections;
the fine office and working arrangement for the staff; the
lovely color decor throughout the building, arranged by
Mr. Perry Marthin; the beautiful abstract murals, one on
the concave wall of the penthouse by Bo Beskow, the other
by Fritz Glarner on the wall of the entrance to the Library; the little auditorium of charming design, the ex-
quisitely designed and tastefully furnished reading rooms;
the periodical reading room; the main reading room and
the Woodrow Wilson Reading Room—all these form part
of a building of near perfection in taste and charm and in
providing services to its users.

The Woodrow Wilson Reading Room, of impressive and
beautiful design honors the name of a great statesman who
labored valiantly, after tragic world conflict, to create a
world organization—the League of Nations—as mankind's
guardian of the peace. He deemed it essential that an organization like the League of Nations should "keep watch
over the peace" and that that organization "should neither
slumber nor sleep."

The Woodrow Wilson Reading Room also represents
the keeping of a trust by the United Nations when assurances were given in 1950 to the Woodrow Wilson
Foundation that the excellent collection of League of Nations documents and books on international topics transferred to the United Nations Library would be so arranged
and serviced as to make them fully available to interested
readers. I believe that we have fully kept that trust.

But, in all probability, we would not be meeting here

on this significant occasion had it not been for the vision and generosity of the Ford Foundation. Although the United Nations Library, thanks to excellent direction and a well trained and experienced staff, and to the development of collections of respectable size and quality, had served its clients well, it was severely handicapped by the inadequacies of the structure in which it was housed. Extensive discussions between officials of the Ford Foundation and the United Nations culminated just two years ago in a decision by the Ford Foundation to grant the funds for the demolition of the old building and the construction, furnishing and equipping of the new Library. The generous gift of $6,200,000 plus accrued interest is now expressed in the beautifully designed, tastefully decorated and efficiently equipped building which we dedicate today.

I repeat the profound gratitude of the United Nations, already officially expressed in the unanimously adopted resolution of 6 November 1959, to you, Mr. President, and to your colleagues on the Board of Trustees of the Ford Foundation, for this magnificent contribution to the work of the United Nations and the important mission of peace and human betterment for which it stands. Your own major objectives are identical with the high purposes of the United Nations. Through your action you have strengthened our capacity to cope with our problems and to advance the tasks that the Charter and the problems of the world lay upon us.

I express to you also our sincere appreciation for the cooperation and understanding which you, your colleagues on the Board of Trustees, and your staff always reflected in all contacts and discussions with the late Secretary-General and his staff. One of many evidences of your effort to be helpful in the most practical and effective way was your employment of four distinguished librarians as consultants to assess our request for funds and to make certain that our needs were fully met in a most professional manner. When the grant was effected and detailed planning of the new Library began, Mr. Hammarskjold retained the same four consultants who continued their invaluable contribution to the problems of planning, arrangements, and furnishing of the new structure.

Only one year ago this month construction began. I pay tribute to all who contributed to the achievement which we celebrate today—to the architects, Harrison, Abramovitz and Harris, who designed the building with beauty, grace and charm of its own, and fitting admirably into the total family of the United Nations buildings; to the general contractor, the George A. Fuller Construction Company, the sub-contractors, the supervisors, engineers, artists, artisans and workers, who labored so effectively and efficiently to bring the building into being in so short a time; and to the staff of the Secretariat who worked zealously with this magnificent team in a tightly coordinated and expeditious effort.

Carved in marble on the entrance to the library are the words, "Dag Hammarskjold Library, Gift of the Ford Foundation, 1961," an inscription flowing from two unanimously adopted resolutions to the General Assembly, a gift that brought this center of learning and research into being, a name that adds purpose and meaning to those who use it.

## DEDICATION OF THE DAG HAMMARSKJOLD ROOM*

First of all let me say how grateful I am to the Association of the Bar of the City of New York for the honor of the invitation extended to me to dedicate the Ham-

* Address delivered at the House of the Association of the Bar of the City of New York, April 30, 1962.

marskjold Room in this House of the Association. I sincerely appreciate the opportunity of performing this task as a tribute to my distinguished predecessor.

Since his unexpected and tragic death on 17 September 1961, a deep appreciation of his work as Secretary-General of the United Nations has been shown by all sections of peoples all over the world. Even those who were critical of his actions, from time to time, expressed their admiration for his unswerving devotion to the principles he held dear and his dedication to the task of strengthening the world organization he headed with distinction for eight years. Today, we have the clearer image of Dag Hammarskjold, who has come to be identified with the very purposes and principles of the United Nations Charter, and who has assumed the symbol of a man relentlessly dedicated to the maintenance of international peace and security.

He had exceptional courage of convictions, and never swerved from the set course dictated to him by his convictions. This gave him a broad consistency. He was convinced of the necessity of developing an international authority within the present world setup. He realized that anything capable of mitigating the present state of tensions would represent a valuable advance. He also realized that the objective of all peace-loving peoples should be an effective world authority like any other governmental system.

I want to take this opportunity of endorsing these convictions and these objectives which were cherished by my predecessor. The greatest problem of our age is to find a system of war prevention that works in our present circumstances. Basically, this is a problem that can be solved only by the willing cooperation of all countries. But many countries will not be brought to operate a limited form of world government unless there is everywhere a growing recognition of the unity of human society. We should therefore be united in our unprecedented need to find a system for living together in peace.

It is now my pleasure and privilege to dedicate this Hammarskjold Room to the cause of world peace through world law not only for our generation but for all generations to come.

# 3

# World Tension and International Relations

## EAST-WEST RELATIONS AND THE UNITED NATIONS*

In taking this subject as my theme this afternoon I have been moved by the consideration that the changing character of relationship between the United States and the Soviet Union has had a major impact, not only upon the contemporary world, but also on the work of the United Nations. I believe that it is timely, and it may be useful, to trace the relationship between these two major powers over the last few decades and then to examine various aspects of their present relationship. Such an analysis may disclose fruitful avenues which may be explored in the future in order to improve East-West relations on which, if I may say so, the future of peace and of mankind depends so much.

When we look at recent diplomatic history, especially during the period after World War II, the shift of alignments between nations has taken place, as we can see, with startling speed. Soviet-American relations are no exception

* Address delivered as the George Huntington Williams Memorial Lecture at Johns Hopkins University on December 2, 1962.

to this generalization. One may recall that the United States maintained its policy of non-recognition of the Soviet regime for well nigh 16 years until, in 1933, President Franklin D. Roosevelt changed this policy. In the period between World War I and World War II, despite the vision, almost utopian, of global collective security which was held by President Wilson, the United States stayed outside the League of Nations. This circumstance, however, did not prevent the United States from being an active proponent of international peace, as evidenced by the conclusion of the Kellogg-Briand Pact for the Renunciation of War (1928), and of the naval treaties of Washington (1921) and London (1930). The Soviet Union entered the League of Nations only in 1934, mainly as a consequence of the rise of the Nazis in Germany and remained a supporter of the League until a few months before the outbreak of World War II.

It was, however, only with the beginning of the Second World War that the United States and the Soviet Union gradually established a relationship which could be described as cordial. This development was, however, the result of the recognition of a common danger, caused by the presence of a common foe, namely the Axis Powers. Although President Roosevelt may have had certain long-range views on the value of improved relations with the Soviet Union, irrespective of the circumstances of World War II, the impression is unmistakable that their war-time friendship contained an element of a "marriage of convenience," which was forced on both parties by the circumstances.

In the 1930's, as in other periods of history, the alignments of nations were based on considerations of national interest and security. The inherent weaknesses of the League of Nations, as shown during this period in more than one crisis, encouraged nations to form alliances out-side the League, which in turn made the League less effective. This process culminated in the inability of the League to prevent World War II. Once the war had started the United States found itself moving away from its traditional isolationism, even before the Japanese attack on Pearl Harbor forced it to become a major participant in World War II. Being immune from the ravages of war on its own territory, the tremendous industrial and agricultural potential of the United States enabled it to become, not only the arsenal, but also the granary of the Allies.

This experience of forced involvement in world affairs, coupled with the pre-eminent position of the United States as the world's greatest industrial power, made it inevitable that the United States should finally abandon its traditional policy of isolationism. The United States was thus instrumental in the signing of the Atlantic Charter in 1941, and was in the vanguard of the movement for the establishment of a post-war international organization. Thus the United States gave up the concept of a "Fortress America" and gradually came to recognize the fact of mutual inter-dependence of nations. The conferences of Moscow (1943), Dumbarton Oaks (1944) and Yalta (1945) were significant milestones in bringing to birth the United Nations as the greatest hope for war-weary humanity.

Thus the United Nations was born at a time when the two great powers were working in close cooperation, and the Charter of the United Nations was framed on the assumption that this cooperation would continue. It was on this basis that the members of the United Nations conferred on the Security Council "primary responsibility for the maintenance of international peace and security," and agreed "that in carrying out its duties under this responsibility the Security Council acts on their behalf" (Article 24). Further the members of the United Nations agreed "to accept and carry out the decisions of the Security Council in accordance with the present Charter" (Article 25). The Security Council was to be "so organized as to be able to function continuously" (Article 28). It was also provided that decisions of the Security Council on all matters other than procedural matters shall be made "by an affirmative vote of seven members, including the concurring votes of the permanent members" (Article 27), thus introducing the well-known principle of the veto, which may be described positively as the principle of unanimity among the big powers.

The Security Council was then envisaged as the most important among the principal organs of the United Nations, vested with primary responsibility for the maintenance of international peace and security. This tremendous responsibility could have been discharged by the Security Council only if the harmony between the two major powers could have been continued. We all know that before long the differences between the USSR and the United States became very sharp, beginning with the controversy over the presence of Soviet troops in Iran (1946), and reaching a climax with the Korean war (1950). This was the beginning of the era of the cold war. Future historians may undertake learned analyses of this period with a view to allocating responsibility, and even blame, for the emergence of the cold war. I wish here merely to note the fact of bi-polarity, which before long characterized the work of the United Nations, and which continues to this day to affect the effectiveness of the United Nations, and in particular the Security Council.

The advent of the cold war and the fact of bi-polarity in international relations generate political tensions not only in the United Nations, but all over the world. Even so, the situation today is less grim than it was before World War II. In the thirties there was one aggressive nation wishing to dominate the world by force—Hitler's Nazi Germany. Today there are *two* Great Powers, neither wanting war, but each so apprehensive of the other that they are convinced they must possess greater military might. Hence the frantic nuclear arms race. A clash between the two would mean the destruction of mankind. This explains why a growing number of nations wish to be non-aligned, to fight for neither side, to keep the two giants apart, to lessen the tension between them and to reduce the danger of nuclear accidents. In this way, the period of two-power predominance within the United Nations gave way to a tri-polar situation.

While this process of tri-polarization was going on in international relations, another significant change was in evidence in the relationship between the two Big Powers. In the late forties and early fifties the political system—and theories, such as the inevitability of war—prevailing in the Soviet Union were increasingly regarded elsewhere as a definite threat to political and economic systems in other parts of the world. In my view the system created and maintained by Stalin was manifestly ruthless and obsolescent even before his departure. Mr. Khrushchev, who is now in control of the reins of government, belongs to a different category of leaders, with a coherent philosophy of the world based on the thesis, not of the inevitability of war, but of the imperative of competitive co-existence. We may or may not agree with his philosophy or with his aims, but we have very good reasons to believe that he does not want war.

The West does not seem to appreciate the full significance of this obvious change of political climate in the

Soviet Union. Throughout the fifties most Western leaders saw the world as a battlefield between two antagonistic systems, militantly expressing the principles of good and evil. Hence compromise was betrayal: evil could be held at bay only by iron-clad alliances, held together by mutual fear and backed by the constant threat of nuclear war. While this attitude could be criticized as a modern version of Hobbesian pessimism, it nevertheless provided a stable and fixed frame of reference in which decisions could be taken.

This concept of iron-clad alliances and this view of the world purely in terms of black and white was, in essence, the Western response to Stalinism. However, this attitude persisted even when the character of Soviet challenge was already changing. This view of the world scene was perhaps partly responsible for many newly-independent countries pursuing a policy of non-alignment. President Kennedy proved himself to be a leader of vision and imagination when, early last year, he proposed a neutral Laos in return for a cease-fire. Thus the President wisely admitted that the attempt to create a series of pro-Western governments in Asia had failed. He accepted the view that the best the West could hope for in Asia—and for that matter Africa—are governments which fear outside inter-ference and subversion as much as they hate colonialism; and that the function of Western policy should be the creation of a framework within which they can exercise their own freedom of choice.

I now revert to my review of the last decade. The Korean armistice of 1953, the Geneva conference on Indo-China of 1954, and the Bandung conference of 1955 brought a new element into the picture, although the last two conferences took place outside the auspices of the United Nations. In 1955, sixteen new nations were admitted to the United Nations in a package deal, including some Asian and Arab countries. The new nations of Asia, while rejoicing in their liberation from colonial rule, took it upon themselves—as already noted—to constitute a third or middle element, anxious to conciliate, to the extent possible, the rivalry between Washington and Moscow. The process was further continued with the admission of three African countries and one Asian country in 1956, one African and one Asian country in 1957, another Asian country in 1958 and 17 new countries (of which 16 were from Africa) in 1960. In 1961 there were 4 new admissions of which 3 were from Africa, and in the current session, we have had 6 new members of which 4 were from Africa. As a result, the United Nations has expanded from a membership of 51 at its inception to 110 today, and the Afro-Asian countries have emerged as one of the dominant groups within the United Nations.

With the rapid growth in Afro-Asian membership we have entered on a new era in which it is no longer true to say that there is a tri-polar situation, but rather a multi-polar situation. As is obvious to anyone who works day after day in the United Nations, it is misleading to think of the Afro-Asian members of the United Nations as a solid bloc: there are any number of alignments within the Afro-Asian group. And, while on certain questions, as for example, colonialism, they maintain a basic accord, on other issues they act quite independently of each other, and, in fact, have on occasion shown considerable rivalry when contesting for seats on the major organs. Thus the simple formula of East-West confrontation, which was replaced by the East-Neutral-West situation, has been superseded by a complex and fluid pattern of international relations.

One result of the increased membership of the General

Assembly, and the emergence of the numerically strong Afro-Asian element in it, has been to give the General Assembly added strength, as the only universal organ amongst the principal organs of the United Nations, in which all members can participate with equal rights, coupled with the fact that the Security Council cannot act effectively on any issue on which the major powers cannot reach prior agreement. The General Assembly has thus become the battleground of the cold war. Both the major powers are anxious to secure the support of the General Assembly for their respective stands on major world issues, and have shown a willingness to accommodate themselves to the views of the uncommitted countries to the extent that their basic positions permit them a little elbow-room. This fact explains to some extent the dissatisfaction with the United Nations, especially on the part of those countries which were used to having much their own way in the past, and now find it necessary to woo the uncommitted countries in an effort to muster the necessary majorities in the Assembly.

Some East-West co-operation has become evident lately in the technological and scientific fields and also in the matter of cultural and other exchanges between the Soviet Union and the United States. Perhaps the most significant development in this regard is co-operation in the field of outer space, but even this is conditioned by the political climate and is subject to the climatic vicissitudes of the cold war.

In difficult areas such as disarmament there is little doubt in my own mind that the introduction of a third element has been very useful. While there was some agreement between the two major powers on broad principles, as reflected in the Zorin-McCloy statement of last year on general and comprehensive disarmament, further progress has been delayed and may be hopefully reached only in the Geneva discussions. The unanimous report of the expert committee on the economic consequences of disarmament has helped to dispel certain misconceptions and apprehensions in regards to economic obstacles in making progress toward a disarmed world. On the question of nuclear tests, too, considerable progress has been made since March last, when the Geneva Conference began; and it is to be hoped that the impasse which now exists in regard to underground tests may be resolved by discussions at the scientific level directed towards reaching agreement on mutually acceptable procedures of verification.

I may say a few words at this point on a subject which has occupied a considerable amount of my time and attention and which was a cause of much concern and even anxiety during the last six weeks. I refer here to the situation in Cuba. It became apparent in late October that there was danger of a direct confrontation between the two major powers, and that every possible step should be taken to avert this confrontation. I gave expression to this feeling in the Security Council, by an odd coincidence on United Nations Day, and I addressed an appeal both on that day and on the next to the Heads of the two Governments, to which I received an encouraging and positive response from both quarters. Most of you may have been familiar with the subsequent developments which have been reported so fully, and sometimes so inaccurately, by the mass media everywhere. In spite of periods when there seeemed to be little progress, the negotiations advanced steadily to a point at which it is now possible to report agreement on certain fundamentals between the two major powers. There may be many who may wish for a more complete and comprehensive solution of the Cuban crisis, but in this imperfect world we have, at least for the moment, to accept less than perfect solutions.

Looking to the future I hope that the spirit of compromise which marked the discussions between the Soviet Union and the United States in the case of Cuba may help the solution of some of the outstanding cold war issues of the world today, both general and local. I have already referred to the question of disarmament and nuclear testing. There are various other issues like Berlin on which it may become imperative to reach solutions on the basis of compromise and the principle of give-and-take on both sides. In all these situations the United Nations is available to the major powers, as it is to all its members, as a channel of friendly contact and informal discussion, and not merely a forum for public debate.

I have already referred to the United Nations as the battleground of the cold war, which is mainly due to the fact that it is the greatest public forum in the world today. In this forum it is possible over the years to debate great issues, and to enlarge the area of agreement and narrow the differences, so that over the years the solution of the most intractable problems may become feasible. For example, no one will question that the work of the United Nations has been in no small measure responsible for the astonishingly rapid emergence of so many African countries as sovereign states and full members of the international community. I would hope that the General Assembly may became even more effective as a public assembly by providing opportunities for friendly personal contacts between the leaders of the world, as also for rational debate on difficult issues, so that the United Nations truly serves the purpose set out in the Charter "to be a center for harmonizing the actions of nations."

I may refer briefly in this context to the increasing use of the United Nations as an organ for pragmatic executive action on behalf of the world community. The United Nations has undertaken, as in the case of West New

Guinea (West Irian), quasi-governmental tasks, in addition to its traditional peace-keeping role in the Middle East, and, more recently, in the Congo.

In this context I would like also to refer to the broad spectrum of instruments for international co-operation which are available in the United Nations in non-political fields and especially in the economic, social and humanitarian fields. The designation of the current decade as the United Nations Development Decade is a concrete recognition of the role of the United Nations and its family of Agencies in the promotion of economic and social development, the importance of which has been stressed even in the Charter. I cannot help feeling that too much attention has been given in the past to the military, ideological and political factors which tend to divide the world into various groups and interest blocs. The time has come for us to direct our attention more to the economic and social structure of society, and particularly to the disparity in the wealth of nations which is one of the root causes of political tension. It is possible, within the United Nations, to stress the common responsibility of nations, rich and poor, in the economic and social fields, and to organize north-south as well as east-west co-operation for the promotion of human welfare.

In this field, the resources available so far to the United Nations have been small, almost marginal, in relation to the resources which have been expended by Governments on a bilateral basis. I believe, however, that the United Nations and its family of Agencies provide a unique opportunity for organizing a global attack on the common problems of mankind. In this way the United Nations can also help prevent the world from becoming frozen into antagonistic interest blocs. In this context, the tendency towards close economic integration of highly organized and developed societies is a factor which causes con-

U Thant, in a photograph taken in November 1961, when he was
Acting Secretary-General

U Thant taking the Oath of Office from Assembly President Mongi
Slim of Tunisia. November 3, 1961

U Thant's family see him sworn in as Acting Secretary-General. (left to right) Tyn Mynt, son-in-law, Mrs. Thant, Tin Maung Thant, their son, and Aye Aye, daughter

The Acting Secretary-General at the tomb of his predecessor, Dag
Hammarskjold, in Uppsala, Sweden, May 6, 1962

U Thant with Muhammad Zafrulla Khan of Pakistan, President of the General Assembly (center), and C. V. Narasimham, Under-Secretary for General Assembly Affairs and Chef de Cabinet, just after U Thant's unanimous appointment as Secretary-General on November 30, 1962

With Dr. Ralph J. Bunche, Under-Secretary for Special Political

The present Secretary-General with the first. Trygve Lie (left) and Foreign Minister Halvard Lange of Norway flank U Thant on pier in Oslo, July 10, 1962

Conferring with representative of the U. S. S. R. and the United States on the Cuban crisis, November 26, 1962. At U Thant's right is Anastas I. Mikoyan, Russian Deputy Premier, and at his left is American Ambassador Adlai E. Stevenson

U Thant talking to reporters at New York International Airport upon his return from Cuba, where he talked with Prime Minister Fidel Castro, October 31, 1962

The Carolinum Hall, Charles University, Prague, as U Thant addresses the asssembled students, September 1, 1962

President Kennedy visits United Nations Headquarters. The President is shown here with (left to right) Ambassador Adlai E. Stevenson, U Thant, Carlos Sosa-Rodriguez of Venezuela, Assembly President, Prime Minister Lester B. Pearson of Canada, and Dr. Ralph Bunche

President John F. Kennedy addressing the General Assembly of the
United Nations, September 20, 1963

U Thant faces Russian Premier Nikita S. Khrushchev at the signing of the Nuclear Test Ban Treaty in Moscow. At Khrushchev's left are Foreign Minister Andre Gromyko and Deputy Foreign Minister Valerian Zorin

Following the signing of the Nuclear Test Ban Treaty in Moscow, August 5, 1963, U Thant makes a statement. At his left are British Foreign Secretary Lord Home, Secretary of State Dean Rusk and Russian Foreign Secretary Andre Gromyko

U Thant with British Prime Minister Harold Macmillan in London,
July 5, 1962

The Big Three at United Nations Headquarters. U Thant meets in his office with (left to right) Secretary of State Dean Rusk, Russian Foreign Minister Andre Gromyko and British Foreign Secretary Lord Home

siderable apprehension among the less developed countries, and it is necessary that special steps be taken to allay this apprehension.

In the important task of breaking down ideological barriers, I believe that non-Governmental co-operation can also be of very great significance. Professional organizations on a global basis, meetings of scientists and technologists from all over the world, youth exchange programs and so forth, may help greatly in the promotion of international understanding. The General Assembly adopted two years ago a resolution on measures designed to promote among youth the ideals of peace, mutual respect and understanding among peoples. It is necessary to promote these ideals, not only among youth, but also, if I may say so, among adults. I believe that the exchange of visits by celebrities in the field of culture, art and sport, by political leaders, by eminent intellectuals and poets, all these may help to create mutual respect and greater understanding.

In the promotion of international understanding, newspapers and journals, radio and television, and other media of mass communication can be of great help. International communication has now been speeded up to an extent which was inconceivable a generation ago. I cannot, however, say that the mass media have played as valuable a part as they are capable of playing in promoting better international understanding. It is important that their reporting should never lack objectivity or a proper regard for facts, even where national emotions have been aroused.

Today the issues involved are so complex, and there are so many diverse interests, that it is a truism to say that every question has many sides. I believe that the mass media are capable of making a special effort to develop more open, receptive and unbiased minds among their readers and audience.

One of the great tasks of education all over the world is

to educate the young for peace because, on the question of peace, no man of goodwill can be neutral. We have not only the task of eradicating ignorance and illiteracy in the less developed countries, but also of correcting the distorted image of foreign countries which prevails so often in advanced countries, if we are to create a basis for durable peace among nations. I would hope that it is not too difficult for the advanced countries, despite their different ideologies, to stress their common aspirations, their similar cultural values and their identical interest in survival.

At this point I wish to address myself particularly to American educationists and leaders of thought. The United States is the one society in which the philosophy of material progress is a spectacular success. Democracy is not inhibited, as it is in Europe, by either the threat of social upheaval from below or the memory of a conservative past. But two world wars and an intervening depression have greatly affected American confidence in the continuity of progress. Political and social changes elsewhere worry most Americans. The revolt of the colonial people, who are in fact the ultimate heirs of 1776, and their desire to fashion their own way of life, seems to be frightening and incomprehensible to the descendants of those who started it all at Lexington and Concord.

It is little use trying to meet this new situation with conventional responses. The attempt to pin the blame on scapegoats and subversives may have been emotionally comforting, but it has probably weakened the confidence of the American people. Nor is more and bigger defense spending the real answer. As we are already witnessing, nuclear power has reduced the traditional influence of military strength on national security. It provides such a devastating armory that the price of a victory could be greater than the sum of all the defeats in past history. The point of diplomacy, therefore, is to avoid a war of such dimensions, and this means that many solutions are now accepted which in previous generations would have been the occasion for war. The less the influence of military factors, the more the strength of the other potent forces that make history.

What has happened is that the revolutionary concept of a meaningful future is, in our lifetime, seizing the minds of the masses. The real challenge to the United States is how to promote this trend towards a better future for all humanity. I believe that this promotion should conceivably be to ensure the proper use of the fruits of wealth, so as to ease the contrast between its own abundance and the poverty of mankind elsewhere.

To illustrate my point, let me cite one glaring instance. In Asia, Africa and Latin America, living standards have largely remained stationary, or have even declined. Throughout the last decade, the fall in the price of raw materials, while priming the affluent societies of the West, has not only cancelled out the sum total of Western aid, but in many cases has led to an absolute drop in national income. One great lesson of this phenomenon is that the world will not live in harmony so long as two-thirds of its inhabitants find difficulty in living at all.

I further believe that the age is past when Governments can claim that each nation by itself provides its own shield of security. The unprecedented scientific and technical progress of recent years has made this concept somewhat outmoded. If we are to survive in this nuclear and space age, we must move forward, however slowly, away from the concept of the absolute freedom of action of the sovereign state, towards the community of ideas and identity of interests that cuts across national, cultural and ideological boundaries.

The United Nations, to me, does not represent a vague ideal of universal peace and brotherhood which has its appeal only to starry-eyed idealists and moralists. Far from it. It is hard-headed, enlightened self-interest, the stake that all humanity has in peace and progress and, most important of all, survival, that dictates the need for the United Nations as a practical, institutional embodiment of the needs of nations on a shrinking planet, as a potent and dynamic instrument at the service of all nations, east and west, north as well as south.

The ideas that I have expressed today are not new. The thesis that all nations share an abiding interest in peace, progress and prosperity, and that relations between nations should accordingly be based on faith and justice is an old and time-honored concept. To illustrate this point, I cannot do better than by recalling President Washington's farewell address when he said:

"Observe good faith and justice toward all nations. Cultivate peace and harmony with all . . . nothing is more essential than that permanent, inveterate antipathies against particular nations and passionate attachments for others should be excluded, and that in place of them just and amicable feelings towards all should be cultivated. The nation which indulges toward another an habitual hatred or an habitual fondness is in some degree a slave."

### A CALL FOR TEMPORARY STANDSTILL AGREEMENTS*

I am very happy to be with the United States Committee for the United Nations, at this luncheon which is its annual membership meeting. The United States Committee has made it its main task to disseminate information about

* Address delivered at the Annual Luncheon of the United States Committee for the United Nations, New York, April 17, 1962.

the United Nations to the American people. This task, which is in itself a task of great importance, has gained added significance these days because of the growing public interest in the working of the United Nations today.

So many of the criticisms one hears nowadays about the United Nations are based on misconceptions or misrepresentations, and it is fitting that the United States Committee should be so active in helping the people understand better what the United Nations *can do* and *has done* to help maintain international peace and security, and to promote the betterment of human beings all over the world.

In particular, I am glad that at the present time there has been a revival of interest in the economic, social, and human rights activities of the United Nations. The General Assembly has designated this decade as the United Nations Development Decade, thus highlighting the important role that the United Nations will play in this decade for the welfare of all human beings. It is our common experience that the smallest political wrangle attracts headlines in newspapers all over the world, whereas some of the most significant work of the United Nations in the economic and social field is hardly ever mentioned. I hope that the United States Committee will give due importance to this aspect of our work.

On the political plane, it cannot be repeated too often that the United Nations can only be what its members make of it. It cannot help but reflect the political realities of the world today, but it would be unfair to blame the United Nations merely because it mirrors the imperfections of the world around us.

In these turbulent times we should well remember a few fundamental facts.

The first task of leaders of men all over the world is to

find the first steps toward a world system of preventing war. Eighteen years ago three men, Roosevelt, Stalin and Churchill, settled by themselves at Yalta the fate of Europe, Asia, Africa and the Middle East. Now, the three most powerful men in the world cannot even decide in any positive way the fate of Europe.

But two of them are masters of the world in a sense that no two men before them have ever been. The President of the United States and the Chairman of the Council of Ministers of the Soviet Union may not be able to make the world behave as they wish, but they have the power to destroy it. The United States and the Soviet Union control between them almost the whole of the world's nuclear arsenal. The process of stockpiling is still going on at a frightening pace. No sane person can believe that either the United States or the Soviet Union will wage a nuclear war deliberately, but there are good reasons to think that the risk of an unintended war is very great. This risk does not depend upon any supposed equality of power between East and West, but upon the risk of accident in the technical measures taken by both sides in the hope of preventing a surprise attack.

The process of replacing men by electronic devices in the complicated machinery of nuclear deterrence now rings new terrors into the so-called balance of terror. From time to time we have been hearing of a nuclear-tipped missile being nearly launched by accident or on false alarm, even by an electrical short circuit. It is common knowledge that both the American and Soviet missiles are at hair-trigger readiness and controlled by electronic devices.

What does this all mean? This means that some system must be found to limit and control the nuclear arms race before it gets out of hand.

Political or territorial disputes such as the future of Berlin or the uncertainties of the Middle Eastern situation, or the highly-charged situation in certain parts of Asia, Africa and Latin America, are serious and urgent, and it is extremely difficult to find solutions to these problems. But it is imperative that the seriousness of these situations does not develop to the point of application of this monstrous nuclear power. If no final solution can yet be found for these disputes, the most sensible and practical course is to insulate them as far as possible from war risks by temporary standstill agreements, while an effort is made to build a more permanent war-free international system.

It is perhaps a Utopian dream when we aspire to create a world in which major war is impossible. In the light of history, it is certainly a Utopian dream, but today, when we live under the shadow of the nuclear bomb, nothing less than that kind of Utopia will do.

The United Nations, despite its imperfections, should be encouraged to grow into a really effective instrument of keeping the peace and preventing war. The only way out of anarchy in any circumstance is through the development of some form of peace-keeping authority. We have today only the United Nations which can play this role, but this Organization is merely an instrument that is as strong or as weak as its members make it. Organizations like the United States Committee for the United Nations could greatly increase the instrumentality of the United Nations by mobilizing public opinion behind it. In this task, as the Permanent Representative of the United States to the United Nations, Ambassador Adlai Stevenson has played a great part and I am happy that he is present today and that he will be addressing you also. Mr. Stevenson came to the United Nations with a great reputation for his liberal and humanistic outlook, and these qualities have been very much in evidence during the last fifteen months that he has been here. They have earned him many friends on all sides as also in the Secretariat. I am sure you will all join me in wishing him well in his difficult assignment.

Mr. Benjamin*, I thank you once again for asking me to join you today and giving me this opportunity to say a few words to you and to the friends of the United Nations assembled here.

---

* Robert S. Benjamin, National Chairman, United States Committee for the United Nations.

# 4

# The Small Nations in World Affairs

Seventeen years ago, when the statesmen of the world gathered at San Francisco and tried to work out a world organization to establish peace on secure foundations, the international situation was very different from what it is today. The Conference was naturally dominated by the three greatest military powers, the United States, the Soviet Union and Britain. There was a wide-spread belief at that time that, if only these Big Three could be brought together in an international organization, there would be no fear of another world war, and even small brush-fire wars could be banished. In the wake of the most catastrophic war in the history of mankind, humanity had a new vision: it saw the glimmer of dawn of a warless world. The tragic history of the League of Nations was still fresh in the minds of these statesmen who realized that the League failed because it did not have sufficient authority

* Address delivered at Uppsala University, Sweden, on May 6, 1962.

to act. There were many in San Francisco who were familiar with the circumstances leading to the collapse of the
League of Nations, and who realized that the League
failed not only because it was lacking in authority but also
because it was lacking in will. The psychological climate in
the Spring of 1945 at San Francisco was one of hope and
even optimism; there was general feeling that the statesmen had learned a bitter lesson of history; the Big Three
had emerged victorious in the colossal war against the
Fascist and Nazi dictatorships at tremendous cost; peace
had been won, and that hard-won peace must endure with
the continued cooperation of the allies.

That hope, that vision and that belief speedily vanished
in the years following the war. The causes of the deterioration in international relations which followed World War
II were mainly political and psychological. After an all-too-
brief period of harmony, the Big Three split among themselves. The United States and Britain were suspicious of
Russian intentions and Russia was suspicious of Western
intention. In course of time, the West moved closer together and established "collective defense pacts." For her
part, Russia too established a cordon of friendly states
around herself and entered into similar "collective defense
pacts." To ask which side started this process would be
unprofitable, since this would generate ceaseless argu-
ments. The relevant consideration in this context is that
fear and suspicion on both sides generated tensions which
came to be reflected in the United Nations. The Big
Powers on the Security Council, which was originally designed as the chief instrument for maintaining peace and
preventing war, have made it an arena of contention and
conflict. The United Nations, like its predecessor the
League of Nations, has had several impressive successes to
its credit, but it has not been an unqualified success in its

essential purpose to establish the rule of law everywhere. One fact clearly emerges out of the debates and discussions on major political questions in the United Nations: ordinarily the Security Council can take effective action only if the United States and the Soviet Union are in agreement.

It is impossible to conceive in our times of a world authority that could physically eclipse the giant states of the United States and the Soviet Union. All that seems possible is to employ the strength of the two giants to support a system of preventing war between other, weaker countries. But how is war to be prevented in disputes between the two giants themselves? This is *the* paramount question of today. In the last resort, there is only the so-called "balance of terror" between them. No doubt there is also a tacit recognition between them that their interest in world peace is greater than any of their other political interests. It is only on this premise that serious negotiations can be based. Herein comes the role of the smaller uncommitted countries like Sweden, which is to develop every means of strengthening this implicit understanding between the Americans and the Russians, thus making "the last resort" increasingly remote.

As far as the United States and the Soviet Union are concerned, the aim for the time being should be to stabilize and, if possible, to reduce arms stockpiles without disturbing the existing "balance of terror"; to eliminate as far as possible the risks of surprise attack or of war by accident; to check the development of new weapons, and the continuous stockpiling of existing ones. In short, the most hopeful approach is through disarmament, starting with the banning of tests under appropriate and effective control and an agreed system of inspection, as the United Nations General Assembly has repeatedly favored.

As far as all other powers are concerned, the aim should

be to develop the peace-keeping authority of the United Nations. A member state such as Sweden could greatly increase the usefulness of the United Nations—and I am indeed very glad to have this opportunity of stating from this forum that Sweden has been playing a very significant role in this direction. Although the moral authority of the United Nations could be built up by channelling international activities through this instrument, its efficacy will always require, ultimately, the supporting enforcement of both the United States and the Soviet Union. In the last analysis it must be a system in which the two giants must be increasingly involved. Such a development of the United Nations would also serve to add another brake to the danger of war between the two giants themselves, and forge a permanent link between them.

I said earlier that the political climate today is very different from that of 1945 when the United Nations was founded. There are still other important differences between 1945 and 1962. The first of these is the increasing use and, indeed, diversion of scientific and technological progress for military purposes. The atom bomb and the hydrogen bomb were not generally known in the Spring of 1945. I do not know whether the scientists at that time who were engaged in this field of research realized that large-scale atomic warfare might so poison the world as to destroy our civilization. Certainly it did not enter into the minds of those planning a new order.

Looking back over the years one would have thought that by now these obvious risks in our present situation would have become apparent to everyone. The best hopes for peace are now placed in maintaining a "balance of terror" but this balance is beginning to look like an illusion. It is surely time to return to the common-sense conclusion that peace and security cannot be achieved without first reaching agreements between East and West to halt the arms race. The arms race not only feeds on itself but creates in every country an attitude of mind which makes agreements impossible. The time has come for statesmen to say firmly that they do not believe in an indefinite continuation of the delicate balance of terror. This balance seems to me to be purely a theoretical conception when considered in the light of political reality. The reality is that neither the United States nor the Soviet Union will deliberately seek a nuclear war, though they may be plunged into one by accident, and the sensible course is to try to prevent accidents by limiting the arms race and reducing the areas of dispute.

Neutralization of certain areas seems to be a welcome trend in international negotiations. In 1955, the Great Powers, including the Soviet Union, signed a treaty which neutralized Austria. In 1960, they signed a treaty neutralizing Antarctica. A year later they were prepared to guarantee the neutralization of Laos.

The importance of neutralization does not lie solely in the creation of buffer states, valuable though that is. Neutralization is a form of territorial disarmament, a partial dismantling of the great military machines whose destructive powers have now become so terrifying. Each act of neutralization, therefore, is a kind of pilot project for the comprehensive disarmament that alone can rid the world of fear and suspicion.

These are among the great issues of the 1960's which were never thought of when the United Nations was founded. Nor had the world's statesmen contemplated the tremendous advance in national self-consciousness first in Asia and then in Africa, the ending of colonialism and the long-existing hegemony of Europe. The world of 1945, like the world of the League of Nations, was essentially the world of Europe, and of the Americas. Asia and Africa were just mere appendages of Europe. Apparently no thought was given at that time to the prospect of emerging nations of these two continents. Today half of the members of the United Nations are from Asia and Africa. One observes a growing nervousness in the West about the rise in membership of the Asian-Africans in the world organization. But surely the best interests of the West are ill served by sour comments about newly independent countries in Asia and Africa. Such an attitude is a poor tribute to the generations of dedicated and idealistic Westerners who worked precisely toward the ultimate goal of independence, even if they did not know it was going to be reached so early. Nor is it fair to expect those countries at their present stage to express frequently and vociferously their gratitude for what the West did for them. Many newly independent countries still retain bitter memories of the past. In some cases independence was too long postponed, causing a mood of frustration and desperation among freedom fighters. If a country has to fight too long and too hard to win an independence which comes too late, then some extreme forces more hostile to their old masters come to the surface and become more dominant. But by and large these new states which now constitute half the membership of the United Nations generally share democratic ideas, including the liberal concepts of objectivity, tolerance and the rule of law, and are rarely attracted by dogmas alien to their way of life. With just a little imagination both the East and the West could find in the building up of the United Nations authority a common platform with these newly-emerging nations, for many of whom this would be the best guarantee of their independence. For the Western powers it would be the rational sequel in world politics to their renunciation of control over their far-flung empires. It would, moreover, pave the way for new techniques of international relationship within the framework of a growing United Nations.

A mature sense of responsibility was first demonstrated by the Asian-African countries in the historic Bandung Conference seven years ago. Nearly half of the 29 countries attending that conference were not members of the United Nations at that time. Surprisingly enough, support for the United Nations was one of the first principles endorsed. The keynote of the Bandung Conference was moderation and a surprising degree of unanimity was achieved in the final declarations. Countries with different ideological and social systems went on record as favoring closer and friendlier relations.

I believe that all small countries everywhere have the same interest in the maintenance of peace and the development of a more effective international instrument for that purpose. The record of Sweden in the United Nations is an unmistakable demonstration of this attitude. Most of the small countries care passionately about peace. Many of them are aroused to furious protest against, say, racial discrimination as against *all* explosions of atomic and hydrogen bombs. For it is all part of the same compassion for humanity and the same commitment to a belief in the future of man. This philosophy which is increasingly in evidence all over the world is an affirmation of community of interest, a mass declaration that human beings must learn to understand one another even if they cannot agree with one another or like one another. It is a challenge to the conscience of the present society—a society characterized by fear, suspicion, frustration and bitterness.

I am in complete agreement with my distinguished predecessor Mr. Dag Hammarskjold when he said that it is the small nations, rather than the Great Powers, which need the protection the United Nations can give. If the West were to set about strengthening the United Nations authority upon the basis of this widely shared common interest, the possibility of effective United Nations intervention for the peaceful resolution of dangerous situations will be greatly increased. Disarmament provides an additional reason why the West should try to prepare the United Nations for a more positive role. Agreed disarmament, which all the major governments profess to want, requires as its inescapable condition the establishment of an international authority with substantial powers. To do so, the first requisite is mutual confidence. The build-up of confidence can be successful only if the United Nations is made to reflect adequately the interests and aspirations of all members large and small. In this context the role of the small nations is still more significant. One of their functions in the United Nations should be to build bridges between East and West—to interpret the East to the West and the West to the East, and thus strengthen the very foundation on which this world organization is built.

Based on these premises let us consider the future of the United Nations.

First we must realize that the world is facing a situation which is entirely unprecedented. The situation of mutual deterrence which has preserved an uneasy peace during the past few years is not in itself likely to produce continuing stability. The more the two Great Powers struggle to perfect their deterrents, the less likely it is that they will dare to use them to deal with anything except a direct attack on themselves. Tension and the dangers of an accidental calamity will rise higher and higher. Lasting security cannot be produced by this policy.

Therefore, the development of the United Nations as a

really effective instrument of preventing war is of primary importance to every one of us. Every man or woman should not only ask himself or herself what he or she is going to do in the world, but also ask, "Will there be a world in which I can live?"

The second great fact of our times is that the whole world is closely linked as never before in the history of mankind. It is not true to say that Russia and the West have no interest in common. Both have the one great overriding interest in preserving peace and avoiding total war. Once that fact is recognized, it may be possible to begin the slow, painful and extremely difficult task of constructing some agreed system of disarmament, inspection and control to replace the present international anarchy. It is not too much to hope that the small uncommitted nations will take the lead in this very necessary historic enterprise within the framework of the United Nations.

Another great fact of our times is the myth of the absolute sovereign state. Up to the First World War, Britannia ruled the waves with a very powerful navy. She was, in fact, more than an absolute sovereign state: she was also the nerve-center of a great empire. The United States, separated from possible aggressors by great oceans, was safe and could afford to be sovereign and isolationist. The same could be said of many other countries with varying degrees of strength and stability.

In San Francisco, seventeen years ago, the assembled statesmen of the world clung to this myth. They still conceived it possible to have a peaceful world consisting of a number of armed sovereign states clinging to their sovereign status without any thought of abandoning one iota of this sovereignty. If the United Nations is to grow into a really effective instrument for maintaining the rule of law, the first step must be the willingness of the member states to give up the concept of the absolute sovereign state in the same manner as we individuals give up our absolute right to do just what we please, as an essential condition of living in an organized society. The individual has to submit to the rules laid down by the authorities, and every one of us has to pay this price as a condition of living. While the sovereignty of each of us is limited to what is necessary in the interest of the community, one retains the domestic rights for the purpose of regulating one's home life.

Similarly, in the community of nations it is increasingly important to restrict the sovereignty of states, even in a small way to start with. This restriction may involve the renunciation of the threat or the use of force as an instrument of policy, the reduction of armed forces and the undertaking to submit disputes to the arbitration of an international judiciary. Even where member states of the United Nations have voluntarily agreed to such restrictions on their absolute freedom of action, the United Nations has no authority at present to enforce them. It seems to me that the United Nations must develop in the same manner as every sovereign state has done. If the United Nations is to have a future, it must assume some of the attributes of a state. It must have the right, the power and the means to keep the peace. In this historic task the small countries have a significant role to play.

In fact, the small nations have more than one role to play in this regard. First of all, as I have already noted, they are to play the part of a bridge between the Big Powers, especially in issues which are of global interest. For example, the Disarmament Conference could not get going for many years, so long as its membership was confined to the principal protagonists in the armaments race. It will be generally agreed that the issue of disarmament is of interest not only to the major military powers but to the entire world; in fact, it is one of the central responsibilities of the United Nations under the Charter. This responsibility was ultimately reflected by the addition of eight countries—outside of the major power blocs—to the Disarmament Conference, and since then there is more hope of progress than there was before. The same is true of nuclear testing, because the effects of fall-out are universal. In all such issues the small nations have a legitimate role in trying to bridge the gap between the extreme positions which are too often taken—for the record, at any rate—by the major powers.

The other role of the small nations is to give expression, so to speak, to the still, small voice. More often self interest, rather than conscience, "makes cowards of us all" and prevents us from speaking out the truth as we see it. It is again a proper role for the small nations to speak the truth as they see it, and let the chips fall where they may. This attitude was shown repeatedly by many of the small nations, and not necessarily the Asian-Africans alone, during the sixteenth session of the General Assembly. I hope that for the future too the small nations will not be either overawed by their more powerful friends, or cowed by threats into silence, and that they will continue to speak out when the occasion demands.

Both these roles—I might even say, functions—of the small nations were exemplified by my distinguished predecessor, the late Dag Hammarskjold. Over the years his role as a bridge builder was so successful that it became a common practice, when any difficult situation came along, for the major organs to say in so many words "Leave it to Dag." His "quiet diplomacy" was one of the most successful ways of bridging the gap between extreme positions, and in his own quiet and unobtrusive way he played the part of bridge builder to perfection.

Even more significant was his role as the authentic voice

of the conscience of humanity. Many times he had to speak out when others were inclined to be silent. Perhaps the most notable example was when he declared on 31 October 1956,

This afternoon I wish to make the following declaration: The principles of the Charter are, by far, greater than the Organization in which they are embodied, and the aims which they are to safeguard are holier than the policies of any single nation or people. As a servant of the Organization the Secretary-General has the duty to maintain his usefulness by avoiding public stands on conflicts between member nations unless and until such an action might help to resolve the conflict. However, the discretion and impartiality thus imposed on the Secretary-General by the character of his immediate task, may not degenerate into a policy of expediency. He must also be a servant of the principles of the Charter, and its aims must ultimately determine what for him is right and wrong. For that he must stand. A Secretary-General cannot serve on any other assumption that that—within the necessary limits of human frailty and honest differences of opinion—all member nations honor their pledge to observe all articles of the Charter. He should also be able to assume that those organs which are charged with the task of upholding the Charter, will be in a position to fulfill their task.

But this was not the only occasion. Increasingly during the last two years of his tenure, which was so cruelly cut short by a tragic fate, he spoke out on major issues and was listened to with respect, even by those who, by implication, disagreed with him. I wish, at this place where he studied and grew to manhood, to place on record this tribute to him and to his memory, and to his great contribution to the international community.

## THE UNITED NATIONS AND THE BIRTH
## OF NEW NATIONS*

I am most grateful to Williams College for honoring me with the degree of Doctor of Laws *honoris causa* and also for giving me this opportunity to say a few words at the end of the commencement exercise.

Only three days ago the General Assembly of the United Nations resumed its Sixteenth Session in order to deal with the question of Ruanda-Urundi and I feel that it might be appropriate for me to say a few words on this occasion on the role of this world organization in bringing new nations into being.

The principle of equal rights and self-determination of peoples is one of the basic principles and purposes of the Charter. The Charter contemplates that non-self-governing territories may gradually emerge as full members of the international community, and has emphasized that those administrations in charge of non-self-governing territories should "recognize the principle that the interests of the inhabitants of these territories are paramount, and accept as a sacred truth the obligation to promote to the utmost . . . the well-being of the inhabitants of these territories and to this end . . . to develop self-government . . . and to assist them in the progressive development of their free political institutions. . . ."

In addition, as you are no doubt aware, the United Nations established, under its own authority, an international trusteeship system with the basic objective of promoting "the political, economic, social, and educational advancement of the inhabitants of the trust territories and their progressive development toward self-government or independence as may be appropriate. . . ."

* Address delivered at Williams College Commencement exercises, June 10, 1962.

As a result of this preoccupation by the United Nations with the attainment of self-government by non-self-governing and trust territories, we have seen a remarkable expansion of the membership of the United Nations during its history of 16 years. Thus, the membership of the United Nations, which was 55 in 1946, stands today at the figure of 104, with the prospect of at least five or six new members joining us before the end of the year.

In this connection I would like to recall that my own country, Burma, emerged as an independent and sovereign state only in January 1948 and became a member of the United Nations in the same year. The 1950's may well be called the decade of Asia because the number of Asian countries who were members of the United Nations at the beginning of the decade was 9 and the number at the end of the decade was 15. Similarly the 1960's will surely go down in history as the decade of Africa, because, of the 22 new members who have joined the United Nations since 1 January 1960, 19 are from the African continent and it also seems fairly clear that in the future the majority of our new members will be African states.

I could, of course, be more specific and describe in detail the role of the United Nations in the birth of new nations, but the facts are too well known to need repetition. It is mainly in the field of trusteeship that the United Nations has direct responsibility, and a number of trust territories which were former mandates of the League of Nations have been guided toward independence under the watchful eyes of the Trusteeship Council and the General Assembly.

Ruanda-Urundi is the latest instance of a trust territory gradually emerging toward independence and before long we will probably have two new independent nations born out of this trust territory.

In addition to such direct assistance, the debates in the General Assembly and in the Trusteeship Council have generally created a climate which is favorable to the emergence of independent nations, after long periods of colonial rule. I am almost certain that, without the pressure of international public opinion which was thus created and developed, many of these newly independent countries might still be only on the road to self-government and would not have arrived at nationhood so quickly. This process, will, I am sure, continue.

While on this subject I would like to refer very briefly to certain aspects of colonialism. A great debate has been going on for decades as to whether the imperialist method has morally justified itself: whether the impact of Western civilization has brought more blessings than disadvantages to the subject peoples. The colonial record can claim, with some justification, to have controlled or eliminated some of the worst aspects of primitive life in certain parts of the world. It has introduced hospitals and better sanitation. It has attempted to combat ignorance as well as disease. It has brought improved methods of transport and communication. Many other material accomplishments can be enumerated.

Nevertheless, against these substantial benefits must be reckoned many features and tendencies which have counteracted these progressive influences. Chief among them is the fact that, in the past at any rate, the primary motive of the colonial power in developing the natural resources of a colony was its own commercial profit. Consequently, the greater part of the wealth obtained from the colony went into the pockets of the colonial investors. Further, the colonies remained essentially as primary producers, with little industrial development.

There is still another disturbing feature of colonialism.

Whatever advantages may have been gained by native societies consequent on the impact of a new civilization, they were offset by the fact that the colonizers often kept themselves aloof from native society. Very few of them bothered to learn the language of the people, or made a real effort to understand the indigenous culture. Wherever it existed, this aloofness and cultural exclusiveness created resentment, particularly in the minds of the educated subject peoples.

One very significant feature of independence movements is that, when independence is too long delayed, a mood of frustration and desperation sets in, and then some extreme forces come to the surface and gain the upper hand. This certainly does not help the cause of healing old wounds, or bridging the gulf between the past and the future. The role of the United Nations therefore should be not only to help expedite the emergence of new nations, but also to create conditions which will help establish friendly relations between the new nations and their former masters as also with other fellow members of the world organization.

While the United Nations can look back with satisfaction on the important role it has played in bringing these new nations into being, this historic process has had important effects on the structure and functions of the world organization. In the first place the emergence of these new countries has placed an additional responsibility on the United Nations in regard to their economic development. These countries, having become masters in their own house, have had to face serious economic problems and have turned for assistance to the United Nations and the international community. It is a heartening feature that in the last decade there has been a greatly increased sense of responsibility on the part of the international community and, especially, the economically advanced countries. During this decade we have witnessed a tremendous increase in the volume of international aid, some of it channeled through multilateral institutions such as the United Nations and its family of specialized agencies including the International Bank, but most of it has been bilateral. Recently the General Assembly adopted resolutions calling upon the advanced countries to set aside 1 per cent of their national income for the economic advancement of the less developed countries. The Sixteenth Session of the General Assembly also decided to designate the next 10 years as the United Nations Development Decade and you will hear a great deal more about what we plan to do to assist the less developed countries in stepping up their economic development at the summer session of the Economic and Social Council.

Apart from the increase of such constructive activity, especially in the economic and social field, the United Nations has been called upon to assume tremendous political responsibilities as a result of the birth of some of these new nations. I have in mind particularly the Congo, which has become one of our most important operations during the last two years. The responsibilities entrusted to the United Nations in regard to the Congo, beginning with the Security Council resolutions in July 1960, were completely novel besides being extremely onerous.

While this is not the occasion for me to deal at any length with the Congo problem, I think it will be generally conceded that the United Nations has played a significant part in preserving the sovereignty, independence, unity and territorial integrity of this new republic located in the very heart of Africa. The Congo is one of the hotly debated issues both within and outside the United Nations and it occupies a great deal of my time and energies, as also that of my colleagues. To those who are dissatisfied with the slow pace of progress in the Congo I would like to say only this: let us just look at the Congo picture today, with the possibility of the peaceful integration of the last of the secessionist provinces, and compare it with the situation this time last year, when practically two-thirds of the country was outside the control of the Central Government and in fact we had no legitimate Central Government to deal with. Today we have a legally constituted Central Government under the able leadership of Prime Minister Adoula, and we have only one province out of six still striving to maintain some form of separate identity. But it is a matter for congratulation that, during the last 22 months, not one member government of the United Nations has recognized this secessionist state, and there are now good prospects that this secession will be ended by peaceful negotiation between the Provincial President and the Prime Minister.

One consequence, of course, of the emergence of these new countries, especially from Africa and Asia, has been that the United Nations has made greater progress toward universality during the last decade than would have been considered possible 10 years ago. This, I am sure you will agree, is a good development. At the same time it has led to all kinds of complaints that the Afro-Asians are now running the United Nations, in fact, running away with it; and there are certain proposals for weighted voting. It seems strange to me that some of these suggestions about weighted voting come from countries which in their own domestic politics attach the greatest importance to democratic principles including the principle of one vote per adult human being, be he rich or poor, strong or weak, learned or ignorant.

It also seems strange that these critics of the United Nations should ignore one of the fundamental principles of the Charter, which states that "the Organization is based on the principle of the sovereign equality of all its Members" as also the principle of "equal rights of nations, large and small." I hope that this criticism of the United Nations is only a passing phase and before long even the critics will realize that the interests of humanity are best served by a universal organization practicing the true principles of democracy on the international plane.

# 5

# The United Nations Development Decade

### THE DECADE OF DEVELOPMENT*

I am very glad to be speaking to you on this occasion on the subject of the Development Decade. It is common experience that political news of any kind is reported fully by the news media while the most spectacular programs of economic development and social progress are hardly mentioned. While this is understandable, I feel at the same time that it should not be overlooked that such development and progress are one of the main purposes of the Charter of the United Nations. The Charter states that the peoples of the United Nations are determined "to promote social progress and better standards of life in larger freedom." The states members of the United Nations have accordingly pledged themselves, for these ends, "to employ international machinery for the promotion of the economic and social advancement of all peoples."

I also feel that it is particularly appropriate that I should be speaking on this subject from this forum. Den-

* Address before the Students Association, Copenhagen, Denmark, May 8, 1962.

mark has been one of the advanced countries which has consistently taken great interest in the economic development of the less developed countries of the world. Within your own shores you have established a pattern of life with the conscious goal that few should have too much and none should have too little. I believe that social justice is one of the great stabilizing forces of the world today, and that it is a good thing if this concept of social justice can be enlarged in scope so that it is no longer national in character, but becomes a global concept.

This year we are beginning a wholly new experiment in human cooperation. Over the next ten years, the United Nations and its specialized and associated agencies are pledged to mobilize their past experiences and coordinate their present efforts in a sustained attack upon the ancient enemies of mankind—disease, hunger, ignorance, poverty—and to lay the foundations in all developing lands for a more modern and productive economy. This is the broad purpose behind the Decade of Development—a coordinated program on which the member governments of the United Nations have set their seal of approval and to which each of the United Nations agencies has pledged enthusiastic support.

Why is this experiment new? The enemies, we all know, are old enough. Throughout human history, men and women have toiled painfully and all too often vainly to give themselves and their children even the simplest elements of decent human living. The sad verdict of philosophers and historians on the general lot of mankind echoes in our ears—Hobbes' definition of the human condition as "nasty, brutish and short," Thoreau's picture of innumerable, anonymous lives lived "in quiet desperation." And in the past, the degree to which the basic sources of human want and misery could be alleviated did in fact remain strictly limited. The resources needed to counter suffering were desperately scarce. And men had not the technological means to expand them or use them better. How could famine be relieved if the oxen who drew the grain carts ate half the food before it could reach the people who were starving? Such were the iron limits of human productivity. And in generation after generation, all but a fortunate few lived in permanent want—undernourished, short-lived, victims of disease, watching their children die, ignorant, bound indeed to a "melancholy wheel" of incurable privation.

I wonder if we fully realize the immense revolution that has occurred in this regard—a revolution that has begun to put an end to the old hopelessness? In the last century, at an accelerating pace, humanity has begun to break out of the old bondage. Science and technology, applied to a wider and wider range of human activities, have unlocked the doors of production. There is food enough to feed all mankind. There is speedy transport to deliver the food to any potential famine area. There are advances in fertilizers, in improved seed, in insecticides which make it certain that tomorrow—or the day after tomorrow—other economies will follow in the wake of the Danish farmer and produce more grain, more meat, more fruit, more fibers from the same acres under cultivation. In energy, in addition to conventional sources, a vast expansion of atomic power hopefully awaits us. And all the time technologies are changing and evolving so that minerals and metals can be substituted for each other and, if one wishes to be fanciful, who knows when we may not mine the planets or, by new chemical formulas, extract our needs out of sun and air?

But there is no need to be fanciful. In most of the developed societies, abundance is not a dream. It is a fact.

Otherwise, how can we explain the astonishing phenomenon that the advanced nations can spend upwards to $120 billion a year on their weapons—and yet achieve rising standards of living for their people, and on top of all that still have surplus industrial capacity lying idle—and some of them still face problems of unemployment at home? Even after all that wealth has been poured into armaments, I repeat, some of the most powerful of the world's economies still have spare labor, idle capacity, vast stockpiles of metals and minerals, and surplus food which can be, and is being, made available to feed needy men elsewhere. I cite these astonishing facts above all to illustrate the degree to which sheer abundance of available resources and *not* a narrow scarcity is the hallmark of this crucial economy, proving that the breakthrough to abundance is the profoundest achievement of the new technology in our day.

A transformation on this scale was bound to have far-reaching repercussions. And I would suggest that one of the most significant political and social changes in the last decade is the realization among more and more people that the relative abundance achieved by more developed nations is not a gift of destiny but a goal which should be available for all. The contrast between rich and poor which used to be confined to domestic society is now impressing itself deeply upon the thinking of mankind as a whole. There are rich nations and poor nations. There is a gulf of poverty and affluence cutting right through the structure of world society. And beneath the surface-play of politics, it is possible that this gulf is the deepest and most vital fact with which we have to deal.

But *can* we achieve this goal? Is it perhaps determined by culture or climate, by the local endowment of resources, by profound causes—both material and historical—over which we have all too little control? Here I would like to point to another significant change which, almost unnoticed, has been overtaking our society since the Second World War. We have become steadily more interested in the *processes* of development and more and more of our trained minds have been devoting themselves to the problem of why development occurs, of what changes and social modifications are necessary to achieve it, of the techniques it requires, the blocks and difficulties it is likely to meet. A whole new field of theory and practice is opening up here and I suggest that although, clearly, we do not know all the answers to the problem of building up a nation's resources, we know more than we did—and I think we are beginning to know it in a more systematic way. Let me give you one or two illustrations of this point.

First of all, few governments now ignore the fact that growth toward greater abundance involves sustained investment. If societies aim at a 5 per cent rate of growth each year—and when population grows by 2 per cent a year, they can hardly aim at less—then they must be prepared to increase domestic saving and investment up to a level of at least 15 per cent of national income. But, of course, an investment ratio tells us nothing about the kind of investments that have to be made, the order in which they should be undertaken, the balance that should be given to this or that sector of the economy, nor any of the deeper social implications of seeking larger savings. However, in all these fields we are beginning to know more.

A country can hardly devote more savings to the development of its resources if it does not know where those resources are to be found. Careful surveys of mineral reserves, of agricultural endowment, of resources in river and territorial waters must precede the formulation of programs for expansion. A "pre-investment" phase in which something like a resource map of the economy is pieced together is a vital tool in the new armory of development; and where such surveys can cover not simply a country, but a group of countries natually linked by some common regional interests—such as a river valley—the survey can itself make a direct contribution to growth on a wider basis.

Again, investment in resources is inseparable from investment in men. We are in the midst, I believe, of new, pioneering work in studying the development of education —in the broadest sense—in its relationship to growth and development in the economy as a whole. The standards and aims laid down at the various regional conferences on education organized by the United Nations Educational, Scientific and Cultural Organization show, I think, a far more systematic grasp of the need to dovetail the training of human beings into the expanding needs of a developing society. The balance between primary and secondary education, the role of vocational and "on-the-job" training, the size and character of the university programs—all these issues are being studied much more clearly in the light of our growing experience and we are perhaps on the brink of a breakthrough in the science of linking human and capital development in an orderly scheme of growth.

This is, in fact, one more example of a wider assertion we can make—that a measure of balance between sectors is a pre-condition of successful growth. For instance, nearly all developing countries have to keep a careful eye on their systems of power and transport. Once an economy begins to grow, its demand for both is virtually insatiable and planners are all too often caught in a series of bottlenecks which have their origins in too many firms chasing too little electricity and too few railway wagons.

But perhaps the most dangerous imbalances occur when

farming is neglected and allowed to lag behind growth in other sectors. Dynamic agriculture, producing more food for a growing urban world, releasing workers to the cities, providing markets for manufactured products, affects the cycle of growth at every turn and societies which neglect it find themselves limping along with the leg of agriculture disastrously shorter than the leg of industry.

And industry too has its pitfalls and imbalances. Nowhere are the implications of indiscriminate programing more intense. Nowhere is it easier to imagine that ten enterprises, all running below capacity and working at a loss, are in some magic way contributing to development. The wrong factory in the wrong place for the wrong product is the besetting danger of every period of growth.

All these facts of imbalance—which our work in development is making steadily more clear—point to a wider need—the need to see developing economies as organic wholes, to devise their pattern of growth systematically through a series of country plans and to accept the disciplines of such a plan in all phases of the nation's economic and social life.

And I think it is at this point that the full significance of our proposed Decade of Development begins to become more clear. For in essence it is an application to our own work, here among the agencies of the United Nations, of the principle of balance, coordination and interdependence which I have been trying to describe. There is not a sector in the developing economies of our world which cannot call upon the work and experience of an international agency. The UN Special Fund, our technical assistance programs and our work directly under the Economic and Social Council are providing unique experience not only over the whole field of economic development but also specifically in such vital areas as pre-investment and the development of human resources. UNESCO is doing pioneering work in the central field of education and the World Health Organization is there to add the extra dimension of physical health. The Food and Agriculture Organization stands ready to fight hunger and to assist in all phases of a dynamic farming program. The World Bank has a magnificent record of supplying capital for power, transport, harbors and highway development in the modernizing countries. It is also building up a corps of professional advisors in the critical field of resource planning. The International Development Association has a growing record of achievement in providing capital for the "infrastructure," for schools, hospitals and communication systems. In addition to its traditional work in various fields the International Labor Organization has expanded its operations and now has numerous training projects in the industrial and management fields. And since developing economies have wholly new problems in the sphere of their relations with other economies, we have the General Agreement on Tariffs and Trade to oversee their flow of trade and the International Monetary Fund to care for the imbalance and capital shortages which can arise in trade relations of such volume and complexity. I have already referred to the imminence of large scale development of atomic power which is the special concern of the International Atomic Energy Agency. And almost at the grass roots level, we have our UN regional commissions—in Asia, in Africa, in Europe, in Latin America—whose special responsibility it is to coordinate effort and correlate experience.

Clearly all these institutions represent a growing combination of immediate practical experience and longer-term research and analysis. And it is essential that their efforts should complement each other. Just as the developing economy itself needs to coordinate its programs and its resources and channel them through a rationally evolved country plan, so, too, it is our hope, during the Decade of Development, to bring about a similar concentration of effort, close liaison and sustained cooperative work among the agencies and thus to achieve our fundamental goal—a rate of growth among the millions of people who live in the developing world which will put them, ten years from now, on or over the threshold of self-sustaining growth.

I would like to remind you that such an effort has never been made before. The United Nations family of organizations has not hitherto proposed to itself any such broad set of goals, aiming, in a coordinated way, at human progress. And I believe that this attempt, in itself, reflects both our growing knowledge of the development process and the growing sense of urgency in dealing with the problems of development. Ten years ago, we probably did not have the experience to make such an attempt. Now the time is ripe, and by adding our efforts to each other's in a cumulative way, our assistance will be more effective, our rate of advance—in both growth and knowledge—will be speeded up, and all the while we shall be learning invaluable lessons on the types of *joint* work and effort which mankind has to undertake if our human experiment is to survive.

Shall we be able to make of this Decade of Development the achievement in human solidarity we hope it will be? We must be realistic. Our agencies represent member governments. In the last analysis, they can go no further and no faster than the nations of the world wish them to go. So it is not enough for us in the United Nations to dedicate ourselves to a Decade of Development. We have to take with us the governments to whom we are responsible and through them we have to reach out to the peoples whom these governments represent. Our Decade of Development cannot ultimately succeed unless it is rooted in the wills and hearts of millions of citizens everywhere. It will not succeed unless it can win their sustained support. It will not succeed unless they see it as a great goal of human endeavor and one which they are prepared to make their own. What are our chances? What are the obstacles? How can we see to it that sustained development is among the aims upheld by "the decent opinion of mankind?"

I think our first task must be to come back to the point with which I opened my address—the availability of resources. I question whether men and women among the wealthier nations of mankind quite realize what abundance is at their disposal or how radically science and technology are transforming and expanding the resources available to man. I have spoken of the spending on arms. Let me repeat it. Something like $120 billions a year goes into the arms effort. Were we sane enough and wise enough to make progress toward disarmament—and I hope and pray we may be sooner or later—much of this vast accumulation of capital would utimately become available to us for human betterment. The tanks could be beaten into tractors, the missiles into rockets for air transport, the metals wasted in mortar and cannon into power plants and laboratories, while the men in uniform could become the instructors, the technicians, the social workers, the artists of a new and richer life of all mankind.

But I would stress with all the vigor at my command that we do not have to wait upon disarmament. Even with armaments, many ecomomies now operate below capacity. Many have growth rates half as great as the big expanders —who go ahead by 6 and 8 and 12 per cent a year. Even if we put the capital needed for the Decade of Development at twice the level normally proposed—not at one per cent but at *two* per cent of annual national income among the richer states—the transfer would still represent no great or unbearable sacrifice.

The truth, the central stupendous truth, about developed economies today is that they can have—in anything but the shortest run—the kind and scale of resources they *decide* to have. If defense gobbles up $120 billions, the resources are provided and economies go on growing just the same. If it takes $40 billions to go to the moon, great nations will go to the moon, creating vast new electronics industries and millions of new jobs, products and opportunities as they go. It is no longer resources that limit decisions. It is the decision that makes the resources. This is the fundamental, revolutionary change—perhaps the most revoluntionary mankind has ever known.

For—make no mistake about it—the revolution brought by science and technology to the developed nations is a revolutionary extension in human freedom. Freedom is choice. Freedom is the ability to act. In the past, it has been wholly limited by the unavailability of so many of the means of action. I cannot feed my neighbor if there is no food and I cannot transport what food there is. Now those old and dreadful tyrannies of shortage are being overcome. A new freedom stares the wealthy nations in the face—the freedom to help or not to help their neighbors who still lie on the far side of abundance and who do not yet command the means to help themselves.

And so, at its profoundest level, the challenge of the Decade of Development is a *moral* challenge. How is the new freedom of our resources to be used? Can our imagination match our abundance only when the ugly, destructive risks of war are at work? Is the only challenge we recognize the challenge of fear—in weapons, in outer space, in international rivalry? Is there no way in which the great constructive and peaceful purposes of man can so grip our heart and conscience that the spending needed to end starvation, to prevent the death of little children, to shelter the homeless and clothe the naked comes to have first priority in the purposes of the human race?

I believe our enemy here is ignorance—ignorance of the scale of our resources, ignorance of the new techniques of growth, ignorance of the possibility of a bold new crusade for humanity's physical liberation. And during this Decade of Development one of our great purposes must be to end the ignorance and liberate the generous and decent instincts of mankind.

This task cannot wait. It becomes more difficult, the longer it is postponed. The secret of getting the job done is to gain early momentum, not only to increase income but to build growth on a self-sustaining kind into the systems of the developing countries. This decade is a crucial time. If we cannot take a great step forward and bring down the number of human beings living in conditions of poverty, disease, hunger and illiteracy, the outlook for all of us is not a happy one.

But I must end with a profession of faith. I am one of those who believe that development assistance to poorer countries is in the ultimate self-interest of the advanced countries themselves. But I would not want to rest my case mainly on that. I believe that ordinary men and women, once convinced of the ability to feed and succour and cherish their fellow men, will not rest until the task is done. The record of the human race is not all of war and horror. It has been sustained through generations by quiet compassion and all-encompassing love. Only the love has been limited by poverty. Today it can be as unlimited as its instincts dictate. There is no greater liberation than this and it is with this fundamental moral imperative that I would end and say, with the poet Auden, "We must love each other or we must die."

### OPENING THE DEBATE ON THE UN DEVELOPMENT DECADE*

It is for me a privilege to attend this summer session of the Economic and Social Council—a privilege enhanced by the occasion to present to you my proposals for the United Nations Development Decade.

This question is indeed more than a broad agenda item. It is, I believe, a program of such significance that, if dealt with appropriately, with vision and resolution, it might make the 34th session of the Council an historic one.

Since the adoption of the resolution by the General Assembly last winter, the United Nations Development Decade has been a major preoccupation in our minds. It has prompted much reflection and soul-searching among us and two months ago I could not refrain from addressing Danish students on this theme, during my visit to Copenhagen. I hope that I shall be forgiven if, in opening your debate on the Decade, I go back to some of the thoughts which I then expressed. This hope rests on the perhaps daring assumption that, when it comes to sharing deep convictions on fundamental issues, the language spoken to government representatives need not be altogether different from that used in addressing a nonofficial audience.

The basic fact, the basic circumstance, which warrants and indeed demands a bold, world-wide approach to economic and social development, is the now demonstrated possibility for mankind at large to create resources rather

* Statement to the Economic and Social Council at Geneva, July 9, 1962.

than depend on them. Endowed as our planet is, and able to take advantage of its riches as we have become, it is no longer resources that limit decisions. It is decisions that make resources, just as, in an economy where growth has acquired enough impetus, acceleration of such growth becomes mainly a matter of effective demand.

As I am not a professional economist, I might perhaps be candid about that notion of effective demand. It evokes the illustration of Keynesian theories inviting us to reflect on the possible stimulating effects on a depressed economy of a mobilization of workers for burying empty cans which could then be dug out, or any other modern version of Penelope's web. I wonder what Lord Keynes would say if he lived in our world of today, in which one and one half billion people suffering from hunger or malnutrition have become pressingly vocal in international forums. Across frontiers he would see, on the one hand, demand for more necessities and greater opportunities; on the other hand, competition for more and deadlier weapons, which I can only conceive as a highly dangerous substitute for the empty can exercise.

In this respect, it is good, and significant of the United Nations' approach, that at the time when the Economic and Social Council is breaking new ground for a momentous long-term program of economic and social development, it is also seized for the first time with the problem of economic and social consequences of disarmament. This may be historically a coincidence, but we should turn it into an opportunity for a broader and deeper reflection on the major problems of our day. Armaments—or disarmament—are a major determinant of the pace, nature and scope of economic and social progress, and they bear in more than one way on the debate which is opening today. At the threshold of the 1960's it is of great importance that a report of the quality of that which is before you should do justice in a decisive way to an alleged and invidious relationship between armaments and prosperity, which may be lingering in the minds of many. By stating categorically, and on the basis of a unanimous finding, that the disappearance of military budgets should not result in the collapse, nor even a serious dislocation of the economies of the industrialized countries, the experts have strengthened our belief that the trend toward increasing armaments is not irreversible and that disarmament, our only durable insurance against the risk of annihilation, is not beyond the reach of the international community. The experts have at the same time drawn attention to the fact, very relevant to this debate on a decade of development, that action should be planned ahead, and preparations made in the economic and social field, for the advent of disarmament. And it is good that we can have confidence that this is being done.

At the same time, I should like to emphasize my conviction that we cannot wait upon disarmament. Mobilizing resoures for economic and social progress is an effort which can and must go forward, whatever happens to military budgets. If the latter were to dwindle or disappear in a near future, as we so keenly hope, the less developed world should, of course, share the savings with the taxpayers of the big powers and additional billions would be available to speed up development all over the world. But let us not make fuller international cooperation contingent upon a particular manifestation of it, however crucial the latter may be.

Is our imagination going to be spurred only by the fear of an international rivalry? Or will the idea that man can change and better his lot become the most powerful driving force of mankind in this century? The latter proposition is the one which we must make come true. What would be the significance, otherwise, of the current process of decolonization bringing to independence so many countries which immediately acquire membership in the Organization by unanimous vote? Political freedom can only render more intolerable the coexistence between the rich and the poor, in the international context just as in any national one.

It is gratifying to see that financial and technical assistance from high-income to low-income countries have become an accepted feature of the international economy, with former colonial powers often accounting for a decisive share in the foreign financial and human resources placed at the disposal of the newly independent countries. But the problem of increasing external assistance and of maximizing its effectiveness becomes every day more acute. In a world shrunken by the progress of communication media, the pressure of underprivileged citizens against national inequalities in levels of living becomes the impatience of entire populations with subnormal standards of nutrition, shelter, education and medical care while billions are spent on, say, space research. I say this because, if everybody is not assured a share in the benefits of the scientific progress which leads us into space, if the fast growing investment capital and technical know-how which are applied to push farther the present boundaries of the kingdom of man are not also fully used to bring better life to all within such boundaries, then the fate of mankind itself is in serious jeopardy. And while, on the plane of tactics, this explosive situation might still allow the interplay of political considerations, on the plane of global strategy it has come to assume the proportions of a compelling moral challenge, in terms of human dignity and human kinship.

It is now a recognized fact that, with present population

trends, the widening of the gap between affluent societies
and low-income economies can only be countered by self-
sustaining and accelerated growth in the latter. To achieve
such growth in minimum time, efforts must, of course,
proceed in the most coherent manner towards pre-deter-
mined objectives. In recent years, the will to get more for
more people at a fast pace has led governments to frame
their major lines of action in the economic and social field
in development plans and today we see the emergence of
this approach on the international scene.

In 1960, the General Assembly requested industrialized
countries to devote at least 1 per cent of their global national product to international aid. In 1961, it has set as a
target a 5 per cent annual rate of growth in the aggregate
national income of less developed countries. Those figures
are very modest ones, and purely indicative of a desirable
minimum. They evidence, however, a definite desire to
project, to organize and phase the work in relation to
clearly defined and quantified targets—an approach typical
of that adopted by an increasing number of governments
for their national economies.

The United Nations Development Decade is a pressing
invitation to member governments to increase their social
and economic investments in a most forward looking, pur-
poseful, cooperative and integrated fashion. But it is also,
and as much, a development plan for the United Nations
family of organizations. In my report, a prospective presentation has been attempted which aims at determining
how the current efforts of our organizations—as distinct
from the sum of those of their members—could best be
pursued and stepped up for a greater effectiveness of our
response to the development challenge. For the numerous
fields of activity and many areas of work in which projects
have been undertaken under the aegis of the United Na-

tions family, indications are given on the ways in which the secretariats concerned see a possibility to increase their catalytic role and usefulness to the community of nations, on the basis of past experience and present expectations.

The analogy with planning exercises conducted in national contexts is not yet carried very far, as attempts to detail our proposals in quantitative terms encounter obvious limitations at this stage. We have endeavored to determine targets, however. Thus, we envisage that the total resources available for United Nations programs in the field of pre-investment and technical cooperation, including Special Fund activities (but leaving aside extraordinary undertakings such as our civilian operations in the Congo) should grow at a minimum yearly rate of $25 million, from the level of $150 million for the year 1962—a level which, we must note, is not yet reached.

One of our most important undertakings in this regard is the United Nations Conference on Science and Technology to be held early in 1963. A glance at the agenda of the Conference evokes the breadth and span of man's imagination and inventiveness which have brought us from subsistence economy to the atomic age. But as we now enter the space age, while entire nations still have to make their industrial revolution, the real challenge for that imagination and inventiveness is to render advanced theory and modern practices valid and effective in less developed contexts. The purpose of the Conference is precisely to assess possibilities and stimulate efforts in that direction. The confrontations, discussions and exchanges which are to take place in these very halls among scientists and experts from many countries at all stages of development should have far-reaching effects.

In sharing ideas and experience about specific development problems, industrialized countries may receive from less developed ones as much as they will give to them. Also, less developed countries will learn one from another in the true spirit of United Nations cooperation, which is characterized by an increasing proportion of expert and training services provided to less developed countries by countries which are themselves underdeveloped. The work of the Conference and the dissemination of its documents should open up new vistas for investment projects. They should stimulate interest in a lasting manner for adjusting different methods and processes to different operating conditions, for modifying concepts, schemes and procedures as required by given changes in milieu. They should inspire scholars as well as foster among experts the desire and ability to diversify their experience and to try out abroad a "know-how" so far proven only at home. And all this should increase the availability of persons professionally and mentally prepared for international service, the human resources on which United Nations programs of technical cooperation are so dependent.

The importance of the human factor is so over-riding that the success or failure of our efforts in the course of the United Nations Development Decade may well depend on our success or failure to carry out properly the training activities which we propose to undertake in the various sectors of the economic and social life of less developed countries. Over the years past, much progress has been made in training methods and techniques. The distinctions between academic and vocational training, between adult and child education, between teachers and students, have become ancillary to the urgent task of enabling every human being to assert himself as an individual and as a productive citizen to the best of his capacities. As if the need for education as an essential support of the dignity of man was not compelling enough in moral terms, we now see, in economic and social terms, that no breakthrough will be possible for less developed countries unless they add fast to their resources in skilled manpower. While training abroad, with its special value from the point of view of international understanding, continues to be of importance, emphasis has been placed on training within the less developed regions and countries themselves. The time is now ripe for an all-out effort. Training on the spot, training on the job, training of the teachers who will train the teachers—everything must be done to achieve the maximum multiplier effect inherent in the dissemination of knowledge and know-how. Without more schools and more institutes such as those on which the United Nations Special Fund spends much of what my colleague Paul Hoffman so aptly calls its "seed money," less developed countries will not be able to turn their population growth from a curse into a blessing.

The United Nations Development Decade is an appeal to our faith in the preservation and in the continuation of economic and social progress by investing in the younger generations who, in addition to education and training, require help to fight malnutrition and disease. Together with investment in industry, large and small, in natural resources and in transport, investment in less developed countries during the Decade must provide for the construction of more than twenty million dwellings in less developed areas and for an increase in food supplies of fifty per cent; in those same countries, expenditure for public health services must double over the period and expenditure on education must rise to an annual rate of 4 per cent of the national product by the end of the Decade—all this in order to meet minimum requirements so interrelated that failure to reach one target in time may jeopardize advances on all other fronts. The complexities of the processes of balanced economic and social development are great, and available techniques for comprehensive planning are far from perfect. But enough knowledge and experience have accumulated already to give our efforts a decisive momentum. We will correct and improve as we go but we must forge ahead in all sectors with mutually supporting programs and projects. For we have passed the time of rising expectations to enter the era of achievements counted upon by billions of people who do not yet enjoy full rights as producers and consumers, or simply as human beings living in the twentieth century.

One very important field in which concrete progress is eagerly awaited is that of international trade. However unfamiliar he may be with the intricacies of its many problems, even the ordinary layman realizes that the possibility to sell more and buy more abroad is a crucial test of international cooperation. The momentum gathered by the work of your Commission on International Commodity Trade, the initiation of intergovernmental action for the development of international compensatory schemes taking into account long-term trends in the demand and supply of primary commodities, carry us well beyond the mere discussion of the compatibility of regional groupings. Encouraging steps have already been taken. Let us hope that, during the Decade, the expansion of international trade will be significant enough for its beneficial effects to be felt in the budget of every household.

So much for the tasks ahead of us. They will no doubt impose a vast additional burden of responsibility on the Secretariat, which over the last few years has already shouldered a significant increase of work in the economic and social field.

To these new tasks I am determined to devote fully all the resources available to me, both in Headquarters and in the four regional economic commissions of the United Nations. The heads of the agencies will no doubt similarly devote the energies of their respective secretariats to the tasks falling within their fields of competence.

The efforts of the organizations of the United Nations family cannot, however, be isolated from the sum of the efforts of their members. For it remains true that the United Nations family can mobilize and utilize no more than the human and financial resources put at their disposal by governments. The extent to which our targets and proposals will acquire value as setting minimum standards of progress, depends on the extent to which they can be implemented, and this again depends on the decisions and pledges of our membership. This Council, for its part, should play a decisive role not only in the formulation of our ten-year development plan but also in its implementation, responsible as it is for evaluating progress from year to year and for seeing that all activities proceed at the right pace and in proper balance in the economic and social field. I am convinced that your discussions and resolutions will contribute much to translating the proposals for the United Nations Development Decade into integrated programs for practical action unfolding gradually and effectively. And may our endeavors be a true reflection and a useful complement of the efforts of individual nations to help each other and, in so doing, to make for a more prosperous and safer world for all.

### THE REPORT ON THE PROPOSALS FOR ACTION*

The report which is being made public today entitled "The United Nations Development Decade—Proposals for

* Statement at a Press Conference at the United Nations, New York, June 14, 1962.

Action" deals with a subject of such extraordinary importance that I felt it desirable to meet and discuss it with you at a press conference wholly devoted to it.

Last December, you will recall, the General Assembly adopted unanimously a resolution designating the current decade as the United Nations Decade of Development. The text of that resolution appears as Annex I to this report. In it, the Assembly requested the Secretary-General to develop proposals which would give more concrete shape to this historic concept.

This report, which has been prepared in response to that request, I hope to present myself to the Economic and Social Council at its session in Geneva next month. It will doubtless be the subject of further action by ECOSOC and by Member States this year. It will also come before the General Assembly at its seventeenth session in September. At each of these stages, I hope the Development Decade will take on new clarity and new momentum.

I know you are all well aware of what the United Nations family has been doing in the field of economic development and technical assistance for more than ten years. And I imagine you are also familiar with the efforts of the various bilateral aid programs, large and small, during the same period. Much good work has been done by all these programs, which do great credit to the generosity of the nations whose contributions have made them possible: but they have all suffered from the same basic limitation. They have had to respond to a need which is so staggering in its dimensions that they have not been able to deal effectively with more than a few segments of it. Now, for the first time, it has been decided to make a concerted attack on the age-old problems of poverty, ignorance and disease, using every resource which is available to us, whether it be national or international in character. Moreover, it has been decided that this concerted attack should be made under the banner of the United Nations itself.

The fundamental facts which underlie the Development Decade are not new to you who are present today. Some of you know them by hard experience. Others have learned them with us here and have reported them in your articles and broadcasts on the basis of the great volume of research and statistical analysis which the various organs of the United Nations have produced in recent years. You will however forgive me if I remind you of some of the factors which have moved governments to embark on this new initiative and to pledge their full cooperation.

First come certain facts about the world economic situation. In the decade of the 1950's the rate of economic progress of at least one-third of the human race—the poorest third who are intent on conquering their own poverty—was dangerously slow. Despite increasing economic development efforts in that decade, their average rise in income per person, when account is taken of their rapidly growing populations, has been less than 1 per cent per year. That means less than one dollar a year of improvement per person, which in human terms is an imperceptible advance. But in the same period the economies of the highly developed countries, starting from a very much higher base, have been growing faster. And thus the already huge gap between their living standards and those of the less developed nations has widened still further.

These material facts are dangerously in conflict with a psychological or spiritual fact: namely, that the peoples themselves who are victims of this situation, and still more their leaders, nowadays look upon the perpetuation of poverty in a world of plenty as morally wrong and politically intolerable. Most of them have only recently achieved sovereign independence, and they are determined to use their new political liberty to escape also from the bondage of want. From this state of affairs arise pressures for change which may build up to dangerous and explosive levels unless they can find a constructive outlet.

Another element in the picture is our knowledge that this situation is no longer unavoidable. It is now within the power of modern man to control and improve it. The investment capital exists, and wisely directed it will multiply itself. The scientific and technical capacities exist, waiting only to be redirected towards new goals and toward the solution of neglected problems. The natural resources and the human potential exist, waiting only to be discovered and put to work.

The ultimate goal of the development decade, as suggested by the General Assembly, is an annual 5 per cent of growth in the national incomes of the developing countries. Given the expected increase in population over the decade, it would represent a 2 per cent increase each year in personal income. Perhaps 2 per cent does not seem very great in itself. It is, however, twice the present estimated growth rate, and it can mean the difference between an economy which is going forward, and one which is standing still. Further, it can mean the difference between order and chaos, and between hope and despair for the millions of people whose earnings, for the most part, fall short of $100 per year.

The document which has been released today contains a series of concrete proposals as to how this goal may be achieved. The methods proposed do not represent any great innovation. They are essentially those which have proved most successful in the past. The proposals call, however, for a steady expansion of existing activities within the context of a better knowledge of what each country requires and what it can realistically achieve. The

United Nations will assume an even larger responsibility than heretofore for helping governments to ensure that their national plans—the core of the program are sound. I hope that the United Nations family will also be able to expand and develop its own assistance programs. It is up to the member states to say how great and how rapid that expansion should be. But the United Nations family— including the Expanded Technical Assistance Program and the Special Fund on a world-wide basis, the regional economic commissions at the grassroots level, and the specialized agencies in their respective fields of competence—has the merit of impartiality and an unrivaled range of technical skills on which it can draw from nations all over the world.

These United Nations assets have already proved themselves in action. They are not in any sense in competition with bilateral national aid, or with established trade patterns, or with private investment; on the contrary, the key activities of the United Nations should be a stimulus to greater and more fruitful efforts in every field which is vital to the total effort.

Perhaps, above all, the United Nations can be a center of coordination, of inspiration and confidence for the enormous complex of efforts on which the Development Decade will depend.

We are barely over the threshold of this adventure of development. We are only beginning to gather speed. It is tremendously important, in the months and years ahead, as the Development Decade takes concrete shape and substance, that the public be aware of its broad implications. In this regard, we shall rely, as always, on the ability of the communications media to distill what is human and fundamental from the complex technicalities and statistical analyses on which the policies and programs of the Devel-

opment Decade must inevitably be based. We on our side
are planning to do what we can to help you by the preparation of suitable materials for wider dissemination.

I know that I can count on the cooperation of you all in
this truly great enterprise which, second only to the safeguarding of peace itself, is the most important task of the
United Nations today.

## INTERNATIONAL ASPECTS OF DEVELOPMENT*

I am very grateful to you for inviting me to say a few
words at this luncheon on the theme of international aspects of development. I see many familiar faces in this hall
and at this table, and I know that many of you have followed with interest the activities of the United Nations in
the field of economic and social development. You must
all, I am sure, be aware of the fact that the subjects dealt
with in this Conference are akin to those discussed in the
various forums of the United Nations. This is, of course,
no coincidence, in view of the aims and outlook of the
Society for International Development. Its concern with
the vital problems of economic and social development,
and of the role of international co-operation in promoting
the development of the growing societies, recalls the determination "to promote social progress and better standards of life in larger freedom" which is so prominently
featured in the Preamble to the United Nations Charter.

I note with interest that you have chosen as the subject
for this, your Fifth World Conference, the question:
"What Makes Development Happen?" This is an equivocal question, and obviously it was intended to be such. Are

* Address delivered at the Fifth World Conference of the Society for
International Development, New York, April 5, 1963.

we to enquire into the motivations which are responsible for the urge to develop, or shall we be concerned only with the workings of the development process? Obviously both exercises are in order, and indeed called for, since a better understanding of the motivations of development can assist us in our efforts to organize ourselves to promote it. While much of the work of this Conference is properly devoted to the discussion by specialists of ways and means to make development happen, I shall, if I may, indulge in a few lay remarks on the circumstances which, I believe, account for the overriding importance of the problem of development in the world of today, and also explain my reasons for hoping that the challenge it poses may be met by our generation.

I have chosen as my theme the international aspects of development, in view of the concern for economic and social development expressed in the Charter itself, under which the United Nations is pledged "to employ international machinery for the promotion of the economic and social advancement of all peoples." One may ask why such an important place was given to economic and social development in an Organization mainly concerned with preserving the peace. I believe that the answer is that the framers of the Charter saw a clear relationship between economic and social development, especially in the developing countries, and the stability and peace of the world. In realizing this inter-connexion, the founding fathers of the United Nations saw far ahead of their own times; they obviously foresaw the tremendous surge of the movement of freedom from colonial rule that we have witnessed in the seventeen years since the Organization was founded. This historic process has lent urgency to the problem of economic and social development, and this urgency was recognized by the member governments of the United Nations when in December 1961 they resolved to designate the 1960's as the United Nations Decade of Development.

I had these considerations in mind in thinking it would be appropriate for me at this Conference to deal with the international rather than the national aspects of development. In so doing, however, let me not be construed as underrating the importance of the national aspects of development. To a group such as yourselves, it is hardly necessary for me to point out that no nation can be made to develop if it is not seized by an inner urge for development. All the external aid in the world and all the efforts of international organizations cannot make development happen without this basic urge.

But the urge alone is not enough. The developing countries have perhaps been too prone in the days of colonial rule to blame their underdevelopment on their lack of political freedom. When they have achieved this political freedom, it does not take them long to realize that development is made up of many factors, and that they are short of both the human and material resources that can make development happen. Basically, nations must pull themselves up by their bootstraps, but a little friendly assistance and encouragement can make the operation easier, and the developing countries are becoming increasingly vocal in requesting such assistance from international organizations, as also from bilateral sources.

The recognition on the part of the economically advanced countries that they have a responsibility to promote the economic development of the less advanced countries is one of the more heartening features of our times. The motivations for giving such assistance to the developing countries are usually many and varied. Whatever the motivations, there is no doubt that the developing countries owe a great deal to this spirit of generosity and this understanding of their problems which the advanced countries have shown. I would like on this occasion to pay a tribute to the advanced countries for this assistance, without which many of the developing countries would have had to put up with an even slower rate of growth.

One may ask, why then has the gap between the richer and poorer countries been widening during the last few years? Why are the richer countries getting more affluent and the poorer countries becoming needier? Some explanation of this phenomenon is due.

One element is no doubt the deterioration in the terms of trade of the primary producing countries. The problem of trade is one with many facets, and various aspects of it have been explored both in and outside of the United Nations. The general question of the progressive decline of the prices of primary products, as well as related issues, such as the problem of evening out violent fluctuations of prices by compensatory financing schemes or commodity agreements, have all been studied in the United Nations. At the same time, we hear the view expressed increasingly that trade, not aid, is the answer to the problem of development.

The developing countries are naturally taking great interest in problems of trade, besides giving attention to national and international programmes of external assistance. This interest has been given concrete expression in the decision of the seventeenth session of the General Assembly to convene a United Nations Conference on Trade and Development. The discussions at this Conference will not only include such familiar problems as terms of trade, but also questions such as trade restrictions and trade discrimination. We already have sufficient indications that these discussions are not likely to be of an academic nature. Judging from the interest that the proposed Conference has already aroused, I feel that the Conference will be regarded in later years as a very significant step forward in working out a new deal in economic international relations. Indeed, I feel that there are few problems before the United Nations which hinge so much on the realization that the disparities between the richer and poorer nations must be tackled in a dynamic and forward looking manner as that of the problem of international trade.

The growing awareness of the widening gap between rich and poor countries, and of the dangerous tensions that such inequities create, to which I have just referred, is accompanied by a growing realization that it can be remedied—not by recourse to charity, nor by calling upon the solidarity imposed on those nations by the shrinking of our planet to the dimensions of a community, nor by sharing the riches which exist, but by maximizing for all the opportunities to reap the fruits of modern science and technology.

The two thousand-odd papers submitted to the major Conference on the Application of Science and Technology recently held in Geneva under the auspices of the United Nations provide numerous illustrations of the fact that methods and processes exist and are continuously improved, for discovering new resources as well as for exploiting existing ones; and that, nowadays, man's ingenuity and inventiveness enable him to derive from his surroundings all that is needed to bring abundance to everyone on earth. The problem is to organize ourselves in such a manner as to apply this ingenuity and inventiveness to the less developed areas, to adapt and innovate so as to set in motion the process of development, and let it gather added momentum where it has already made a start. The Conference was focused on this problem and I find it most encouraging that so many scientists and technicians from all parts of the world were conscious of its importance and stimulated by it.

I referred a moment ago to the issue of trade versus aid. When one examines the question of aid in depth, one is struck by the fact that the resources so far made available to the international programmes, including the relatively large funds available to the International Bank and the International Development Association, are modest in comparison to the big programmes of bilateral aid. In the United Nations itself, while additional resources were placed at the disposal of the Organization with the establishment of the United Nations Special Fund, we have been able only to advance from pure technical assistance to pre-investment assistance. In spite of our limited resources, however, I believe we can make a substantial contribution to the economic development of the less developed countries in two important fields, namely, planning and industrialization.

Not so long ago, there were quite divergent views in the membership of the United Nations about the desirability and wisdom for governments to set targets and adopt national plans or programs. Today, in spite of the wide differences in political philosophy and ideology obtaining among the 110 nations represented in our General Assembly, there is a broad measure of agreement about the usefulness of projections, planning and programming as practical tools for economic and social development, while the controversy about the relative merits of private enterprise and public undertakings is transcended by the realization that the most important aim of development is to bring about expansion and change for the benefit of all.

Of course, planning by itself cannot make development happen. A nation has the responsibility, as I already mentioned, to set its own goals and to adopt and enforce the policies, measures and reforms which are to lead towards those goals. But the fact that planning techniques have proved their worth under different economic and social systems, and also in countries at very different stages of development—as the experience of France, India and the USSR bear witness—leads us to recognize the value of planning as a flexible concept in the strategy of development, especially where growth does not take place as a result of the spontaneous action of producers operating in a well established institutional context. The plan allows the Government to see its role in perspective, and this is particularly important in an underdeveloped economy where the public sector has to act as the spearhead. In drawing up the plan, the authorities have to ascertain the wishes of their peoples and the implications of those wishes; in executing it, they benefit from a better understanding of the obligations and sacrifices being imposed, which would seem greater and less fair, were they not part of a scheme reflecting the long-term aspirations of the community.

If we go into this problem a little deeper, we find that planning consists essentially in establishing functional relationships and, whether the setting is that of a developed or less developed economy, it implies the same logic, the same need to achieve maximum coherence, the same compulsion to take full cognizance and advantage of the interdependence of all the factors and sectors of economic and social life. In a highly industrialized economy, as in a less diversified one, any attempt at planning presupposes that progress in a particular area is conditioned by progress in another; that weak spots should be strengthened with the help of resources generated in the strong ones; that the growth of the whole can be greater than the average growth of the components if the proper interactions among the latter are fostered; that a sacrifice accepted here and now may yield great benefits in a broader outlook and in the longer term.

This awareness of the great law of interdependence has found an outstanding occasion to assert itself in the efforts undertaken everywhere to promote industrialization in the less developed areas. While, at first sight, industrialization evokes the opportunity to apply or adapt science and technology, it soon becomes a question of defining pre-requisites, of striking a proper balance with the modern-ization of agriculture, a balance between heavy and light industry, between resource-based complexes and scattered establishments, between capital intensity and labour in-tensity, etc. A wide and intricate network of inter-relation-ships soon forces us to conceive of industrialization as but one aspect of the process of development, which involves everybody far and near. Success in this process depends not only upon the composition of the various forces dormant or at play within the nation, but also on the co-operation which can be achieved with other nations to give concrete and constructive expression to their mutual dependence.

Once it has been recognized that economic development implies industrialization, it becomes obvious that allow-ance must be made for the diversification of international trade. I have already said something on the subject of terms of trade. Sooner or later, the less developed countries will have to decide that they should diversify their econo-mies, to produce and export larger quantities of processed and manufactured goods. Failure to adopt in time the right commercial policies may thwart progress everywhere, because of the interdependence of suppliers and customers. Again, the only recourse is co-operation, an international co-operation rather than one conceived solely on a regional basis. Indeed, it is interesting to see that, just as sectoral programming breeds comprehensive planning, the tendency toward regional groupings, which manifests itself increasingly in less developed as well as in industrialized areas, does not alleviate but in fact strengthens the need for discussions of broader scope, the striving for ever-widening arrangements such as those which can be arrived at in extra-regional consultations and with the ambit of global organization.

An increasing share of the resources of the United Nations is devoted to the promotion of international cooperation for economic and social development. If to what we are doing, both through central organs and regional bodies, we add the activities of the other organizations of the United Nations family in their specialized fields of work, the resulting picture is, I believe, an encouraging one. True, the world organization has not yet brought about an organized world, and the effectiveness of the United Nations is often less than that of regional groupings. But where the latter are not outward looking enough, the universality of our membership gives special significance to everything which is proposed or undertaken by the United Nations. We are increasingly called upon to act not as a mere forum for debate but as a focal point where world opinion takes shape, colour and life.

I am not neutral in the fight for the reduction of North-South tensions, which reveal themselves as more fundamental than the East-West ones, and I may not be altogether objective when it comes to evaluating the usefulness and importance of the Organization which I serve. Yet, I am fully aware that it can do little without the active support of the peoples in whose name our Charter has been written. The awareness of the realities and necessities of our times is not yet present in all minds. Powerful forces of inertia or resistance are still latent or at work. In underdeveloped areas, self-help, initiative and the sense of purpose must be stimulated. In industrialized countries, the industrialist must move to the new fields opened up by scientific progress, and accept the competition of the developing nations in the traditional ones; while the taxpayer should be better informed about the worthiness of the investment he is called upon to make through his government's contributions to schemes of international aid. Everywhere international understanding must be promoted. In all these tasks, the contribution of non-governmental bodies and dedicated individuals may be decisive. Through organizations like the S.I.D. and meetings like the present Conference, I believe that much can be accomplished toward enlightening the citizens of the world and mobilizing their good will.

The battle for economic growth and social change must be waged on many fronts, but the objective is not beyond the material and spiritual means of our contemporary society. The paramount importance of accelerated training, pre-investment work and basic capital formation is now generally understood. The spectacular achievements of numerous developing countries, as well as the steps already being taken on the road toward closer international cooperation, make me believe not only that development does happen as a process but also that, as a concept, it has captured the mind of man and will help him not only to visualize, but also to achieve, a world of plenty for all. Such a world, may I hope, will also be a world of peace for all.

### FREEDOM FROM HUNGER*

I feel it a great privilege to be able to participate in the World Food Congress. The Congress is a major event in the Freedom-from-Hunger Campaign, which in turn forms part of the international effort to make the United Nations Decade for Development a reality.

The objectives of the Congress and the Freedom-from-Hunger Campaign are among the objectives of the Charter of the United Nations itself, which calls for the promotion of higher standards of living, full employment, and conditions of economic and social progress and development. But they are far from being vague or abstract objectives; they are very concrete; and they cannot fail to stir the imagination and arouse the enthusiasm of all men and women of goodwill.

Many of us come from countries where hunger is no stranger, but an ever-present reality, seen on the roadside and at street corners. FAO has provided us with the stark facts; it has put figures to the paradox of poverty in the midst of plenty, of famine or near-famine side by side with surpluses, a paradox which represents, let us admit, such a reproach to our present-day world.

In times past, there seemed little one could usefully do to meet this challenge except by way of charity or temporary relief, but in recent years we have come to realize that the paradox can be resolved, and that we have the technical knowledge required to eliminate hunger from the face of the earth. This is the extraordinary challenge facing our generation, a challenge which has been taken up by the Freedom-from-Hunger Campaign, and which forms the theme of your Congress.

* Address before the World Food Congress, Washington, D. C., June 4, 1963.

President Lyndon B. Johnson arrives to address the General Assembly. He is shown here with U Thant and (left) Assembly President Carlos Sosa-Rodriguez and Under-Secretary Ralph J. Bunche (at Mr. Thant's left)

View of the General Assembly as President Johnson addresses the delegates on December 17, 1963

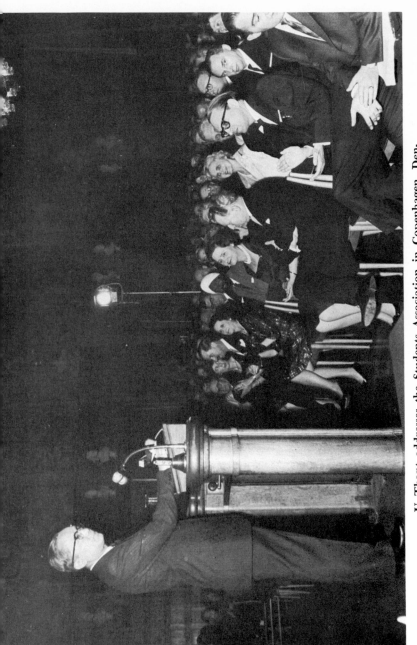

U Thant addresses the Students Association in Copenhagen, Denmark, on May 8, 1962

A visit to Florence. The Secretary-General is shown leaving the Palazzo Vecchio in the Italian city on July 1, 1956

The Secretary-General inspects a Guard of Honor during his visit
to Kingston, Jamaica, in February 1963

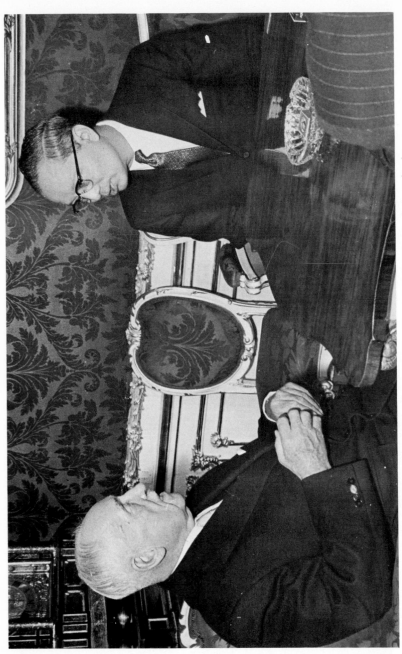

U Thant in a discussion with President Adolf Scharf of Austria, in
the Imperial Palace in Vienna, September 3, 1962.

In Kultaranta, Finland, U Thant visited President Urho Kekkonen,
July 19, 1962. Mrs. Kekkonen is at the President's right

In London, Hugh Gaitskell, Leader of the Labour Party, greeted Mr. Thant in the House of Commons, July 5, 1962

U Thant with King Olaf V of Norway, on a pier in Oslo, where they are about to embark on the Royal yacht "Norge," July 10, 1962

Ambassador Adlai E. Stevenson entertaining the Secretary-General and Mrs. Jacqueline Kennedy at luncheon in the United Nations Headquarters, on February 7, 1963

Attorney-General Robert F. Kennedy meets with U Thant at United Nations Headquarters upon his return from the Far East, January 28, 1964

The King and Queen of Denmark entertain U Thant at Fredensborg Palace, Copenhagen, May 8, 1962. At Mr. Thant's right is Princess Margarethe

The Secretary-General at the Quirinale Palace, Rome, with President
Antonio Segni of Italy, July 10, 1963

President Eamon de Valera of Ireland greets U Thant in Dublin, July 14, 1961. At right is Irish Foreign Minister Frank Aiken

The Secretary-General welcomes President Tito of Jugoslavia and Mrs. Tito to United Nations Headquarters, New York, October 20, 1963

U Thant with British Prime Minister Home (at that time Foreign Secretary), in London, May 20, 1963

I hope that your discussions will serve to lay out a strategy for our attempts to solve the problem, and that the Congress as a whole will bring home to world opinion the tremendous importance of the issues at stake.

Hunger today affects mainly the developing countries. The most important line of attack is, of course, to increase food production in these same countries. But the achievement of useful results is rendered both more urgent and more difficult by the rapid population increase in these areas to which the President of the United States has referred a moment ago; an annual increase of 2 per cent to 3 per cent in food production is needed merely to feed an expanding population at the present woefully inadequate levels. To make a serious impact on the problems of hunger an annual increase of the order of 4 per cent to 5 per cent is consequently needed.

How can such a target be reached? One does not need to be either a scientist or a farmer to realize that the best hope lies in the widespread adoption of scientific techniques in agriculture that have already produced startling results in the advanced countries.

We have tried to contribute to this objective through the recent United Nations Conference on the Application of Science and Technology for the Benefit of the Less Developed Areas, which was held in Geneva last February. One of the main items on the agenda was agriculture; all the resources of agricultural science and technology were laid out in 516 papers, the greatest number submitted to the Conference on any subject.

This wealth of material, together with the conclusions to be drawn from discussions at the Conference itself, is available to the developing countries and FAO is taking vigorous steps to ensure that it is used to the best advantage. The extension within the developing areas of such modern techniques as the use of fertilizers and improved seeds, the extension of irrigation and double-cropping, the provision of suitable tools and machinery, and in the case of livestock a scientifically designed breeding programme, improved feeding and the control of disease, such measures seem to me to offer the best hope for large-scale success.

Economic and social development can be aided, and critical shortages can be relieved, by contributions of food from surplus stocks held by certain of the advanced countries. Indeed, the extension of food-aid programmes, and notably the recent inauguration under the joint auspices of the United Nations and FAO of the World Food Programme, convince me that the existence of what are referred to as "surpluses" has become an established feature of the contemporary world economy.

And this must surely bring us to realize that surpluses can, within certain limits, be translated from economic liabilities into social assets. I believe, indeed, the time may have come for a new look at the entire problem of agricultural surpluses and especially for redefinition of the word "surplus" itself, because, properly used, "surpluses" may be of the greatest benefit to mankind.

I have talked, so far, mainly about food production, that is to say, about measures to make enough food available to under-nourished populations. But this is only the first half of a solution, for the populations in turn must have enough income to be able to buy the food that is offered to them. The millions of poverty-stricken town-dwellers, for instance, can only hope to buy more food if they have regular employment, and employment must be provided to them by the establishment of industries. A growing urban market, in turn, is necessary to ensure the farmers of an outlet for their expanding production.

The town cannot live without the countryside, nor can

the countryside hope to prosper without the town. Thus, the problem of eliminating hunger rejoins the complex process of general economic and social development, which is the target of the United Nations Development Decade as a whole.

All the agencies in the United Nations system are working in their different spheres of activity for the objectives of the Decade. Of primary importance for the problems of hunger and malnutrition is, of course, the work of FAO, the sponsor of the present Congress. The work of other specialized agencies is also of great relevance, as you will be hearing in subsequent statements.

The contribution of the United Nations itself takes a variety of forms, embracing as it does the work of the Special Fund, the Expanded Programme of Technical Assistance and UNICEF. Among the various fields of specific concern to the United Nations, I have referred already to industrial development, and we also have particular responsibilities in the development of water resources, which, of course, are essential for agriculture.

And I should like to refer to a subject of special importance right now, namely, international trade. The United Nations Conference on Trade and Development will take place in the early part of next year and, indeed, the Preparatory Committee for the Conference is meeting at present in Geneva.

It is hoped that the Conference will produce measures that will permit the developing countries to achieve expanding exports at stable prices. An increase in their export earnings would in turn enable them to finance extended development programs, which are so vitally necessary to raise the standards of living of their populations.

I have spoken already, in connection with agriculture, about our recent Conference on Science and Technology.

The material provided by the Conference also covers many other sectors of the development process, some of which are relevant to the problem of food. For instance, an economic method of desalinizing sea water would revolutionize the agricultural prospects of large areas of our globe. We are paying increasing attention to these major questions, and have prepared a series of proposals for action by the United Nations.

I should like before closing to pay two tributes. The first is to our host country, the United States of America, whose President we had the privilege of hearing a few moments ago and whose kind references to the work of the United Nations and Specialized agencies are very much appreciated. This country has long been in the vanguard of the attack on the problem of world hunger and malnutrition, and I am convinced that, in the critical period that lies ahead, its support will be given as unstintingly as in the past. My second tribute is to FAO, which I should like to congratulate on its twentieth anniversary.

The years that have elapsed since the United Nations Conference on Food and Agriculture at Hot Springs, Virginia, in 1943, have seen sweeping changes come over the face of our planet. Our understanding of present-day problems of agriculture, and the mobilization of international efforts to resolve them, are due in no small measure to the work of this organization and its distinguished Directors-General, past and present, and in this context, I want to pay special tribute to the present Director-General for the wonderful work he is doing.

In recent years, we have enjoyed a particularly close and fruitful co-operation with Dr. B. R. Sen, under whose leadership FAO has come to play an ever more vital role in a key sector of the world economy. I am confident that in coming years the work of FAO will be still further intensified for the benefit of mankind.

Ladies and Gentlemen, our first and foremost responsibility in the United Nations is "to save succeeding generations from the scourge of war." Yet success in this endeavour would be a hollow victory if half the world's people were left hungry. Peace can only assume its true meaning if it is accompanied by at least minimum level of general well-being. And freedom from hunger is surely a fundamental condition of human welfare. It is with this thought that I take pleasure in wishing your Congress every possible success in its task.

# 6

# Science, Technology and Outer Space

SCIENCE AND TECHNOLOGY FOR UNDER-DEVELOPED AREAS*

This vast gathering was first conceived in the winter of 1960, a period of acute tension within the United Nations itself, as an act of confidence in the fundamental solidarity of all peoples and nations. It is my first and pleasant duty to pay tribute to the vision and the wisdom of those who originated this undertaking and laid the ground for it: the members of the Scientific Advisory Committee, Dr. Homi Bhabha, Sir John Cockcroft (later replaced by Sir William Penney), Prof. Vasili Emelyanov, Dr. Bertrand Goldschmidt, Dr. W. B. Lewis, Prof. L. C. Prado and Dr. I. I. Rabi, together with my predecessor, the late Dag Hammarskjold. In preparing and working out the details of such a complex project, the international officials concerned and the members of the Scientific Advisory Committee were assisted by the Scientific Advisory Panel under the able chairmanship of Mr. Hedayat, and to them also I extend my gratitude.

* Message to the United Nations Conference on the Application of Science and Technology for the Benefit of Less Developed Areas, Geneva, February 4, 1963.

No doubt neither the nineteen-hundred-odd papers which have been prepared for the Conference nor the discussion which will take place in the course of the Conference sessions can claim to offer a complete account of the actual and potential benefits of applied science and technology for the less developed areas, a subject which touches on all scientific disciplines and almost all aspects of modern society. But each and every one of those here present, whether he be a scientist, a statesman, an economist, an administrator, an international official, or a representative of a non-governmental organization, will draw from this Conference an answer, or part of an answer, to some of the specific problems which are the fabric of his professional life.

The idea of holding the Conference was, of course, no sudden inspiration, but arose naturally out of two trends that have in recent years marked the efforts of the United Nations in the economic and social field. The first of these trends was the drive to promote and accelerate, by every means at out disposal, the economic and social development of the poorer countries—a drive that is epitomized in the United Nations Development Decade. The second trend was the increasing concern of the United Nations to stimulate scientific and technological investigation and exchanges. This concern had been reflected, for example, in the calling of the International Conferences on the Peaceful Uses of Atomic Energy in 1955 and 1958, the establishment of the International Atomic Energy Agency, the calling of the Conference on New Sources of Energy in 1961 and the survey of recent advances in scientific research undertaken, under the auspices of the Economic and Social Council, in the years 1958 to 1960.

These trends have marked the efforts in the past few years not only of the United Nations itself but of the whole United Nations family. At the staff level, the preparations for the present Conference have been a joint enterprise of the United Nations, the International Labour Office, the Food and Agriculture Organization of the United Nations, the United Nations Educational, Scientific and Cultural Organization, the World Health Organization, the International Telecommunication Union, the World Meteorological Organization and the International Atomic Energy Agency. These agencies have made a major contribution to the thinking that underlies the planning and organization of the Conference's work; they have contributed moreover by preparing the agenda items within their fields, by providing technical and other staff and by the submission of papers. Their executive heads are on the platform with me this morning and to them I should like to pay a warm tribute. It is on their behalf as well as on my own that I extend greetings to the Conference.

We must approach our task in a spirit of humility. We suspect that science and its applications may be the major instrument of change in the contemporary world. We know at least that it is one of the principal agents of modern history. Yet we have surely not yet given sufficient thought to the relationship between science and society.

Moreover, with all its triumphs, science today is on trial. It is on trial, in the first instance, because of the vastly increased powers it has given to the forces of war and destruction, to the point that, for the first time, humanity may now be threatened with instant and toal annihilation. Equally important, in my view, is the fact that in its boldest and most far-reaching experiments, science seems to have lost contact with society. Its processes have at times become so involved in mathematical abstraction, and its preoccupations centered on areas so remote from daily life, that, to the common man, the scientists may appear today to live in a secluded world of their own. In some way, in the unfolding of its unavoidably complex processes, science must be made to remain aware of its human origin and its human destination.

The Conference may, I feel, contribute to this by focusing the attention of the scientific world on one of the most urgent needs of contemporary society, the need to combat poverty, chronic disease and illiteracy, the need to raise more than two-thirds of the world population to a condition compatible with human dignity. These are objectives which have now been clearly identified and which, for all of those entrusted with some responsibility in public affairs, have developed into a kind of "categorical imperative." But it is far from certain that the scientific world is as yet so concerned with those over-riding objectives that it applies to the pursuit of them all the energy and resources that are potentially available.

It is also clear that those directly responsible for the progress of their nation are often not adequately informed of the advances that could be realized by the application of modern science and technology. The scientists of the world and the leaders of the developing nations together hold one of the keys to a better future. It is essential that they be enabled to meet, converse and help each other. Such closer contacts may assist the scientists to find their true place in society, by stimulating their concern for results of early and practical benefit to their fellowmen. It will also provide the leaders of the developing countries with fuller knowledge of the instruments which are at their disposal for overcoming rapidly the obstacles to economic and social development and will thus help them in the great task of giving a maximum content to political freedom.

I hope that by the end of our meetings we shall all have a clearer view of some of the fundamental aspects of the question with which this Conference is concerned and be ready to chart new courses of action, national and international.

The first aspect which might, I suggest, be brought forward is the need for new research to deal successfully with some of the most pressing problems of the new nations. Many of these problems have either ceased to exist or perhaps have never existed in the very different environment of the countries which have now reached a high level of development. Scientific research on any extensive scale is still a privilege of a minority of countries, and because it is so directly conditioned by the local environment obtaining in these countries, it tends to bypass problems which are crucial in other parts of the world. As a result, the more advanced countries are as yet not adequately geared to certain of the tasks which are inherent in their desire to co-operate with the developing nations. Scientific research is one of these tasks, and we should now seek to fill the gap. The first, and in my view the easiest, step is to identify the areas where new research specifically designed for the needs of the new nations should be undertaken and pushed forward. This requires only an effort of organization, of directing existing knowledge, talent and resources to certain neglected problems. I see no reason why it could not be carried forward successfully.

The second aspect of the broad problem before us which you may wish to ponder is how science and technology can be absorbed effectively by the developing countries. This is a far more complicated and difficult matter, for it involves an organic process about which we know very little. It is often said that development may nowadays be telescoped by applying all the technological knowledge already acquired, that the trials and errors and the turmoil through which industrialization and social improvement took place in the advanced countries during the nineteenth century may be avoided. There is some truth in this, and this is one of our reasons for hope. But let us not deceive ourselves with the illusion that what is at stake is just a simple transfer of technological device. Let us be aware of the disruptions which may be caused by a superimposition of modern knowledge and the techniques on a society whose habits and thinking, methods of work and way of life are often entirely unprepared for them. And let us tackle the vast problem of education with more vigour, for a general rise in the standards of education is surely the most effective means of achieving—and maintaining—those social transformations that are necessary.

In the course of the preparation of this Conference, the title "Scientific independence as a corollary to political independence" was suggested for one of the general sessions. This title was not retained, because it was felt that it could be mistaken for an advocacy of self-sufficiency in science and technology as a proper objective for each and every one of the new nations. This, in a way, would have belied the great act of solidarity which this Conference represents. But the suggested title embodied a fundamental truth. In my view, the development of certain scientific institutions and the training of at least a small number of scientists in some of the advanced disciplines is by no means a luxury for any of the new nations. On the contrary, it is an immediate need in every country. When countries are planning their own economic and social development, and in the practical day-to-day business of acquiring machines and equipment from abroad, or entering into long-term arrangements with foreign concerns and technicians for the development of their resources, or when concluding loan agreements, they must—if they are to have a minimum of self-confidence—be able to call on at least a small number of their own citizens who are conversant with the ways of science and technology.

It is clearly of the greatest importance that the momentum generated by this Conference should be maintained. One of the objectives we should undoubtedly set for ourselves, and seek over the coming years to realize is the establishment of scientific and technological programmes and institutions in the developing countries. This, it seems to me, might now be recognized and accepted as a new international responsibility, which our system of organization could help to shoulder by various means—for example by keeping the progress made under review, by arranging for exchanges and discussions, and possibly by furnishing some technical assistance if this were desired. Such a task would also represent a contribution to the process of "decolonization" and emancipation, which has emerged as a major objective of the world of today, inseparable from that of the maintenance of peace.

Finally, let me recall that the Conference has been conceived as a major event in the United Nations Development Decade, as likely to have a significant impact over the coming years in raising standards of living in the underdeveloped areas of the world. That it may achieve such an aim is my earnest hope, and in this spirit I wish you all success in the great task that lies before you.

## TO THE COMMITTEE ON PEACEFUL USES OF OUTER SPACE*

The United Nations has entrusted to this Committee the protection of the common interest of mankind in furthering the peaceful uses of outer space. In the service of that common interest, it has laid on the Committee the

* Statement to the Committee on the Peaceful Uses of Outer Space, New York, March 22, 1962.

urgent responsibility of devising means to promote and strengthen international cooperation in this important field.

I need not review the earlier efforts of the United Nations to organize such cooperation nor the reasons why it could make only partial beginnings in furthering it. Happily, earlier difficulties have now been overcome. I need not stress that the world looks to you to develop agreement on the means of realizing the principle that outer space should be explored and used only for the betterment of mankind and for the benefit of states irrespective of the stage of their economic or scientific development. Indeed, the composition of this Committee reflects that principle.

My hopes, the hopes of all who seek to calm the turbulence of our times, are raised higher by the evidence we have had in the last two days of the willingness of the Soviet Union and the United States, the leaders in this field, to explore practical steps to develop international cooperation in space activities for peaceful purposes. The messages exchanged between the President of the United States and the Chairman of the Council of Ministers of the USSR contain a series of suggestions of specific projects of cooperation which could be of inestimable value to mankind and on which common actions seem feasible. In addition, there are indications of an interest in discussing areas of possible cooperation lying beyond the more immediate projects.

What is important at the moment is that we have solid evidence of willingness to cooperate. This can only be welcomed. It could portend that the world is turning the corner in the direction of that peaceful adjustment to the breathtaking changes accompanying the scientific and technological revolution of our times, which is urgently needed.

What must give this Committee and indeed all the

members of the United Nations a sense of gratificaton is that the Soviet-American exchange of views is to occur within a United Nations context thus affording recognition of that common interest of mankind which is the first principle of international cooperation in this field as in others.

It is clear that the states with the greatest achievements in outer space should provide a lead to the rest of the world. As they themselves have acknowledged, their preeminence rests, however, on scientific foundations laid by men and women from every part of the earth without distinction of great and small, weak and strong. In the International Geophysical Year the world has already had evidence of the results to be achieved by pooling the intellectual resources of all its peoples. The world will be well served if the spirit of universal cooperation which animated the IGY marks the activities of this Committee and of its leaders also. For the Secretariat I may pledge our best efforts to assist the Committee and its members in their endeavors in the noble cause which they serve.

## ON PEACEFUL USES OF OUTER SPACE*

On this occasion, I should like to convey to the Scientific and Technical Sub-Committee on the Peaceful Uses of Outer Space my best wishes for the success of this session. I trust that it will be no less fruitful than your first session.

Last year, your Sub-Committee presented a series of recommendations on the exchange of information, the encouragement of international programmes and the creation of international sounding rocket facilities which offer,

* Message to the Scientific and Technical Sub-Committee of the Committee on the Peaceful Uses of Outer Space, Geneva, May 14, 1963.

as I noted in my report to the General Assembly, a basis for practical and useful action. Perhaps as significant as the recommendations themselves was, as many delegations remarked in the main Committee and the General Assembly, the spirit of co-operation which made them possible.

During the year, steps have been taken to translate your recommendations into action. Valuable information on national space programmes has been furnished by many countries and has been circulated by the Secretariat to all Member States.

In addition, the printed material supplied by some countries and organizations has been included in the collection of documentation in the reference library on the exploration and use of outer space which is being established in the Outer Space Affairs Section at Headquarters in New York.

The attention of Governments has been drawn to the activities of COSPAR and to the scientific community's plans for the International Year of the Quiet Sun and the World Magnetic Survey.

In their respective fields, the specialized agencies have pressed forward with their plans to promote international co-operation in the peaceful exploraton and use of outer space, bearing in mind the contribution that can be made to the progress of the developong countries as envisaged in the United Nations Development Decade program.

Thanks to the efforts of the Government of India, your Sub-Committee's imaginative and far-sighted proposal for the establishment of an international equatorial sounding rocket facility under United Nations sponsorship is nearing realization.

In the course of the year, the space achievements of the USSR and the United States have continued to command the admiration of us all. Such feats as the team flight of two

Soviet cosmonauts, the Venus and Mars space probes, and the successful demonstrations of the possibilities of long-range communication via satellite are further landmarks in man's conquest of space.

Concurrently, the two countries have made further progress in their bilateral talks on co-operative space projects. The recently announced Rome agreement between Dr. Dryden and Academician Blagonravov is an encouraging and practical embodiment of the desire for co-operation expressed in the exchange of messages between Chairman Khrushchev and President Kennedy, brought to the attention of the Outer Space Committee at its first session.

I need not say that if the two delegations desire to continue their talks at Geneva, the Secretariat will be happy. to provide any services required.

The process of building and strengthening international co-operation in outer space is not a simple one. It cannot be completely abstracted from terrestrial difficulties. Nor can one be blind to the fact that space exploration is potentially a source of immense danger, as well as of benefits.

But, as a distinguished space scientist, Sir Bernard Lovell, has said: "There is scarcely a major scientific advance of the century which does not carry with it the powers of good and evil, and in every generation there are voices which, in the face of the ever-recurring crises, will either assume an attitude of passive pessimism or will seek to dam up the outlets of man's insatiable curiosity. It is hard to believe that these attitudes are in any sense constructive. . . . On the contrary, it seems likely that civilizations which survive are those where the challenge of scientific and technical progress is accepted, thus providing the driving force enabling the community to pass rapidly through the years of crisis without self-extermination."

Through your Sub-Committee, the United Nations is, I believe, making a contribution towards meeting that challenge, and helping to ensure that the exploration and use of outer space shall be a growing point of co-operation, rather than a new area of conflict and mistrust.

## THE UNITED NATIONS CONFERENCE ON
## SCIENCE AND TECHNOLOGY*

The United Nations Development Decade could be a phrase conceived in hope, but destined only to lead to a cycle of debates, resolutions and reports; or, it could be a period of action that improves the lot of the general run of mankind to a greater extent than during any comparable period. I know that all of us want it to be the latter. All representatives of Governments here today, and all other persons, wherever they may be, who understand the gravity of the issues that are posed by the widening of the gap between the rich and the poor nations, undoubtedly hope that the will and the means can be found to meet the great challenge which was laid down by the General Assembly in its resolution on the United Nations Development Decade.

In one section of that resolution 1710 (XVI), the Secretary-General was requested to develop proposals for 'the intensification of research and demonstration as well as other efforts to exploit scientific and technological potentialities of high promise for accelerating economic and social development'.

Let me illustrate what this could mean, and its relationship to international co-operation. Suppose that the world

* Address delivered to the Economic and Social Council in Geneva, July 8, 1963.

had a way of producing electric energy, economically and safely, in any village, by means of small generating units utilizing power from the sun or from any other source. When this technological point is reached, a demand would arise for several millions of dollars of capital aid, for the purpose of locating such an energy unit in every village. Additional demands for capital would soon also arise from the impetus that the wider availability of electric power would give to economic development and, especially, to industialization. Training courses would be urgently required for the persons who would operate and maintain these units once they were installed. Here, we are again reminded that the development of human resources, surely the true aim of technological advance, is also an essential condition for it.

But it is not just a question of being put in a position of needing *more* capital and *more* training. Once the new technological device is ready for adoption, capital can be embodied in more useful forms and training courses can become more useful than before. By the same token, earlier programmes of capital and technical aid may become superseded. National development plans, too, may need revision; as also economic projections.

I have purposely chosen an unusually dramatic example. Most technological advances, however, are relatively small —a slight improvement in a plow, a machine that reduces the amount of heavy manual work in a factory, a new cost-saving way of managing an operation or organizing the layout of work. Thus, even while we recognize the cumulative effect of the many smaller improvements in techniques that can undoubtedly be made in every field, we must also be prepared for the revolutionary impact to be expected from some of the larger break-throughs. If we are to realize the aims of the Development Decade, we have a job to do that will not be easy. Therefore, to strengthen our resolution, let us proclaim in a high, rather than a low key, the inspiring possibilities. Technology can be the most powerful force in the world for raising living standards, and our task is to harness it for that purpose.

You have before you in documents E/3772 and in E/3772/Add.1 a summary report of the United Nations Conference on the Application of Science and Technology for the Benefit of the Less Developed Areas. An account of the genesis, preparation and organization of the Conference appears in the main report. One aspect to which I wish to call special attention was the extremely solid and valuable support which was given from the beginning by the entire United Nations family of agencies. The co-operation of our colleagues from ILO, FAO, UNESCO, WHO, ITU, WMO and IAEA was outstanding, both in arranging for the Conference and in contributing to the substance of it, and we return sincere thanks to them.

The body of the main report, largely made up of short summations of the written and oral discussions in the 12 major subject sections of the Conference, draws heavily on a report which was submitted to me by the Conference Secretary-General. A wider range of inquiry would be hard to imagine. Map-making, preferably by photogrammetry, was stressed as being often a needed first step for developing countries. The implications of rising population pressure were debated; thus, the prospect was noted of arable land per head of population falling, by the year 2000, to roughly half an acre, as against 1.18 acres in 1959, and the need was recognized for strenuous efforts to conserve water. Some attention was given to the resources of the seas, especially to fisheries and other food possibilities, and to demineralization to help relieve water shortages. If I may digress at this point, could it not be envisaged that our scientific knowledge would some day reach a point where it would be possible to launch a comprehensive, co-operative project to develop the varied and almost un-limited resources of the seas for the benefit of all mankind?

Some other questions taken up were: the challenge to devise processes and plants for the heavy chemical industry that will reduce the minimum size of economic operations below the level in the advanced countries; and the some-what contrasting situation in the iron and steel industry, where relatively small plants can already be built and operated economically, requiring in general only the transfer of known technology from the advanced to the developing countries. This list could be very much ex-tended and still not begin to reflect the breadth of the discussions—let alone, of course, their specific content and depth. Indeed, the whole report should be read as merely a brief introduction to the substance of the work of the Con-ference. However, in an eight-volume report, which is ex-pected to be available in printed form by the year's end, an attempt will be made to provide a definitive account of the written and oral proceedings, readably presented and rea-sonably priced to commend it for wide perusal and use. In addition, the papers that were contributed to the gen-eral and the specialized sessions, as well as the reports of the Conference Secretary-General on the individual ses-sions and the reports of the rapporteurs, will continue to be available in their original form.

Our objectives are practical ones. The Conference was intended to have a practical effect. The participants in the Conference having ably discharged their function, it re-mains not merely to preserve an accurate record of the information they brought, and the views they contributed, but also to follow up. Certain steps have already been taken with the aim of determining what the follow-up action should be. On this question, I have had the benefit of consultations, both at the Government level and in the Administrative Committee on Co-ordination, and my views are summarized in Part Three of the report which is before you. I solicit your consideration of those views. They are in no sense final, but they do indicate, I feel, the direction in which a start should be made.

Today, I think you would wish me to speak only of the main considerations, which I believe are three. *First,* it is necessary to build centres of scientific and technological strength in the less developed countries. *Second,* it is necessary to focus more resources, in the advanced countries, on science and technology for the benefit of the less developed countries. *Third,* it is necessary to make a judicious assessment of priorities.

Under "centres of strength" I include several different things, which are all vital if science and technology are to strike roots in the soil of the less developed world—roots without which they cannot be expected to grow. Science and technology cannot be exported or "pushed" out from their habitat in the advanced countries; they have to be imported or 'pulled' in by the developing countries themselves, when and as the most forward-looking and qualified people of those countries feel the need, and are able to define it.

Every developing nation undoubtedly requires its own scientific and technological "establishment." The heart of an establishment is people. There is no country that does not need at least a minimum number of its own highly trained scientists, to help assure its intellectual independence and dynamism. Moreover, the developing countries need to expand very rapidly the numbers of their middle-level technicians. We thus come back to the problem of finding practical ways to accelerate education and training.

UNESCO, of course, has considerable interest where basic science is involved, while the ILO, the United Nations itself and all the agencies of the United Nations family are concerned with various aspects of technology. Apart from training, Member Governments should also keep in mind the crucial question of incentives. Middle-level careers, essential for national development, are today too often regarded as unrewarding for the individual.

An establishment will also include institutions and resources. Each developing country needs laboratories and other research facilities. It also requires some organization, such as a national science council or research council, to help guide research and formulate policy. Working closely with the Government's national planning body, that organization can ensure that the importance of promoting scientific advance is not overlooked or underestimated when the plan is drawn up, and it can also reduce the risk that the plan may allocate scarce resources, without first taking foreseeable technological changes into account.

Research facilities are as necessary to the developing countries as facilities for training, with which they can often be advantageously combined in a local university. I hope that research facilities in the advanced countries will be placed more and more at the disposal of the developing countries. However, it is also essential to establish more adequate and better oriented, as well as more numerous, research institutions in the developing countries themselves, as was, for certain purposes, suggested by the United Nations Conference on New Sources of Energy two years ago. These then should be linked up with research institutions in the advanced countries, so that there may be a continous exchange of knowledge and of scientific staff.

There is urgent need for such research facilities in the developing countries. Some problems can only be properly investigated in the under-developed world—for example, problems connected with diseases or with plant life peculiar to the tropics. Other problems can be studied in the advanced countries up to a point, but the final stages of research and the pilot operations should be carried out close to where the results are to be applied, so as to assure successful adaptation. Consequently, and because research institutions can become centres of great strength for the developing countries, I believe that we have here a subject for emphasis in the programmes of the United Nations family of organizations in the immediate future. The Special Fund has had useful experience in this field already, and could logically serve as a main support for a broader attack on the problem if it were to be provided with adequate resources.

Not all of these research institutions should necessarily be conceived of as national institutions; some might advantageously be established on a regional, or even an inter-regional, basis. This is obvious where the problems are common to all humid regions in the tropics, or to all arid regions; but it may apply, too, to some other investigations. Multi-national research institutions should make it possible to economize skilled manpower and financial resources, encourage wider use of the findings, and especially benefit small countries unable to proceed with the research on their own. Such regional and inter-regional research institutions should, in my view, be linked in some appropriate way, with the United Nations regional economic commissions, directly or through the three newly created development planning institutes.

The second essential is to focus more resources in the advanced countries on science and technology for the benefit of the less developed countries. The purposes of the Development Decade require the deep involvement of the

energies and assets of the less developed countries themselves, and also a substantially increased transfer of resources to those countries, by way of additional co-operation from the advanced countries, many of which have
already been extremely generous in their co-operation.
But, when we count not only the cost of developing the
applicable new methods—and preparing the people to receive them—but also the cost of the new equipment with
which to carry the new methods into practical effect
throughout the under-deveolped areas, the total resources
required will certainly be large. In other words, the application of science and technology in the poorer countries
will be an expensive operation. No useful purpose would
be served by disguising that fact.

It is not a question of money alone. The scientific community will have to become much more deeply involved in
the whole development effort, both individually and
through its scientific organizations. Many scientists have
already left their ivory towers to engage in practical activities, but the institutional means through which they can
serve the cause of the development of the less developed
areas have not been perfected, and their actual involvement in such work is still rather marginal. Fortunately,
some of the best scientists and technologists are now being
associated with the work of the United Nations and its
related agencies, as members of advisory committees and
panels. This kind of arrangement has proved very useful to
us, and I hope it has been mutually profitable. In this
context, I would like to acknowledge with gratitude the
assistance rendered to me by the United Nations Scientific
Advisory Committee, as also the help rendered by the Scientific Advisory Panel in connexion with the organization
of the Conference. However, still more needs to be done
along these lines.

Let me revert now to material and financial resources. In a seriously undertaken programme of international co-operation for bringing the benefits of science and modern technology to those who do not yet share in those benefits, the rewards will be great, but so also must be the input of resources. Otherwise, as the Council cannot but be aware, the nations whose representatives voted for the resolution on the United Nations Development Decade—as all did— will have sown fine words and reaped a harvest of very meagre results.

To say that the United Nations and its related agencies should be enabled to dispose of some part of the necessary additional resources is surely no radical doctrine. As I have mentioned already, it would seem entirely reasonable to seek ways of channelling larger resources in this endeavour through the Special Fund and the Expanded Programme of Technical Assistance. It would, however, seem to me desirable that a larger portion of the budgets of certain of the international organizations should be devoted to this field and, furthermore, that the budgets themselves should be strengthened, so as to enable these organizations to play their part on an expanded basis more nearly in consonance with the need. As far as the United Nations itself is con-cerned, it would be proper to enlarge the provision for those of its activities as are most directly related to indus-trial and other technology. If I am not proposing this immediately, except to the limited extent that it may be possible to make internal adjustments within our present means, it is only because of the overriding financial crisis of the United Nations, of which you are fully aware.

At the same time, I would emphasize that an important part of the role of the United Nations family must be the catalytic role. It will be necessary to keep the possibilities for useful further action under continuing and detailed review—but often try to get others to take that action. The major contribution of resources must be looked for, at present, from bilateral arrangements; this includes private action—by foundations, industries, and so on—as well as public action. One instrument is, of course, the bilateral aid programmes as such. Another might be a whole array of going programmes not tied to the aid programmes in any formal sense. For example, a practice of devoting special attention to the technological problems of the developing countries, or of a particular developing country, might spread among the agricultural colleges and their associated research laboratories and experiment stations in the advanced countries. Much benefit could result from this. The same applies to teachers' colleges, public health organizations, and other centres of technical knowledge and skill, so numerous in the advanced countries.

It may also be that the research and development programmes to which some Member Governments are devoting large financial resources could be of help. Within them, there may be certain activities that could, without any detriment to the work for which they have been authorized, yield also the answers to certain technical problems confronting the less developed countries. The concept of an accidental by-product benefit to civilians from defence or space research, sometimes referred to as the spillover effect, is already familiar. Conceivably, if thought were to be given to the matter, there could be some effort consciously to seek concurrent joint-product effects that would help to accelerate development in the less developed countries. I would hope that some Member Governments might wish to examine their research and development program from this new point of view.

To call assessment of priorities the third essential is not to suggest that the technological needs of the less developed countries are confined to any one sector or area. In fact, technological improvement is co-extensive with the development process itself—almost if not quite the essence of it. That is a major reason why it would not seem practicable to establish a new United Nations agency for science and technology. All the agencies have tasks to perform in this field, which they are especially well equipped to perform, and the best assurance of a vigorous, unified and consistent effort lies in intensifying their individual action, while at the same time perfecting the co-operation among them, and seeing that any gaps are closed, through the mechanism of the Administrative Committee on Co-ordination. Steps have in fact now been taken to establish a Sub-Committee on Science and Technology of the ACC, to which reference is made in the ACC's report to the Council (Doc. E/3765), as well as in my own report. But obviously, within each field of activity, resources would be spread too thin if no decisions were taken on priorities and points of concentration.

Our Department of Economic and Social Affairs has started to review its varied work programmes at Headquarters and in the regions, from the point of view of the scientific and technological issue. The largest and most important single concentration point for the Department, undoubtedly, is the technological work directly related to industrialization and natural resources—water, energy, minerals. Cartography goes with it, and transport must also be added. What is needed might in part be achieved by substantially accelerating the program of building up technological institutes to which I have already referred. We are also now beginning to make some headway, through our Centre for Industrial Development and our Resources and Transport Branch, in assembling a body of engineering and industrial economic skills which can be made available on request in such areas as manufacturing, mining, power, roads, railways and water. We plan to continue to develop, on our staff and within our auxiliary services, such a corps of engineers and related technical experts. For example, it may be possible to regularize the establishment of panels of individuals willing and able to serve from time to time on suitable assignments, and also to enter into agreements with institutions and firms under which they will furnish us with qualified personnel for such assignments at our request.

Other parts of our work have their concentration points, too, for the application of science and technology. In housing construction, new techniques to reduce costs are greatly needed. Community development work has an important part to play in transfer and adaptation at the grassroots levels, as distinct from the level of the university, laboratory or experiment station in the developing country itself. The techniques of training in public administration and of development planning may also be mentioned as illustrations.

Finally, in widest perspective and with a view to invigorating the whole follow-up to the Conference, I suggest that there might be established an agreed special list of new inventions, adaptations or cost-reductions, each having a potential developmental effect of extraordinary dimensions, directly or through its ultimate repercussions. The automobile was clearly an invention in that class for the Western world. Would a new kind of car or truck, tailored in price, durability and other specifications to what developing countries can afford, qualify for a place on such a list? Certainly, better roads, more mechanical-mindedness and many other desirable things might follow almost automatically once such a vehicle came into general use. Would the small energy unit to which I re-

ferred earlier be another example? Would economical
desalinization plants for areas short of fresh water be another? Would the mass application of certain new teaching
aids and techniques, such as a system for using radio and
television for greatly accelerating all kinds of education
and training, be yet another? In the field of physical or
mental health, would there be some particular piece of
technical research that should go on even a short list of this
kind?

These questions cannot be answered today, but further
study of relative needs, on the one hand, and of the feasi-
bility of achieving a break-through in the different areas of
need, on the other, might yield some answers, with experts
from the less developed countries playing an active part in
advising both on needs, in the larger sense, and on technical specifications. The final stages of research and field
testing would also, in each case, be carried out in one or
more of the less developed countries, with the help, for
example, of a regional or inter-regional research institution, so as to assure acceptability of the product in the
actual location where it was to be used. Thus, transfer and
adaptation would be a built-in, integral part of the technical solution itself. It is my belief that, in addition to
bilateral governmental and United Nations resources, it
will be possible to obtain the support of foundations and
similar private institutions to bring designated special
priority research tasks to a successful conclusion. For my
part, I would certainly be willing to lend my full support
to seeking such additional assistance.

May I in conclusion offer certain suggestions to the
Council, as regards action it may wish to consider taking at
this session for following up on the Conference on Science
and Technology.

*First*, it would be useful if the Council's discussion could indicate how much importance the Council itself attaches to scientific and technological work—its place among the services that the United Nations and the related agencies can and should render during the Development Decade.

*Second,* the Council's guidance would be appreciated with regard to any of the specific programme suggestions I have advanced, particularly the research intitutions in the less developed areas and the recruitment of stand-by auxiliaries to perform missions in industrial and other appropriate technical fields.

*Third,* the Council's help is needed in finding the best ways of securing for the United Nations and the related agencies such additional resources for scientific and technological work as may appear to the Council to be necessary.

*Fourth,* it has been suggested, in my report and in the report of the ACC, that the Council may wish to establish an Advisory Committee on Science and Technology. Suggestions were also included on how, if that were the case, the Committee might be constituted and how it might report to the Council, with a view to achieving the closest possible relationship with the work of all the international agencies concerned. Decisions in relation to the need for such an Advisory Committee appear to be in order.

Should the Council decide to establish an Advisory Committee in this field, that Committee could clearly play an important part. For example, if the concept of a list of especially important research items finds favour, then the drawing up of such a list will have to be taken in hand. Again, if the Council considers that regional and inter-regional institutions, as well as national ones, need to be established and strengthened in the less developed areas, then it would be logical to draw up a scheme for an effective and reasonably complete network of such institutions for the less developed world as a whole, and a phased plan for bringing them into operation. Arrangements for examining these or other matters, and preparing recommendations on them, could no doubt be worked out by the Council's Committee, in conjunction with the United Nations Scientific Advisory Committee and the principal scientific and technological committees of the specialized and related agencies.

The United Nations Conference on the Application of Science and Technology for the Benefit of the Less Developed Areas has focussed attention on the sort of practical approach by which the whole effort of the United Nations Development Decade could be accelerated. Much will depend on decisions to be taken now by the Council.

# 7

# The United Nations as a Force for Peace

TO THE PEOPLE OF SWEDEN ON THE UNITED NATIONS
AS A FORCE FOR PEACE*

It is a matter of regret to me that the responsibilities of my office, which quite often make unanticipated demands upon my time and movements, have kept me from coming to Sweden, at the time, as planned. But I take this opportunity to convey to all of the people of Sweden the substance of the remarks which I intended to make. They relate to peace, which must be the most vital concern of peoples everywhere, whatever their political leanings. Peace, in my view, knows no party lines.

In our time there are new and compelling reasons why we should seek peace, and the conditions which make it possible, with more determination than ever before.

One could simplify the functions of the United Nations in this search by saying that it was an association of sovereign States devoted principally to remedying and liquidating the grievances and injustices of the past, to adjust-

* Message delivered on May 1, 1963.

ing and solving the tensions and dangers of the present and to laying the foundations for a more stable and happy future. It is with the second of these main streams of activity that I propose to deal in this message, for if we do not devise means of tackling and making safe the violent antagonisms which sometimes arise in the world in such a way that they do not spread and infect the community of nations, then all our efforts to improve on the past or to plan for the future will be in vain.

These activities are also of particular interest to you here in Sweden who have contributed so much to these pioneering efforts. In saying this I am not only thinking of my predecessor and your great compatriot, Dag Hammarskjold, who unquestionably did more than any man to develop the machinery of the United Nations so that it could with increasing effectiveness meet its awesome responsibilities for world peace, and who, in his tireless and fearless pursuit of his duty, met his tragic death. I am not only thinking of Count Folke Bernadotte, who gave his life as United Nations Mediator in Palestine in one of the earliest efforts of the United Nations to keep the peace. I am also referring to the officers and men who have served the United Nations bravely and loyally in the Middle East and in the Congo, and to the many Swedes who have served and are serving as international civil servants in one capacity or another throughout the world. It would be difficult to think of any other country showing greater practical support for the United Nations than Sweden—a support expressed not only in the loyalty of its Government to the ideals of the United Nations but also in the service of its citizens.

The United Nations has responded in a practical way to a variety of crises in its 18 years of existence, and has, in the process, developed practices and precedents which have greatly enlarged its capacity to deal with emergencies. I mentioned the great contribution of my predecessor to this evolution. Another very important factor has certainly been the necessity, recognized by all concerned, of dealing with certain dangerous situations effectively without involving them in the stresses and strains of East-West struggle. A third factor has been the increasing reliance of the smaller nations upon the United Nations, the increasing influence of their moderating voice in the United Nations, and their loyal support of its efforts to keep the peace. These efforts have also entailed an increased responsibility and workload for the Secretary-General and his staff and a growing recognition, in most quarters, of the value of the Secretariat as an objective international civil service. This too is a most significant institutional development.

One of the most encouraging of the pragmatic developments that I have mentioned has been the increasing use of the military personnel of Member States for the maintenance of the peace in various parts of the world under United Nations auspices and the adaptation of the military art to the task of maintaining the peace.

Methods of using military personnel productively on a far smaller scale than is envisaged in the Charter have been evolving since the early years of the United Nations. These relatively modest enterprises have all been directed to the control of explosive situations before they get out of hand and spread. In Greece in 1947 and 1948 the military attaches of the members of the United Nations Commission proved themselves invaluable as an observer group in checking on infiltration into Greece from her northern neighbours. In Kashmir, an observer group of military officers was formally set up by the Security Council and is still operating.

The first truce agreements in the Palestine war in July

1948 were enforced on the ground by some 700 United Nations military observers working under the United Nations Mediator and his Chief of Staff. This team later developed into the United Nations Truce Supervision Organization after the conclusion of the armistice agreements between Israel and her Arab neighbors in 1949. This organization played, and is still playing, a vital role in keeping the peace in the Middle East and in regulating frontier incidents in such a way that they do not develop into much more serious conflicts.

A far larger scale and more unusual international peace-keeping organism was evoked by the critical situation which arose in October 1956 following the armed intervention in the Suez Canal area of the forces of Israel, France and the United Kingdom—the creation of a United Nations police and peace-keeping force, the United Nations Emergency Force in the Middle East, which allowed for a peaceful withdrawal from Egyptian soil of the armed forces of France, the United Kingdom and Israel, and the clearance of the vital waterway—the Suez Canal. The Force still watches over the peace on the once troubled frontier between Israel and the United Arab Republic. It presents one major problem—it is so useful and necessary that it is hard to envisage a date when it can be withdrawn from the area.

The Lebanon crisis of 1958 evoked another kind of United Nations military organization, a corps of 600 observers to watch over the borders of Lebanon for foreign infiltration, but it was in July 1960 that the United Nations was confronted with its most complex and pressing peace-keeping task to date. So much has been written about the Congo and the United Nations involvement there in the past two and a half years that I shall do no more here than to mention the general proportions of this problem, which have a tendency to be obscured by a wealth of dramatic and controversial detail. On the appeal for help by the new Government of the Congo, the United Nations, literally at a few hours notice, undertook to be the guarantor of law and order, and the watchman against external interference from many sources. It also became the counsellor of a newly independent State which had had little preparation for independence, on all the problems that beset a country the size of Western Europe, which occupies a vital, strategic and economic place in the world, and which, by its very potential wealth and possibilities, is a target for a bewildering variety of foreign interests.

There is still a long and difficult road ahead both for the Government and people of the Congo and for the United Nations which is assisting them, but given the fearsome complexity of the problem and the cross-currents and conflicts of interests at all levels, from the global level to the tribal level, which afflict the Republic of the Congo, it is remarkable that this pioneering effort by the community of nations has not only saved one of its members, the Congo, in its time of trial, but has turned a situation of great potential danger to Africa and to the world into a most promising experiment in world responsibility. Sweden has done more than its share in the support of this historic effort.

Another operation, also involving an unprededented role for the United Nations, has meanwhile passed off peacefully and successfully and, as is the rule with successful peace-keeping operations, has attracted virtually no publicity whatsoever. It has in fact been successfully and formally concluded on this very day. I refer to the transfer of West Irian from Dutch sovereignty, through an interim period of United Nations administration safeguarded by a United Nations force, to the sovereignty of Indonesia, the entire operation taking place with the mutual agreement of the parties concerned. This is the first time in history that an international organization has assumed direct administrative authority for a territory in the process of historic transition.

In certain situations the United Nations and the Office of the Secretary-General can provide a useful middle ground on which the parties may meet without any loss of face or prestige, and accommodate their differences in a civilized and dignified manner. I like to think that the United Nations played a useful role of this kind in the resolution of the Cuban crisis last October, a crisis which for a few days seemed to bring the world very near to the nuclear disaster which all men dread. There are situations of a less portentous nature in which also the course of mediation and moderation can be of assistance to the parties. I refer, for example, to the differences between Somalia and Ethiopia and between Thailand and Cambodia. There are times when the world community, through the United Nations, may usefully keep a watchful eye on a potentially dangerous situation and lend its support to the efforts of those concerned to solve outstanding differences in a peaceful and constructive way. Such a situation existed prior to the independence of Ruanda and Burundi, and it is a source of gratification to find that the difficulties foreseen have, for the moment at least, apparently evaporated. Such situations exist today in Yemen and in South-East Asia.

In such situations the technique of quiet diplomacy—a technique in which my predecessor excelled—can make the difference between a disastrous breakdown of understanding and communication and a constructive advance towards a resolution of differences.

I have voiced a guarded optimism on the potential of

the United Nations as a force for peace and of the achievements which are already to its credit. It would be unrealistic if I did not also mention the practical basis upon which alone such activities can continue. Your country has, I have said, made great contributions to the efforts of the United Nations, both in men and in resources. There is, nonetheless, at the present time a very serious financial crisis facing the United Nations due to the failure of some members to pay their contributions towards the peacekeeping operations of the Organization. The International Court of Justice has recommended that the expenses of the peace-keeping operations of the United Nations should be part of the normal assessment of the member states. I hope very much that the time will soon come when all members of the United Nations will find it possible and, indeed, desirable to respect this opinion of the World Court.

I have said nothing of the great basic problem of disarmament or of the special preoccupations of the great powers. I hope that the United Nations operations I have mentioned may, in their modest way, be a pointer in the right direction and an encouragement in the constructive future use of the military art. They are the first gropings, imperfect admittedly, towards the kind of international authority which is one of the inescapable conditions of agreed disarmament.

I said last year at Uppsala that the United Nations must ultimately develop in the same way as sovereign States have done, and that, if it is to have a future, it must eventually assume some of the attributes of a State. It must have the right, the power and the means to keep the peace. We are only in the beginning and the process will surely take several generations. But the peace-keeping operations already conducted by the United Nations provide the hope that we are on the road to these essential developments.

## EDUCATION FOR PEACE*

A little while ago Carleton University honored me by conferring on me the degree of Doctor of Laws, *honoris causa,* and you have now honored me further by asking me to deliver an address to this convocation. I deeply appreciate this dual honor, as also this opportunity to say a few words on a subject with which all thinking men today are rightfully preoccupied.

I recall that the first honorary degree conferred on my distinguished predecessor, Dag Hammarskjold, was by Carleton University in 1954. In your letter inviting me to accept the degree of Doctor of Laws, Mr. President, you mentioned that Carleton is a young and rapidly growing university in the capital of Canada. You also mentioned that my speaking on this occasion at your university in the capital of Canada would further strengthen the feelings that most Canadians have for the United Nations.

I feel therefore that it is appropriate for me not only to speak on the most crucial subject of this age, but also to address myself particularly to the younger generation. The Charter of the United Nations begins with a reference to determination of the peoples of the world "to save succeeding generations from the scourge of war" and "to unite our strength to maintain international peace and security." This preoccupation with peace is, however, not in any sense recent; it is in fact as old as recorded history. Throughout history men have fought and at the same time yearned for peace. All the great religions of the world have peace among men as their basic purpose.

At the same time I have often pondered, as I have no doubt many of you might have, on that truth which is so

* Address delivered at Carleton University, Ottawa, Canada, May 25, 1962.

simply stated in the constitution of the United Nations Educational Scientific and Cultural Organization, "since wars begin in the minds of men, it is in the minds of men that the defenses of peace must be constructed." Thus the teachers are the true architects of minds and the students are the true builders of peace. If the teachers instruct the younger generation in the ways of peace, not only will their work succeed, but the basic idea of peace in our time will triumph. If we lose the minds of men, no matter how hard we may propagate the idea of peace through the United Nations and through collective international action, the idea will fail, leaving us in a lawless and disorderly world, if indeed a world should continue to exist.

The burning issue today is this battle for the minds of men, and here we have the phenomenon that each of the major ideologies is convinced not only that it represents the true philosophy of peace, but that the other system is bound to fail. As a result of this preoccupation with ideology and dogma, and on the general assumption that history repeats itself, we have mistrust and fear which is the source of all our problems and the basic fact behind the cold war.

Historians have concluded that many wars in the past were inevitable, and from this they proceed to infer that, given a similar set of circumstances, wars in the future will similarly be inevitable. But nothing is more fallacious than the generally accepted assumption that history repeats itself. The plain fact is that history does *not* repeat itself.

It seems to me that historical developments are conditioned by a peculiar set of circumstances prevailing at a particular time and place. At Munich, British Prime Minister Chamberlain tried, with extraordinary patience and almost in desperation, not to repeat the events of 1914, with results which were worse. Disillusioned by the tragic failure of Mr. Chamberlain's policy of appeasement, another British Prime Minister, Sir Anthony Eden, eighteen years later, embarked on a tough Suez policy which ended in failure. There was a considerable body of opinion in Britain in 1956 that history would repeat itself and that a policy of appeasement would be disastrous. The thesis turned out to be false, with unfortunate consequences.

The same obsession with the past seems to me to govern the thinking of the Big Powers today. Russia's obsessive fear of encirclement probably has its roots in her memories of 1919, and leads her to think in terms which are no longer valid in this thermonuclear age. The United States of America, too, seems to me to be a prisoner of her past. She was rudely dragged into the center of the world stage, much against her will, by the unprovoked attack on Pearl Harbor. It seems to me that the fear that such a catastrophic surprise attack will be repeated dominates the thinking in Washington, and a surprise attack is seen in the United States as the supreme risk. This fear stems from the same assumption that history will repeat itself.

It is therefore our first task to allay, if not to remove, this fear and mistrust, and to do so we need two things. First we need to try and understand each other's point of view. We also need to realize that it is no longer true to say that there are two sides to every question; in fact, there are many sides. It is accordingly meaningless to present the problems of our complicated existence in simple terms of black and white and to overlook the infinite gradations in between, or the whole spectrum of colors outside of these two basic hues.

This need for mutual understanding is reinforced by the amazing technological progress of our time. We live in an age when men are not content to circle the globe in a matter of minutes, but are aiming literally at the stars. The fantastic developments in the methods of transportation and communication have reduced the universe to the size of a simple country. In such a world it is essential that we realize the identity of interest that binds us together and not exaggerate the issues that divide us, however big the issues and however deep the divisions. We have to think of the world as a unit in the same way that we think of a city or county as a unit whose inhabitants, as I said, have a complete identity of interest, and especially the interest of survival.

And that brings me to the next point, that the same technological progress which has shrunk the world is also responsible for the development and perfection of inventions with a capacity for destruction which no one could have dreamed possible a generation ago. Today the major powers have the power literally to extinguish all life on this planet. It is perhaps true that over any period of history, notwithstanding its catalogue of wars, nations have never waged war lightly but only when there seemed no other way out of national danger. Today the chapter of wars in the pages of history may have to be closed, not by the exercise of moral judgment that war is bad, but by sheer necessity—the imperative of self-preservation. Surely there can be no material stake so important as to lead one to undertake the total destruction of his enemy, especially if, a the same time and in the same process, his own destruction is involved.

I have said elsewhere, and I repeat, that the great danger to our world today is that peace is preserved by the precarious balance of terror, with the ever-present possibility of global nuclear war by accident.

The development of nuclear weapons, it seems fairly obvious, has added a new dimension to the concept of war. War itself loses its utility as a consequence of uncertainty. War is not just violence. It is the controlled use of violence for attainable ends. But how can anyone control a war when he has no means of knowing whether his first nuclear strike has been effective or not? The whole conduct of military operations, whether by land, sea or air, is based on getting back information on what has been achieved in the first stage of operations. All that one can be certain of with a nuclear strike is that it has killed a lot of people and destroyed a number of installations over a wide area.

But you cannot be certain that you have killed the right people and destroyed the right buildings or installations. All that is certain is that the object of the war—the defense of your own country or territory—will be foiled by the very operations undertaken to achieve it. What is called strategy will be a kind of chess game played blindfold. Quite literally, the players do not know what they are doing, for they have no previous experience of their moves. Disarmament, therefore, is not only a very desirable alternative to war, but it is the only possible alternative if the human race itself is to survive.

It is for this reason that I advocate that we discontinue the piling up of armaments, and the mistrust and fear which is as much a cause as a consequence thereof. In fact, if war is no longer desirable, one might well ask: why armaments? Why this astronomical expenditure on weapons of such terrible destruction that they are in fact stillborn because they can never be used? Let us hope that this is only a passing phase and a temporary paradox, and that before long we might see the first steps toward the halting of the arms race, beginning perhaps with nuclear disarmament.

I referred earlier to the fact that men are now aiming at the stars. I do believe that, while disarmament may come about in our time and nuclear engines of destruction may be dismantled, the exploration of space will proceed with increased momentum. Indeed, we may be on the threshold of adventures in the universe which go far beyond the navigation of uncharted seas and the discovery of new lands that our ancestors undertook only a few centuries ago. Let us hope, however, that the kind of national claims and counterclaims, colonialism and imperial wars which characterized the discovery of the earth will not mark the exploration of outer space. For this reason I attach great significance to the coordination of work in the development of outer space which is taking place within the aegis of the United Nations.

There is one other area where a better understanding of each other's point of view can mean increased prosperity for all. This is also the result of the same technological progress to which I referred earlier. I said in Copenhagen the other day that the basic fact of our time is the fact of abundance. This abundance, this embarrassment of riches in the advanced countries, exists side by side with deep unfulfilled needs elsewhere, so that the problem is not one of production, to use the language of the economists, so much as of distribution.

I am one of those who are distressed by the attempt of nations as of human beings, to exploit each other because, truly, such exploitation is so unnecessary. I believe it is unnecessary because I do not think it is true any longer that one nation can become rich only by beggaring its neighbor. I believe that it is possible for the advanced countries, for example, to contribute to the economic development of the less advanced and in doing so to gain greater prosperity for themselves.

The concept of taxing the rich according to their capacity to pay, in order to cater to the poor according to their needs, is now well established as a simple canon of social justice in all democratic countries. It requires only a little imagination to lift this concept to a higher plane, namely the international plane, and to extend its scope from the country to the universe. Surely it is not too difficult for educated people to raise their sights a little in economic matters, as they do so easily when they turn their minds skywards into outer space.

This is the century of the common man and it is at the United Nations, through governments big and small, strong and weak, politically mature and inexperienced, that the common aspirations of mankind find a voice and an expression. Our task in the United Nations is thus to bring about a real international democracy so that the common man everywhere may live free from fear and want. But nations are made up of human beings and, as I said at the beginning, the real task is to build peace into their minds.

If this task is to be successful, then our young and educated men must have minds which are independent and objective, detached and inquiring. It quite often happens that an issue arises in a country, or even in a neighborhood, which is deemed vital to its security or prosperity, and at that point pressures develop which make it doubly important for people to preserve an independent, objective, detached and inquiring attitude of mind.

One of the ways of preserving these attitudes is the search for the basic concepts and the underlying principles from which men of various races and creeds draw their inspiration in the pursuit of the higher life and the ultimate goal of human endeavor. Such a search is most likely to end in a sharing of our beliefs, in civilized conduct and generous behavior, the spirit of tolerance, of live and let live, and of understanding the other man's point of view. This is the essence of all great religions and I believe that it holds the key to the solution of the most pressing problems of our time.

The young men and women who are here with us today have the opportunity, and the responsibility, to help in developing and maintaining such an attitude of mind, so that we might have a world which is made up of societies whose doors are as open as their hearts and, most important of all, societies which are made up of people with open minds.

## PROGRESS TOWARDS PEACE*

I am grateful to you, Mr. Rector, for this opportunity to say a few words this evening at the University of Warsaw, on the subject of "Progress towards Peace."

I know that the University has played a significant role in influencing your country's thinking, in promoting its literary, scholarly and scientific achievements and, to some extent, even in shaping your political development. I also think it is fair to say that the vicissitudes of your University are a fair reflection of the diversity of your country's history itself.

I understand that when the University was re-opened most recently in 1945, it had to begin almost from scratch as so many of its staff members had been killed, and so much of its equipment and facilities destroyed, in the course of World War II. Today I see here a flourishing establishment representing all the basic faculties of a modern University, and the facilities are being expanded.

I understand that there are some 10,000 students at the University, and that there are also a number of Asian and African students receiving scholarships while studying

* Address delivered at the University of Warsaw, Poland, August 31, 1962.

here. In view of the limited accommodation available in the University for students from your own country, I commend your readiness to admit so many students from Africa and Asia.

I have given this address of mine the title "Progress towards Peace" because I am one of those who are convinced that peace can be obtained only through progress; and by that I mean, not only economic and social progress, but also political progress and progress in mutual understanding.

The Charter has recognized the important role of economic and social progress in maintaining world peace and stresses in the preamble itself the need "to employ international machinery for the promotion of the economic and social advancement of all peoples." I have repeatedly stated that I am gravely concerned with the growing gap between the living standards of the wealthy countries with their affluent societies, and the conditions in the poorer countries with societies for whom existence is a continual struggle.

It is a phenomenon of the postwar period that so many of the underdeveloped countries of the world have been able to free themselves from colonial rule. In some respects the position of Asia and Africa is similar to Europe's immediately after World War II.

In Europe, after the great war, productive capacity had been destroyed and halted. In Asia and Africa, where colonialism held sway for hundreds of years, productive capacity outside of agriculture had hardly existed and had to be established for the first time. Unlike Europe, however, Asia and Africa have no sufficiency of skilled manpower nor of managerial, administrative and organizational capacity, and last but not least—they also lack capital.

In Europe the Marshall Plan took three and a half years

and cost approximately $13 billion. A similar program for under-developed Asia and Africa will no doubt take a longer time and probably will cost more.

Nationalism and the urge to be free had spurred the peoples of Asia and Africa to struggle for independence. To millions of peoples in these two vast continents, independence was regarded as being synonymous with progress.

It must have seemed to their leaders on the threshold of freedom that, once they were masters in their own homes, it would be possible for them to accelerate their economic and social progress. This unhappily has not been so.

Most of these countries have come face to face with the problems of economic development for the first time and they have discovered that the road to economic progress is uphill all the way. They have made some progress, but much of it has not been reflected in improved living standards because of the concurrent growth of population. At the same time their rates of economic growth has been lower than that of the advanced industrialized societies, and as a result the gap between their respective living standards has widened.

If this continues, a new element of tension will be introduced in the relations between these countries, just at a time when the grievances of the underdeveloped countries against their old masters under the colonial rule are gradually being forgotten.

The advanced countries have themselves realized the inherent danger and explosive nature of the situation and have therefore initiated large-scale programs of bilateral assistance. In fact, one of the by-products of the cold war has been a kind of competition between the two great world powers in giving assistance to the less developed countries.

While this assistance may be politically motivated, it has beyond all doubt benefited the developing countries, and especially those which have set up the necessary administrative and planning machinery to use this assistance to the best national advantage.

At the same time, multilateral programs have also gathered momentum, and the resources available to the United Nations and the specialized agencies for rendering economic aid and technical assistance to the less developed countries have been gradually increased during recent years.

Even so, the assistance available to the less developed countries is proving inadequate, particularly when account is taken of the continued weakness in the prices of raw materials on which so many of these countries depend. In all the circumstances, I feel that, in the long run, it may well be to the advantage of the developing countries to undertake greater efforts toward international economic development.

The United Nations solemnly decided at its sixteenth session to designate this decade of the sixties as the Decade of Development. I hope that during this decade most of the developing countries will be able to register significant increases in their gross national product as well as in their per capita incomes and living standards. I feel that progress in this regard would be an important contribution toward peace.

The idea behind this program is to achieve substantial results in the sphere of public welfare and living standards in underdeveloped areas. The means to do it exist. The knowledge exists. The technique exists. All that is required is a decision on the part of the developed countries to dedicate their energies to this most constructive and exciting venture of our times.

It lies within our power, within the coming decade, to stamp out diseases which unnecessarily kill millions of humans each year and debilitate many more millions. It lies within our power to open up the avenues of knowledge to hundreds of millions of people by making illiteracy a thing of the past. It lies within our power to harness our rivers, to improve our agriculture, to develop our industries, to house our peoples decently, and to raise the physical and social well-being of the almost sub-human two-thirds of the human race.

Such a cooperative effort through the machinery of the United Nations could capture the imagination of the whole world. It could provide an outlet for the fulfillment of man's longing to engage in creative works of peace and progress. And perhpas it is not too much to hope that in cooperative, constructive work above the clamor of political conflict, beyond the reach of clashing ideologies, the tensions which plague us today might recede and be forgotten in the joyous task of working together for the good of humanity.

In the long run it is arguable, of course, that the underdeveloped countries should be able to get their foreign exchange requirements by trade rather than by aid. Speaking as one coming from an underdeveloped country myself, I can say without fear of contradiction that no country likes to be a beggar. It is, however, a significant economic fact that over the years the terms of trade have been favoring the advanced and not the developing countries. This again is an indication of the economic weakness of the less developed countries and their relative lack of staying power and bargaining strength.

As for private foreign capital, all the studies made on this subject go to show that external capital flows more freely from one advanced economy to another, rather than from an advanced economy to a developing economy. Therefore, deliberate transfers of capital have to take place on a governmental or institutional basis, and this fact is now commonly acknowledged even by the countries which are the main exporters of private capital.

I said earlier that it may well be to the long-term advantage of the advanced countries themselves to assist the economic development of the developing countries. This statement may or may not be accepted by economists, if considered in purely economic terms. Whatever differences of opinion there may be amongst them, there is, however, no doubt in my own mind that such assistance would make a contribution towards world peace.

It seems to me ironic that, when something like $120 billion a year is spent by the great powers on armaments, it is so difficult for the advanced countries to decide to set apart 1 per cent of their national income for the economic advancement of the less developed countries. If the great military powers should decide, even pending disarmament, to set aside 5 per cent of the national expenditure on armaments for such a purpose, the capital requirements of the less developed countries could be largely met, while the relative strength of the major military powers would not change very much.

In fact, I would go further and say that most of the capital requirements of the less developed countries could be met even without any progress in disarmament, in view of the embarrassing abundance of consumption goods in the advanced countries and the ease with which some of it could be switched over for producton of capital goods which the underdeveloped countries need.

What a happy world we will be in, if only the present competition for arms supremacy gives way to another kind of competition, to raise the living standards of the common people and to encourage peace and harmony in this turbulent world!

So far, I have traced the connection between the economic and social progress of the less developed countries, and progress toward peace. I would now like to turn to political progress.

I referred earlier to the great national movements in the postwar era on the part of many countries under colonial rule to obtain their freedom, not only their political freedom, but their freedom of action in the economic field. This has been the most significant political development of the postwar period which began with Asia and which is culminating now in Africa, much more rapidly than seemed possible five years ago.

This development has produced a considerable addition to the membership of the United Nations and I personally believe that, as a result, the Organization is more truly representative of world opinion today than it was at any time before.

I also believe that the newly independent countries will soon forget their grievances arising from their colonial past and concentrate on the tasks ahead. I am convinced that they can play a significant role in bridging the gulf between East and West. Their influence has already been evident in the work of the eighteen-nation disarmament committee in Geneva.

In this complex world of today which is dominated by the two giants, there is a useful middle role to be played by these smaller countries, many of whom may have neither the resources nor the technology to sustain great armies or armaments but who, for that very reason, can approach with objectivity such major issues as war and peace.

I hope that this progress toward universality of the United Nations will continue until all countries of the world are members and are able to make their contribution to the peace of the world.

The issue of disarmament and nuclear weapons has necessarily been one of the major preoccupations of the smaller countries. They know that if nuclear war should break out, it will not be the major powers that will be the only sufferers.

Even if nuclear war could be avoided, as we all hope, they realize that nuclear testing presents an equally grave danger since fallout is no respecter of frontiers. I feel that here, too, progress has to come by stages.

I do not believe that it is possible to reach general and complete disarmament overnight, because the arms race is merely an external manifestation of a deep-rooted feeling of mistrust and lack of confidence. This mistrust has built up over the years and will not die a sudden death.

Progress toward its removal is one of the major tasks, not only of statesmen but also of men and women of good will all over the world. In this task of making progress toward better understanding of each other, I feel again that the nonaligned countries can play a valuable role.

In particular I feel that one of the first steps in making progress in this direction is the cessation of nuclear testing. Equally important is the prevention of the spread of nuclear weapons.

It is a sad commentary on the situation of the world today that the means for the extermination of the human species is now in the hands of the three or four great powers. In due course, it will pass into the hands of many governments, large and small.

There was a time when only the United States had nuclear weapons. This was followed by a time when only the United States and the Soviet Union had such weapons. Later the United States, the Soviet Union and Britain possessed them. And now France has joined the nuclear club. It seems likely that one or two other countries may shortly manufacture these terrible weapons.

It is also obvious that during the next few years the manufacture of engines of mass destruction will become cheaper and easier. There is no end to this process until many states will be in a position to inflict incalculable destruction on the rest of mankind.

As I have stated on a previous occasion, if all sovereign states were governed by rulers possessed of even the rudiments of sanity, they would be restrained from committing such colossal crimes. But experience has shown that, from time to time, power in one country or another falls into the hands of rulers whose sanity is clouded by the pursuit of individual or national glorification.

There is still another hazard to mankind that stems from the sheer number of people who handle these weapons of mass destruction. I have no doubt that the designers and manufacturers of nuclear weapons have attempted to install in them certain mechanical safeguards against accidental firing or explosion.

There are, however, no final or foolproof safeguards against the possibility of human or mechanical failure. The danger of war by accident is therefore ever present. This is one aspect of the problem on which there can be no two opinions.

No one in his senses can maintain that testing of nuclear weapons can contribute to human happiness. We must bend all our energies to put a stop to these tests. Time is already running short, and every day's delay entails untold risks. The greatest risk lies in doing nothing, in wasting time in hair-splitting and meanwhile in piling up nuclear and thermonuclear weapons. The hydrogen bomb is a greater evil than any evil it is intended to meet.

One fact clearly emerges out of the negotiations and discussions both inside and outside the United Nations. This fact is that action can be taken on major issues only if the United States and the Soviet Union are in agreement.

Disarmament, the cessation of nuclear weapons tests, and the prevention of spread of nuclear weapons are problems which call for an immediate solution. Only a spirit of trust and understanding by both sides can lead to a satisfactory solution of these pressing problems and thereby meet the greatest challenge of our time.

### COMMENTS ON POPE JOHN'S ENCYCLICAL "PEACE ON EARTH"*

It is with a deep sense of gratification that I have read the Encyclical "Peace on Earth" issued today by His Holiness Pope John XXIII. No doubt because of the universal significance of peace, the message has been addressed not only to the members of the Catholic Church but to all men on earth.

I can well understand the profound emotion which Pope John XXIII has said he felt when signing this document of far-reaching significance, for in addressing his thoughts to the peace of the world in this nuclear era, he was indeed appealing for man's survival, for the application of human knowledge not to death but to life and for the dignity of man in a community of understanding.

The Encyclical, among others, calls for a strengthening of the United Nations—thus focussing attention to the fact that peace is an international responsibility. At the same time, it calls for such specific measures as a reduction of arms stockpiles, a ban of nuclear weapons and a general

* From a press conference, New York, April 11, 1963.

agreement on progressive disarmament and an effective method of control, which is a primary responsibility of the big nations. To the voice expressed in favour of these measures by the overwhelming majority of nations and peoples of the world has now been added this heartening and noble call by His Holiness Pope John XXIII.

The contents of the Encyclical are certainly in harmony with the purposes and objectives of the United Nations. They come as a timely reminder that the fate of mankind still hinges precariously in the deadly balance of nuclear devastation, and will contribute very significantly to intensify the efforts of all those who are confident that the human race has enough wisdom to preserve its own species —a species with a record of splendid achievements in the realms of art, science, literature and religion.

Let me take this opportunity of offering my respectful homage to His Holiness for his great wisdom, vision and courage in ceaseless endeavours for the cause of peace and human survival.

# 8

# Education and the United Nations

## EDUCATION IN OUR CHANGING TIMES*

You have just honored me by conferring on me the degree of Doctor of Laws *honoris causa,* and I am deeply grateful to you for it. I appreciate even more your kind invitation to me to deliver the Commencement address on this occasion, as it gives me an opportunity to share with you a few thoughts on a subject which concerns all of us vitally. I have chosen to speak to you today on the subject of "Education in Our Changing Times," not just because it is an appropriate theme for a Commencement address, but even more because I feel that the present generation has a great responsibility to educate itself, not only to ensure its own survival, but the survival of mankind itself.

We are all aware of the ringing pledge of the Charter "to save succeeding generations from the scourge of war." Today it is not simply a question of saving succeeding generations from the scourge of war, it is more a question of saving mankind itself from total annihilation. With the progress we have made in the development of nuclear weapons and long-range missiles, with the ushering in of

* Address delivered at Mt. Holyoke College, South Hadley, Mass., June 2, 1963.

the era of push-button warfare, and with all the dangers that the world faces of war by accident even more than by design, I feel that I am not over-stating the case when I put the choice before the present generation in these striking terms.

In this second half of the twentieth century, I consider that the primary task of the educationist everywhere is to dispel certain age-old assumptions. It seems to be assumed, for example, that there are no more than two sides to a problem. As a matter of fact, almost every problem has more than two sides. It is also fallacious to paint human beliefs and human societies in terms of pure black and white. There are various shades in between.

Basing himself on these new principles, the educationist should be concerned primarily with the greatest question before us—the question of human survival. War, which has often been in the past an instrument of national policies, should no longer feature in the settlement of disputes. With the advent of the atomic age the very concept of war has undergone a tremendous change. War no longer means the controlled employment of violence, with defined targets and limited objectives. It means an uncontrolled unleashing of weapons of mass destruction, probably resulting in the annihilation of all that human ingenuity and effort has built over the years.

The United States and the Soviet Union now control between them almost the whole of the world's nuclear arsenal. Their common interest is to ensure that existing restraints on the use of this devastating power are not weakened, but strengthened. This means that some system must be found to limit and control the nuclear arms race before it gets out of hand through the spread of weapons to more and more powers, or through the development of weapons which are uncontrollable.

In seeking proper remedies for war, one must be clear
about the causes of the disease. Disparities in wealth and
living standards between nations no doubt affect the stability of the world; and while programmes to assist developing countries in their efforts to reduce these disparities
are urgently necessary, they will not in themselves dimin-
ish the risk of global war; in fact, the devastating wars
which "twice in our lifetime" have "brought untold
sorrow to mankind" were started by wealthy and advanced
countries. Nor does the creation of larger regional blocs
or even a federation of nations make wars less likely—
except perhaps between the members themselves. The
level of armaments and relative military strength between
States does not itself make war more or less probable. Nor
are ideological differences the fundamental cause of war;
there have been fierce wars between ideologically similar
States.

All such factors—economic, military, ideological—may
contribute to the causes of wars. What turns these factors
into wars is the psychological or emotional frame of mind,
which replaces rational thinking. This state of mind, fed
daily by mass media propagating sensationalism and suspicion, develops into a condtion bordering on obsession,
which renders peaceful settlement of disputes difficult if
not impossible, and leads us nearer to thinking in terms of
a solution by force, which means international anarchy.

The only way out of anarchy in any circumstance—
whether local, regional or world wide—is through the creation of some form of government. Between nations, this
has been done peacefully by voluntary union or forcibly
by conquest. But in the present world situation neither of
these procedures offers hope of a solution.

A voluntary union, or even federation, is possible only
between states of roughly similar internal character; it

cannot be expected—and may not work—between ideologically different groups of States. And conquest is almost equally unimaginable; war has ceased to be practicable, except on a tiny local scale, as any large-scale military action would probably end as a suicidal adventure.

This leaves us with the necessity of having to try to form a world authority within the limitations of the present world set-up, across the barriers of the cold war. But to be worth having, it need not be complete or flawless. Anything capable of mitigating the present anarchy would represent a valuable advance.

An effective world authority, like any other governmental system, must be based on power. It cannot grow out of a paper constitution or a Charter or the formation of international agencies in specific fields, though all these in themselves may make useful contributions. As nation-states grew out of the unifying power of the stronger feudal lords, so must a society of nations grow out of the needs of its largest and most powerful constituent members.

It is impossible to conceive in our day of a world authority that could physically overawe the giant States of America and Russia. All that seems possible is to employ the strength of the two giants to back a system of preventing war between other countries. But how is war to be prevented in disputes between the two giants themselves? It seems to me that one of the first steps to be taken is to attempt to do away with the cold war which has been such a marked feature of international relations since the end of World War II.

We in the United Nations are all too familiar with the cold war. The curious thing about the cold war is that it is not a battle for more territory, or even for more political power. As it is waged in the United Nations, it is a battle for the votes of the uncommitted and for the minds of the unconverted. History is full of examples of religious intolerance, but the ideological fanaticism that we see today seems to me sometimes to be even more implacable, and certainly more deadly and dangerous to the human race, than the religious fanaticism which marked the history of past centuries and occasioned such extreme instances of man's inhumanity to man.

One remarkable feature of the cold war is that each side is so completely convinced of its own rightness. The doctrines of capitalism and communism have, in fact ,undergone some subtle changes since the major exponents of these theories expounded their dogmas. There is no doubt that some of the theories of communism, for example, were influenced by the conditions of extreme laissez-faire of private enterprise, the ruthless exploitation of labour, including the labour of women and children, and the accumulation of wealth and power in the hands of a few, that marked the rise of capitalism in the eighteenth and nineteenth centuries. While communist dogma may still speak of capitalism as though it has remained unchanged over the last century, in fact, capitalism has undergone a change. Even in the capitalist countries, society has awakened to the dangers of unrestricted private enterprise, and the societies practising the most advanced theories of private enterprise have found it necessary to adopt, at the same time, stringent laws to avoid the danger of extreme concentration of economic power in the form of monoplies. Far from labour being exploited, united labour has learned its own strength. Small men and women everywhere have in a way become capitalists, with a stake in the development of their own societies. Social welfare legislation has made sure not only that child labour is outlawed, but that children are given opportunities for education and for choosing their own careers.

On the other hand, while some captalists may not wish to concede this point, I believe that communism too has undergone many changes. For example, there are many communists in the world today who do not believe in the inevitability of war between the two rival systems of society. In the Soviet Union the leaders talk in terms of competitive co-existence. I can well understand why they should wish to compete with the capitalist societies to provide better standards of living for their own people, since they believe in the inherent superiority of their system and this would be the surest way of demonstrating it.

While thus the practice of capitalism and of communism has perhaps come a little closer than the extreme antithesis assumed by dogmatists in the past, there is still the ideological fanaticism to which I referred, and which complicates our existence. Each side is convinced that it alone represents the true philosophy of peace, and that the other side is a warmonger. Both sides mistrust the intentions of the other, and are also very much afraid that one side might achieve some technological break-through in the field of missilery or nuclear warfare, or even defence systems against nuclear attack, which gives it an advantage over the other. If this atmosphere of mistrust and fear continues and if, meanwhile, the stock-piling of nuclear arms and the development of more deadly engines of destruction should continue unchecked, surely the danger of total annihilation of mankind to which I referred earlier is becoming "nearer, clearer, deadlier than before."

It is in this context that I feel that I should address myself today mainly to the younger generation. Those of you who are leaving this institution of learning today will in due course be responsible as citizens, as mothers, and as enlightened members of the public in shaping not only the policies of your country but—what is even more important—the minds of the young. Your first task, I think, should be to try to understand each other better and to remove in this process the fear and mistrust that characterize the attitudes of the major protangonists of the cold war.

I believe that the prime need today is this need for better understanding, especially the better understanding of the other man's problems and of his point of view. We live in an age of technological miracles. The other day we saw an astronaut take off at 9:00 a.m. and return to the earth at 7:30 p.m. the next day, after having completed 22 orbits around the globe. Some months earlier we had the fantastic spectacle of two astronauts, one of whom was in orbit for four days, and the other for three days, practically in tandem. Now there is a race to the moon. Already the aeronautical industry is talking in terms of aircraft which will travel at two to three times the speed of sound. In a world which is thus shrinking, it is essential that the human mind must open out, and that we must realize that we all have a common interest in survival and that this interest binds us together.

Some ten days ago there was an epoch-making conference in Addis Ababa of the Heads of State and other officials of the independent countries of Africa. It was a matter of great personal regret to me that, although I had been invited in a personal capacity to attend this historic meeting, I was not able to do so. Most of the countries represented at this conference had achieved their independence only during the last decade or so. The Heads of State assembled in Addis Ababa were naturally concerned that the African people still subject to colonial rule should obtain their independence soon. But even more striking was their concern with their interdependence, and their emphasis on the establishment of a machinery for regular consultations and concerted action on common problems. This meeting has an important lesson for us—for individuals as well as nations—the lesson of our mutual interdependence.

One fact of our interdependence is our common interest in survival, which can be realized only by better understanding, because such understanding is the key to the solution of our most pressing global problems. As I pointed out earlier there are very few international issues today which can be settled on the basis of a clear-cut judgement that one side is right and the other is wrong. International problems have become so complicated, and so many different elements enter into them, that a simple clear-cut judgement in terms of black and white is no longer possible. Nor can these issues be settled by the imposition of the will of the stronger on the weaker. For history shows that no issue can be settled on a permanent basis by superior force. This in fact would be a good reason for outlawing war, because wars do not solve any problems; in fact, they leave more problems unsolved in their wake, and give rise to more new problems as the years go by, than the problems that they were supposed to solve.

How then can we solve the issues of the world today? We can do so only by creating an atmosphere of confidence to replace the present atmosphere of mistrust. We can solve great issues only by discussion and debate, by negotiation and give-and-take, by conciliation and compromise. It is only in this way that these problems will remain solved and not raise their ugly heads again, as they surely will if they are suppressed rather than solved.

The solution of these great issues is, of course, one of the primary functions of the United Nations. I would be the first to concede that the United Nations is far from being perfect. But I also feel that people often criticize the United Nations because of a basic misunderstanding of its nature. The United Nations is not a world government, nor is its General Assembly a world legislature. It is, in a sense, of course, the parliament of mankind, as it gives opportunities for the large and the small countries equally to have their say on major issues, and this is the original meaning of a parliament. But it is not a world legislature with the authority to pass laws binding on all member governments; its resolutions are more in the nature of recommendations than of statutes. But the United Nations does offer a machinery for multilateral diplomacy, which did not exist before. As it makes greater progress towards universality over the years, it enables its Member Governments to hold a simultaneous conversation with the rest of the world, which would not be possible through the normal channels of bilateral diplomacy. And the means it adopts to solve the issues, big and small, which it faces are the very means of persuasion and negotiation which I advocated a moment ago.

I believe that one of the major tasks of education in our changing times is to create in the young the willingness to tolerate differences of opinion and the desire to try to understand different points of view. There was a time not so long ago when religious fanaticism was so great that the hatred of the Saracen for the Christian was no less than that of the Christian for a heretic in his own faith. It is only during the last century or so that religious tolerance has more and more come into its own. Today what we need to do is to practise the cult of political tolerance so as to reach the goal of ideological co-existence, as the first imperative of survival on our planet. Because truly the only alternative to co-existence is no-existence.

In the search for better understanding, we also have to minimize differences of race, colour and nationality. I am an Asian who has lived for some time in the Western world. I think I can say without fear of contradiction that, while we may have a different sense of values, we do not have a different concept of civilization. A civilized Asian is no different from a civilized European or American. But each of them is very different from his own uncivilized compatriots. If we can minimize these differences of race and colour and nationality at the same time that we make an effort for better understanding, we shall find it easier to live together on this planet.

There is only one more thought that I should like to share with you. I said a moment ago that the Asian and his Western counterpart may have a different sense of values. I believe that this is particularly true in the field of education. While one has to take all generalizations with reservation, I think it is safe to say that the main aim of education in the West is the development of the intellect. The massive progress of science and technology has tended to stress the intellectual rather than the moral and spiritual values. In Asia, if I may say so, the traditional aim of education is to impress on the young the importance of the mind rather than the body, and even more basically, the importance of the spirit rather than the mind. Education thus becomes inward looking, and the aim of education is the discovery of one's self rather than the discovery of things external to us. Today I feel that both approaches are inadequate, and that it is not enough to stress in education either purely moral and spiritual or purely mental and intellectual values. Education cannot mean merely the development of our intellect or of all our potentialities, for there are potentialities for evil in us as well as for good. Nor can it mean mere preparation for life, but rather to make the world a better place to live in. Our educators should realize as clearly as possible what kind of potentialities they are to develop in their students; what kind of life they are to educate young people for. The ideals and values which constitute the essential elements of culture must first be clearly understood and appreciated.

What we therefore need is a synthesis of these values—spiritual and moral as well as intellectual—with the aim of producing a fully integrated human being who is inward looking as well as outward looking, who searches his own mind in order that his nobler self may prevail at all times, and at the same time recognize his obligations to his fellow men and the world around him; because while the world is shrinking, humanity is multiplying, and each of us has to recognize his essential kinship to every other member of the human race.

# 9

# Issues Before the United Nations

## SOME MAJOR ISSUES BEFORE THE UNITED NATIONS*

I certainly feel it a privilege to have this opportunity of addressing the Economic Club of New York, and I am most grateful to this important organization for the opportunity thus afforded to me.

The subject of my talk today is "Some Major Issues before the United Nations." It is obviously a topic of very wide range and interest, and it will be hardly possible for any one to deal with it adequately in the space of twenty-five minutes or so. But I shall attempt to deal with the more important aspects of the major issues confronting the world organization today.

As you are no doubt aware, the functions of the United Nations can be broadly classified into three categories: political, economic and social, and trusteeship activites. Before I deal with these main functions, I should like to comment briefly on the United Nations financial problem which, I believe, has been widely publicized, but little understood, over the past few years.

* Address before the Economic Club of New York on Tuesday, March 5, 1963.

The financial difficulties of the Organization had their origin in the Organization's undertaking to maintain peace in the troubled area of the Middle East between Israel and Arab countries, and as a result of its efforts to help the Government of the Congo, among other things, to maintain the territorial integrity and the political independence of the Republic of the Congo, to prevent the occurrence of civil war and to maintain law and order in that country.

In essence the problem is a political one which reflects on the one hand the dissatisfaction of some Member States with the basic objectives of these peace-keeping operations or with the manner in which the directives of the Security Council and the General Assembly have been carried out, and on the other hand the dissatisfaction of some other Members with the method that has been employed to apportion the costs of large-scale peace-keeping operations among the member governments. There was also uncertainty in the minds of some Governments as to whether the assessments for these activities represented legal and binding obligations for the governments concerned.

As a result, a considerable number of governments have thus far failed to pay their assessments to the budgets for the Middle East and Congo operations with the consequence that the Organization's deficit has grown steadily during recent years.

At the beginning of this year this deficit, representing the difference between the Organization's current obligations and its current resources, stood at approximately $72 million and may be expected to increase to about $127 million by the end of June. The deficit would have been far greater had it not been for the sale of 40 Governments during 1962 of $121 million worth of United Nations bonds.

While the financial position of the United Nations has been a matter of deep concern to me, I have high hopes that we will find it much improved during the course of the present year as a result of the following four factors. Firstly, the General Assembly's decision last December to accept the advisory opinion of the International Court of Justice which was to the effect that expenditures authorized for the United Nations peace-keeping operations in the Middle East and the Congo constitute "expenses of the Organization" within the meaning of Article 17, paragraph 2, of the Charter of the United Nations.

Secondly, the decision last December of the General Assembly to appoint a Committee of twenty-one member governments, which is currently meeting, to consider and report to a Special Session of the General Assembly on methods of financing large-scale peace-keeping operations such as those in the Middle East and the Congo and on means of dealing with the problem of the arrears in the payment of past assessments.

Thirdly, a determined effort to collect contributions that are now in arrears and to sell additional United Nations bonds up to the limit of the $200 million authorized by the General Assembly. For this purpose I have requested Mr. Eugene R. Black, former President of the International Bank for Reconstruction and Development, to serve as my Special Financial Consultant and he has kindly consented to act in this capacity without remuneration.

And fourthly, a sharp reduction in the costs of the United Nations operations in the Congo, which should be possible now that the military phase of that operation may be considered at an end.

We must, of course, anticipate some continuing costs in both the Middle East and the Congo, for some time to come. It should not be beyond our capacity, however, to find the means to cover these costs if Governments give the problem their most earnest and urgent consideration. For, in the final analysis, their success in finding a common measure of agreement on future action will help determine whether the United Nations can continue to be an effective force for peace.

Now, coming back to the three main functions of the United Nations, let me take up the trusteeship activities first.

One of the most remarkable achievements of the United Nations has been its contribution to the emergence of a large number of independent countries particularly in Asia and Africa. The present membership of the world organization is 110, compared to the original membership of 51, and the United Nations played a similar role in the birth of many of these new members, particularly from Africa.

The drive toward independence, which in our time has swept dramatically through so many parts of the world, is an irreversible process parallel to other great historical events of the same character, particularly those which occurred in the American Continent—North, Central and South—at the end of the eighteenth and the beginning of the nineteenth century. Then, as now, a large group of colonial territories—one of them the United States—became independent nations in a relatively short period of time.

As the experience of practically every country has shown, accession to independence is not enough by itself to make such independence meaningful. Many of the states emerging from dependent status are lacking in adequate numbers of trained personnel, whether at the administrative or technical levels; their economic and financial life is generally precarious; their educational advancement is far from high and they are often plagued by political instability. This is true of many newly independent nations but such a situation was not unknown to countries which are now powerful and developed but whose backwardness in many respects at their time of their emancipation did not, and in fact could not, have prevented their emergence as free nations.

The task ahead in this increasingly interdependent world of ours is clearly to help the new countries in resolving their main deficiencies. To this end the United Nations and its family of agencies can play and in fact have been playing for many years now a constructive role. They provide assistance to the developing countries without strings attached and offer channels which can be used in such a way as to avoid injecting political issues or subjecting the assistance to conditions other than the benefit of the recipient countries.

The emergence of many newly independent countries in Asia and Africa and the absence of democratic trappings in the set-up of many of them disturb some older members of the United Nations. In this connection it is worth remembering that all the independence movements in Asia and Africa are led by a class of people who are staunch nationalists. Through a variety of circumstances these nationalists fight at the vanguard of independence movements, and the transfer of power in most cases goes to this class. It will be a mistake to assume that the political institutions in most of the newly independent countries will be of the same type as those prevailing in the United States or in Britain, or that there will necessarily be two main parties competing against each other for the votes of the people. In many newly independent countries it is most unlikely that there will be a two-party system for many years to come. The nationalist movements are going to be very powerful indeed; they will control the government without there being any effective challenge to them from within. And any challenge from outside will only strengthen them. It will take time before any issues arise in the new countries on which it will be possible to build a real opposition organization. It is worth remembering that the democratic system of government, though most desirable, is at the same time a highly sophisticated and difficult form of government to operate, particularly in newly independent countries.

I wish I could dwell at some length on the economic and social activities of the United Nations. But considerations of time at my disposal and of more pressing and urgent political issues compel me to be very brief in dealing with this category of UN activity. The issues confronting us in the economic and social fields are not less important than the ones which are labelled political. Indeed, they are more fundamental. The peoples determined to "save succeeding generations from the scourge of war," as our Charter goes, are not merely asserting their will to preserve the mere existence of the species but also their aspirations to a better life. They fear less the loss of what they have obtained than the loss of what they hope to achieve.

Regardless of our political credo, religion or philosophy, a peaceful world is not one in which we can have peace of mind as long as some are affluent and others destitute. True, the problem of wealth and poverty among individuals and nations is as old as mankind itself and, in fact, one may feel that its very existence bears witness to one of the major forces driving the world, namely, the desire of every one to improve his lot.

The Charter of the United Nations explicitly states that one of its primary functions is "to employ international machinery for the promotion of the economic and social advancement of all peoples." With this in view the United Nations General Assembly has launched what it terms Development Decade.

We are now entering a new year of the United Nations Development Decade. Some of you may recall the proposals which I put forward last summer, and which were endorsed by the Economic and Social Council, outlining a programme of action by the United Nations family of organizations for the attainment of the objectives of the Decade. This work was carried forward during the recent General Assembly meetings in New York.

Since then a number of important steps have been taken. As an integral part of the expanding endeavours of the United Nations in the Development Decade, the World Food Programme was launched on 1st January this year. It is a joint program of the United Nations and the Food and Agriculture Organization, with the co-operation of other United Nations agencies.

In January, the Governing Council of the Special Fund approved 42 new projects with a total cost of over $96 million. These projects, geared to priority goals of the Development Decade, may be expected to make major contributions to the economic development of countries in Africa, Asia and Latin America.

The new United Nations Committee on Housing, Building and Planning has outlined a future plan of work which should enable the United Nations to provide stronger and more specialized leadership for the expansion of housing and related programs in the low-income countries during the Development Decade.

A major step in another crucial area is being taken by the Preparatory Committee for the United Nations Conference on Trade and Development which met here a few weeks ago. I need scarcely underline the potential impor-

tance of that Conference or how essential it is to do everything possible to ensure its success.

Meanwhile, all the agencies of the United Nations family are co-operating with me in preparing detailed proposals for early action by the United Nations family under the
inspiration of the Development Decade.

In addition to Headquarters' activities I must mention
the constantly expanding activities of the regional commissions. The Economic Commission for Africa met last
month in Leopoldville. This very day the session of the
Economic Commission for Asia and the Far East was
opened by President Macapagal in Manila, and this will be
followed in April by the Economic Commission for Europe and in May by the Economic Commission for Latin
America. We are relying greatly on these meetings, which
reflect so directly the problems and needs of the different
regions of the world, for guidance in our forward planning.

Last in this brief list of activities, but certainly not least,
is the United Nations Conference on the Application of
Science and Technology for the Benefit of the Less Developed Areas, which took place in Geneva last month. I have
every hope that through this great Conference, and the
intensified co-operation generated by it, a major contribution will be made over the years to come to the attainment
of the goals of the Development Decade. The attainment
of these goals, it is my sincere belief, is crucial to the well-
being of humanity and to the peace of the world.

Now, let me deal with some major political issues before
the United Nations. As you are fully aware, the world organization responded to the call of the Central Government of the Congo to undertake certain activities, nearly
three years ago. Recent events have shown the correctness
of the United Nations policy in that unfortunate country.

It is true to say that but for the presence of the United Nations in the Congo, the country would have gone to pieces by now and become a major arena of the cold war. Thanks to the United Nations, the sovereignty and the authority of the legitimate Central Government have been upheld and the territorial integrity of the Republic preserved. The United Nations has been able to assert its right to complete freedom of movement in the whole territory of the Congo. It has also been able to assist the Central Government in maintaining law and order over the vast territory. The success of the Congo operation has been made possible by the co-operation of the countries which provided men, money and materials required for this operation.

For the future we have to think in terms of gradually disengaging ourselves from the Congo and enabling the Republic to stand on its own feet. There will have to be a shift from military assistance to civilian assistance. The nature and size of assistance will of course depend on the availability of funds and its operation within the context of the resolutions adopted by the various organs of the United Nations.

Last year the United Nations was able to contribute to the solution of a long-standing dispute between the Netherlands and Indonesia regarding West New Guinea (West Irian). This was a major trouble spot and a potential threat to peace in South East Asia. Thanks to the spirit of co-operation shown by the two countries concerned, and the wise and patient guidance of Ambassador Ellsworth Bunker, who kindly deputised for me during a delicate phase of negotiations, it was possible to reach an agreement on the future administration of the territory, providing for a transitional stage of administration over the territory by the United Nations Temporary Executive Authority.

The period of this Temporary Executive Authority is due to end on 1st May this year, and recently Mr. C.V. Narasimhan, my Chef de Cabinet, visited Indonesia and West Irian to finalize the arrangements. I hope that everything goes smoothly between now and 1st May, and that the United Nations will be able to transfer the administration of the territory on that date in good order to Indonesia, in conformity with the terms of the Agreement arrived at between the Netherlands and Indonesia on 15th August 1962.

That Agreement is unique in more than one respect. It is the first time that the United Nations has exercised executive authority over a vast territory. For the first time also the principle was established that the two main parties to the Agreement should bear the entire cost of the operation in equal parts. I am sure you will agree with me that this is a useful precedent to follow for the future.

At this moment the United Nations is directly or indirectly involved in the restoration of law and order in several other parts of the world, one of the most delicate being the border areas between Israel and Arab countries. I need hardly explain the historic role the United Nations has been playing in that part of the world. There is a general consensus everywhere that, but for the United Nations, that area of the world would have long been a scene of ugly clashes perhaps developing into wider entanglements. The Earl of Home, Secretary of State for Foreign Affairs of the United Kingdom Government, said in the House of Lords on 20th February last, "This action (United Nations presence in the Middle East) has really worked extremely well, and has been on the whole efficiently conducted, and, I would say, has certainly con-

tributed to the peace in that area, in that it has prevented
border clashes developing which could have led to a wider
war."

In another area of the Middle East, Yemen, there have
been, in recent weeks, developments which caused us considerable concern. After consultation with the Government of the Republic of Yemen, I sent Dr. Ralph Bunche,
an Under-Secretary for Special Political Affairs, to Yemen
to confer with Government leaders, and to report to me on
his findings. He is still in that area.

In the limited time at my disposal, it is hardly possible
for me to dwell, even briefly, with other issues before the
world organization. However, there is one problem of
tremendous magnitude standing head and shoulders above
others and which in fact is *the* problem not only before the
United Nations but one which involves all mankind—the
problem of disarmament. I do not propose to go into the
background of the negotiations now being conducted in
Geneva nor to assess the respective positions taken by the
powers primarily concerned with disarmament. However,
I want to bring home certain salient points connected with
this greatest of all problems facing mankind.

Just a year ago, pursuant to a decision of the General
Assembly, a group of international experts from ten different countries co-operated in the preparation of a unanimous report on the economic and social consequences of
disarmament. This report indicated that the world is
spending roughly $120 billion annually for military ex-
penditures, which is equivalent to 8 to 9 per cent of the
world's annual output of all goods and services. They concluded that this expenditure amounted to almost the entire national income of all the under-developed countries.
An examination of the recent budgets of the great powers

shows that this tremendous diversion of the world's resources to armaments is increasing from year to year.

Because of differences in budgetary systems and practices, it is not possible to make direct comparisons between
the budgets of the different countries, but the fact emerges
very clearly that each of the great powers is expending an
enormous proportion of its national income for military
purposes and that from year to year these figures are increasing. Just to cite one big power, the United States
budgeted $47.5 billion in 1961 for national defence rep-
resenting over 50 per cent of its national budget of $85
billion. In 1962 the military budget increased to $51.1
billion representing 58 per cent of the total budget of
$87.8 billion. For the current year the defence budget has
been increased to $53 billion.

It is far from my intention to pass judgement on the
national policies of member states, large and small, but I
want to speak on this subject, not as the Secretary-General
of the United Nations, not as an Asian, not as a Burman,
but as a human being, a member of that species, the *homo
sapiens*, whose continued existence is in the balance. The
world is full of conflicts: racial, ideological and political.
Fortunately, religious conflicts which were a feature of
human society hundreds of years ago are no longer a serious problem. Human beings have successfully developed a
sufficient degree of tolerance toward religious differences. If
one remembers the mood of Christians and Moslems
during the Crusades and subsequent religious wars in
Europe between the various Christian sects resulting from
proselytizing zeal and other religious conflicts in certain
parts of Asia, one must conclude that in the twentieth
Century religious tolerance is more or less an accomplished
fact.

However, the spirit of tolerance is still lacking in regard

to political or ideological issues. Almost everybody who is politically conscious has strong feelings about one or more of these issues. In the past two hundred years or so, wars were fought not so much on religious issues but largely on non-religious ones—mainly political or colonial. In our lifetime we witnessed two world wars. The first world war was fought mainly in Europe, but its repercussions were felt all over the globe. The second world war, fought with weapons twenty years more modern than their predecessors, spread to three continents, Europe, Asia and Africa. It was also fought on a more intensive scale at sea and in the air. The destruction and damage done in the second was very much greater than in the first, both in absolute and relative terms.

We have already come to learn from the first two world wars that war solves none of the world's problems; that the problems which they leave in their wake are usually worse than those which they were intended to solve. We had already begun to realize that in modern war there is no such thing as victor or vanquished; that there is only a loser, and that loser is mankind.

All these facts were realized by thinking people even before the advent of the atomic age. They would have been sufficient in themselves for man to want to outlaw war. Indeed, he tried to do so after the first world war, in the formation of the League of Nations. Even before the termination of the second world war he was seriously thinking of a world organization which, he hoped, could prevent further wars from breaking out. The United Nations was formed immediately after the war with the primary objective of "saving succeeding generations from the scourge of war, which twice in our life-time has brought untold sorrow to mankind."

No mention of atomic weapons is made in the United

Nations Charter. It was, I think, Dr. Einstein who, in reply to the question, "What weapons will be used in a third world war?" answered he did not know, and added that what he knew was which weapons would be used in a subsequent fourth world war—the sling. These words by a man who was not only a great scientist but also a philosopher, and whose scientific discoveries contributed so much to usher in the atomic age, were meant to point out the almost total devastation of the earth, such as to reduce any survivors to a prehistoric state.

I have said earlier that almost everybody who is politically conscious has strong feelings about one or more of these issues; but let us set aside such feelings for the moment and consider ourselves only as members of a biological species which has had a remarkable history and whose disappearance none of us can desire. The plain fact is that all of us—Americans, Russians, Burmans—are in peril, and if the character of this peril is understood, there is hope that we may collectively avert it. We have to learn to think in a new way. The most pressing question facing all of us is: What steps can be taken to prevent a military contest of which the issue must be disastrous to all sides?

I must say that most of us have not fully realized what could be involved in a war with hydrogen bombs. The general public still thinks in terms of the obliteration of cities and the destruction of installations. It is well understood that the new bombs are more powerful than the old. No doubt in a hydrogen-bomb war great cities would be obliterated. But this is one of the minor disasters that would have to be faced. For we know now that hydrogen bombs can gradually spread destruction over a much wider area than had been supposed. Most scientists agree that if many hydrogen bombs are used, there will be universal death—sudden death only for the fortunate few—but, for the majority, a slow torture of disease and disintegration.

Some time ago a world-wide controversy arose among scientists regarding Strontium-90, man-made radio-active poison released by nuclear explosions. The final effects of Strontium-90 are still in dispute, but what is not in dispute is the fact that it is eaten and drunk and is built into the bones as a substitute for calcium. It is present in the bones of every Atomic Age child. At the United Nations Atoms-for-Peace Conference a few years ago, and in scientific publications since, concern has been expressed about the effects of such radiation on the lower organisms on which the food-cycle of mankind ultimately depends. We know just enough to know that we do not know what the biological effects will be of the diffusion of radio-active substances into our environment. We do not know the actual biological chain-reaction.

Here, then, is the problem, stark, dreadful and inescapable: Shall we put an end to the human race, or shall mankind renounce war? Most people will not face this alternative because it is so difficult to abolish war. The abolition of war will demand distasteful limitations of national sovereignty. It requires certain psychological adjustments to meet the greatest challenge of our time. It also requires some form of collective action within the framework of an international organization like the United Nations. The Disarmament Conference currently in session in Geneva on the banning of nuclear tests has not made sufficient progress to warrant optimism. Although concessions have been made by both sides regarding the principle of international inspection, the agreement is centred around the question of number. Surely with a little good will and a little give-and-take, it should not be impossible to reach an early agreement on what has become a game of arithmetic!

As geological time is reckoned, man has so far existed

only for a short period, perhaps half a million years. What he has achieved, especially during the period of recorded history is something all of us should be proud of. For countless ages the sun rose and set, the moon waxed and waned, the stars shone in the Milky Way, but it was only with the coming of man that these things were understood. Man has unveiled secrets which might have been thought undiscoverable. Much has been achieved in the realm of art, science, literature and religion. Is all this to end because so few are able to think of man rather than of this or that group of men? Is the human race so destitute of wisdom, so incapable of tolerance, so blind even to the simple dictates of self-preservation that the last proof of its progress is to be the extermination of all life on our small planet? I cannot believe that this is to be the end. I cannot believe that humanity is so bereft of commonsense as to launch universal suicide.

What is most needed in these tense times is the will to compromise. In human affairs, no one group is 100 per cent right and another 100 per cent wrong. In international relationships, pure white and pure black are rare. Various shades of grey usually predominate. That is why every international agreement represents a compromise of some kind, except where the terms are dictated.

To my knowledge one of the wisest mottos for every one of us is enshrined in the UNESCO Charter. It says "Since wars begin in the minds of men, it is in the minds of men that the defenses of peace have to be constructed."

There is no peace in the world today because there is no peace in the minds of men.

## UNITED NATIONS STAND-BY PEACE FORCE\*

I am deeply grateful for this opportunity to address the annual meeting of the Harvard Alumni Association on this Commencement Day. I have chosen as my theme a subject to which governments, as well as individuals, have been giving considerable thought, namely, the peace-keeping role of the United Nations, and the means to strengthen it under present conditions.

The development of an international order, enshrined in an accepted code of world law and guaranteed by an effective world police force, has long been a human aspiration. This dream is based upon the very reasonable idea of projecting the stability and orderliness of a well-governed state onto the relations between nations.

In the history of most nation-states, there came a time when the feuding of a few powerful interests or personages, in disregard of the welfare of the majority, and the ensuing chaos and disaster, became intolerable. From this situation, there was the evolution in due course of a strong central authority, based on popular representation, a sound system of law and a reliable police force. In our world, we reached a similarly intolerable situation many years ago and have twice in this century paid a terrible price for having failed to draw the necessary conclusions.

Most sensible people now agree that some reliable system of ensuring world peace is essential. But, as in most situations involving great and conflicting interests and very large numbers of people, there is all the difference in the world between the need and the practical fulfilment of the need. That fulfilment will be a long and complicated process, requiring a degree of confidence and under-

* Address delivered before the Harvard Alumni Association, Cambridge, Mass., June 13, 1963.

standing which we have not yet established in our world.

Few would deny that, if we are to look forward with confidence to the future, we have to take a great step forward in regulating the relations of nations and produce workable institutions for that purpose. One should not, however, under-estimate the difficulties of such a step or the inevitable risks which attend it.

Nations and governments, taking a great step forward, face imponderables and unknown dangers which no research or scientific test can resolve, for these unforeseeable events will be the result of the actions, reactions and interactions of hundreds of millions of human beings, and the human mind and human behavior are still perhaps the most mysterious and awe-inspiring force in our world. Statesmen are wise, therefore, to view the future with caution and to examine proposals for fundamental change with more than usual care.

While we are making this step forward towards a new world order, we need guarantees, we need moderating influences and we need some commonly operated and accepted agency to share the risks and make the necessary tests and experiments, and even mistakes. Certainly we need an agency through which the necessary confidence and contact among nations can be built up and maintained. The United Nations is the nearest thing we have to such an agency, and I believe that it is beginning to play an important role of the kind I have just described.

It is no doubt true that there are certain great problems, such as the struggle between the greatest powers and the related problem of disarmament, which may be with us for a long time and which, perhaps, cannot be tackled head-on by the United Nations. We must, of course, do everything that we can to avoid adding fuel to the great power struggle.

There are, however, a large number of important problems and situations which *can* usefully be tackled and, if this is done, the greatest problems themselves can be isolated, if not resolved. We should, in this process, begin to develop the necessary institutions and practices by which, at a later stage, a more stable world order can be ensured.

I am going to talk today about one particular aspect of our problems, namely, peace-keeping and the use of international peace forces by the United Nations. Due partly to the lack of unanimity among the great powers ever since 1946, and partly to the radical change in the nature of war resulting from the development of atomic and hydrogen weapons, there has been a gradual change in thinking on questions of international security in the United Nations.

There has been a tacit transition from the concept of collective security, as set out in Chapter VII of the United Nations Charter, to a more realistic idea of peace-keeping. The idea that conventional military methods—or, to put it bluntly, war—can be used by or on behalf of the United Nations to counter aggression and secure the peace, seems now to be rather impractical.

There has also been a change in emphasis from the use of the military forces of the great powers, as contemplated in the Charter, to the use, in practice, of the military resources of the smaller powers, which has the advantage of not entangling United Nations actions in the antagonisms of the cold war.

Although there has been one collective action under the aegis of the United Nations—Korea—and although in 1951 the Collective Measures Committee, set up by the General Assembly under the Uniting for Peace resolution, actually published in its report a list of units earmarked by Member States for service with the United Nations in actions to counter aggression, actual developments have in practice been in a rather different direction.

The nature of these developments is sometimes confused, wittingly or unwittingly by an attempt to relate them to the use of force to counter aggression by the Security Council provided for in Chapter VII of the Charter. In fact, the peace-keeping force I am about to describe are of a very different kind and have little in common with the forces foreseen in Chapter VII, but their existence is not in conflict with Chapter VII. They are essentially *peace* and not fighting forces and they operate only with the consent of the parties directly concerned.

In this context, it is worth noting that *all* of the permanent members of the Security Council have, at one time or another in the past 15 years, voted in support of the creation of one or other of these forces, and that none of them has in any case gone further than to abstain from voting on them.

Since 1950, the United Nations has been called on to deal with a number of critical situations of varying urgency. The most urgent of these have been what are sometimes called "brush-fire wars," meaning, I take it, small conflagrations which, unless controlled, may all too easily ignite very much larger ones.

If we briefly look through the United Nations experience with this kind of operation, we can see that from small and informal beginnings a useful body of precedent and practice has grown up over the years of using military personnel of Member States on peace-keeping operations. In Greece in 1947, the United Nations Special Committee on the Balkans found that professional military officers were invaluable as an observer group in assessing the highly complicated and fluctuating situation. The Security Council itself set up an observer group of military officers in India and Pakistan to watch over the Kashmir question. This observer group, which was set up in 1948, is still operating.

A much larger use of military observers by the United Nations was made when, in July 1948, the first truce agreements in the Palestine war were supervised on the ground by some 700 United Nations military observers working under the United Nations Mediator and the Chief of Staff. This team developed into the United Nations Truce Supervision Organization after the armistice agreements between Israel and her Arab neighbors were concluded in the period from February to July 1949.

This organization of officers from many countries still plays a vital role in keeping the peace in the Middle East and in reporting on and dealing with incidents which, though small in themselves, might all too easily become the cause of far larger disturbances if not dealt with. Its indefatigable members in their white jeeps are now a familiar and welcome part of the Middle Eastern landscape.

A peace-keeping organization of a different nature made its appearance as a result of the Suez crisis of October 1956. Confronted with a situation of the utmost urgency in which two of the permanent members of the Security Council were directly involved, the General Assembly voted for the urgent creation of a United Nations force. This was essentially *not* a force designed actively to fight against aggression.

It went to Egypt with the express consent of the Egyptian Government and after the other parties concerned had agreed to a cease-fire. It was designed not to fight but rather to allow those involved to disengage without further disturbance. It allowed for the peaceful resolution of one of the most dangerous crises which had faced the world since the Second World War. It also, incidentally, allowed for the clearance by the United Nations of the Suez Canal, which had been blocked during the previous military action.

The United Nations Emergency Force in the Middle East has for six years watched over the borders of Israel with the United Arab Republic in the Gaza Strip and through the Sinai Desert. It also watches over the access to the Gulf of Aqaba and to the Israeli port of Elath. What was once a most troubled and terrorized frontier has become peaceful and prosperous on both sides, and the very presence of the United Nations Force is both an insurance against a resumption of trouble and a good excuse not to engage in it. It presents us with one serious problem. To maintain an army of over 5,000 men costs money, but at present the parties concerned have no wish to see it removed.

In 1958 another very tense situation, with quite different origins, occurred in Lebanon. After the success of UNEF, there were suggestions in many quarters that another United Nations force should be collected and dispatched to that country. Here, however, the problem, though aggravated by external factors, was essentially a domestic one.

The Security Council therefore set up a three-man observer group and left the Secretary-General considerable latitude as to the methods to be employed to make this group effective in watching over the possibilities of infiltration from outside. A highly mobile group of 600 officers was quickly organized to keep watch from ground and air, while the crisis itself was resolved by negotiation and discussion. By the end of 1958, it was possible to withdraw the United Nations Observer Group from the Lebanon altogether.

The greatest and most complex challenge to the United

Nations in the peace-keeping field arose a few days after the Congo gained its independence from Belgium on 30 June 1960. The general proportions of this problem are sometimes obscured by a wealth of dramatic detail and are worth restating. Harassed by mutiny, lawlessness and the collapse of public order and services from within, and afflicted by foreign military intervention as well as by ominous threats of other forms of interference from without, the new Government of the Congo appealed to the United Nations for help.

The Security Council committed the United Nations to respond to this appeal and thus made the Organization not only the guarantor of law and order and the protector of the Congo against external interference from any source, but also the adviser and helper of a newly independent State which had had virtually no preparation for its independence.

By filling, in the space of a few hours, the very dangerous vacuum which existed in the Congo in July 1960, the urgent danger of a confrontation of the great powers in the heart of Africa was avoided and the territorial integrity of the Congo preserved. The new leaders of the Congo have been given at least a short breathing-spell in which to find their feet. Despite its shortcomings, which must be judged in the light of the fearsome complexity of the problem, the United Nations Operation in the Congo is, in my opinion, a most promising and encouraging experiment in international responsibility and action.

The blue helmets of the United Nations Force are known throughout the Congo as the symbol of security. Its soldiers have given protection at one time or another in the last three years to almost every Congolese public figure and almost every group, both African and non-African, when danger and violence threatened them. It is worth noting that, now that the withdrawal of the United Nations Force in the Congo is in sight, the deepest regret, and even alarm, is expressed by the very groups who used to be its most hostile critics and detractors.

In the Force, soldiers from other African countries work side by side in this vast tropical country with those from farther away. Their loyalty to the United Nations, their team spirit and comradeship have been an inspiration to all those who value the peace-keeping role of the United Nations.

I will end my catalogue with two more operations, one of which has already been successfully concluded, and which also involved an unprecedented role for the United Nations. I would like to refer first to the transfer of West Irian from Dutch rule, through a temporary period of United Nations executive authority, backed by a United Nations Security Force, to the administration of Indonesia. This entire operation has taken place with the agreement of the parties concerned, and in consultation with them.

The second is the dispatch to Yemen of an observer team as a basis for the disengagement of the United Arab Republic and Saudi Arabia from the affairs of Yemen. This operation will be paid for by the two parties concerned, and has been undertaken at their request and that of the Government of Yemen.

Although these are peace forces, service in them is hard and can be dangerous. In the Middle East, the United Nations has registered casualties not only from accidents and disease, but from mines. Both there and in West Irian, as also in Yemen the terrain and the climate are inhospitable. In the Congo, we have had, unfortunately, serious casualties from unwanted fighting as well as from other causes, and I very much hope that we shall have no more.

I have only mentioned here the peace-keeping activities

which have involved the use, in one way or another, of military personnel. If I were to mention the many other tense situations in which the United Nations, and my office in particular, have been used as a metting-ground and as an instrument for mediation and peaceful settlement, the list would be much longer.

To sum up, we have now had experience of three major peace-keeping forces and a variety of military observer and truce supervisory operations. Each of the three forces has been different in composition, nature and task, but they have shared certain common characteristics.

All three were improvised and called into the field at very short notice; all three were severely limited in their right to use force; all three were designed solely for the maintenance of peace and not for fighting in the military sense; all three were recruited from the smaller powers and with special reference to their acceptability in the area in which they were to serve; all three operated with the express consent and co-operation of the States or territories where they were stationed, as well as of any other parties directly concerned in the situation; and all three were under the direction and control of the Secretary-General acting on behalf of the organs of the United Nations.

These facts may now seem commonplace; it is a measure of the progress that has been made that even ten years ago they would have seemed very unusual.

By the standards of an efficient national military establishment, these forces have considerable disadvantages. Obviously, a force put together only after the emergency with which it is to deal is in full swing, will inevitably have some shortcomings. There is difficulty in recruitng at very short notice exactly the right kind of units for the work in hand, and in operating a force whose units and officers meet each other for the first time in the midst of a delicate operation. There are differences not only of language and traditon but of training, equipment and staff procedures. There are differences in pay and emoluments which, if not handled carefully, can cause considerable problems of discipline and morale. Staffwork and command are especially difficult where every decision has important political implications.

Although these contingents from member states are under the operational control of the United Nations, disciplinary powers are still vested in the national authorities and this could be, although in fact it never has been, the cause of very serious difficulties for the United Nations Force Commander and for the Secretary-General.

The fact that the military establishments of the permanent members of the Security Council cannot be used cuts us off from the most obvious sources of equipment and personnel. The improvised nature of these operations also gives rise to various problems of logistics.

In our experience, these difficulties, which are inherent in the pioneering nature of these operations, have been offset by the enthusiastic co-operation of Member States and by the spirit and comprehension of the officers and men of the contingents which have made up the United Nations forces. It is an incouraging thought that in the military establishments of some 30 or more countries in the world there are now large numbers of officers and men who have served the United Nations with distinction in one or other of these operations and have added thereby a new dimension to their military experience.

The improvised approach also makes it possible on each occasion to make up the United Nations force from the countries which are, politically and in other ways, most suitable for the operation in hand, and at least the United

Nations is not afflicted with the age-old problem of having on its hands a standing army with nothing to do.

In my opinion, a permanent United Nations force is not a practical proposition at the present time. I know that many serious people in many countries are enthusiastic about the idea, and I welcome their enthusiasm and the thought they are putting into the evolution of the institution which will eventually and surely emerge. Many difficulties still stand in the way of its evolution.

Personally, I have no doubt that the world should eventually have an international police force which will be accepted as an integral and essential part of life in the same way as national police forces are accepted. Meanwhile, we must be sure that developments are in the right direction and that we can also meet critical situations as and when they occur.

There are a number of reasons why it seems to me that the establishment of a permanent United Nations force would be premature at the present time. I doubt whether many Governments in the world would yet be prepared to accept the political implications of such an institution and, in the light of our current experience with financial problems, I am sure that they would have very serious difficulties in accepting the financial implications.

I believe that we need a number of parallel developments before we can evolve such an institution. We have to go further along the road of codification and acceptance of a workable body of international law. We have to develop a more sophisticated public opinion in the world, which can accept the transition from predominantly national thinking to international thinking.

We shall have to develop a deeper faith in international institutions as such, and a greater confidence in the possibility of a United Nations civil service whose international loyalty and objectivity are generally accepted and above suspicion. We shall have to improve the method of financing international organization. Until these conditions are met, a permanent United Nations force may not be a practical proposition.

But we have already shown that, when the situation demands it, it is possible to use the soldiers of many countries for objectives which are not national ones and that the soldiers respond magnificently to this new challenge. We have also seen that, when the situation is serious enough, Governments are prepared to waive certain of the attributes of national sovereignty in the interest of keeping the peace through the United Nations. We have demonstrated that a loyalty to international service can exist side by side with legitimate national pride.

And, perhaps most important of all, we have shown that there *can* be a practical alternative to the deadly ultimate struggle and that it is an alternative which brings out the good and generous qualities in men rather than their destructive and selfish qualities.

Although it is perhaps too early, for the reasons I have already given, to consider the establishment of a permanent United Nations force, I believe there are a number of measures which could be taken even now to improve on our present capacity for meeting dangerous situations. It would be extremely desirable, for example, if countries would, in their national military planning, make provision for suitable units which could be made available at short notice for United Nations service and thereby decrease the degree of improvisation necessary in an emergency.

I take this opportunity publicly to welcome and express my appreciation for the efforts of the Scandinavian countries in this direction. Denmark, Norway and Sweden have for some time now engaged in joint planning of a stand-by force comprising various essential components to be put at the disposal of the United Nations when necessary. It would be a very welcome development if other countries would consider following the lead of the Scandinavian countries in this matter.

At present, the activities of the United Nations are overshadowed by a very serious financial crisis, a crisis which stems directly from the costs of the special peace-keeping operations in the Middle East and the Congo and from the failure of some Members to pay their assessments for those operations. Although the sums of money involved are small in comparison to the sums spent by many countries on military budgets, they do, nonetheless, present a very serious financial and political challenge to the stability of the United Nations.

The United Nations is the sum of all its members and, to develop in the right direction, it must maintain this global character. On the other hand, I am convinced that the Organization must maintain and develop its active role in keeping the peace. I therefore view with the gravest concern the prolongation of the financial crisis of the United Nations with its very serious political overtones, and I trust that we may see a solution of the problem before too long.

I am concerned at this financial crisis more particularly because I see, in the long run, no acceptable alternative method of keeping peace in the world to the steady and sound development of the peace-keeping functions of the United Nations. It is no longer possible to think rationally in terms of countering aggression or keeping the peace by the use of the ultimate weapons.

However improvised and fumbling the United Nations approach may be, we have to develop it to deal with the sudden antagonisms and dangers of our world, until we can evolve more permanent institutions. There has been already a great advance in the world towards co-operation, mutual responsibility and common interest. I have described some of the pioneering co-operative efforts made by the United Nations to keep the peace.

I believe that these efforts constitute vital steps towards a more mature, more acceptable, and more balanced world order. We must have the confidence and the means to sustain them and the determination to develop out of them a reliable and workable system for the future.

I am a firm believer in the organic development of institutions. I also firmly believe that, if the United Nations is to justify the hopes of its founders and of the peoples of the world, it must develop into an active and effective agency for peace and international conciliation by responding to the challenges which face it. May we have the courage, the faith, and the wisdom to make it so.

## INTRODUCTION TO THE ANNUAL REPORT 1961-1962*

### I

The year covered by the present report has been a critical period in the life of the Organization. Amidst its efforts to resolve the continuing and urgent problem of the Congo, the United Nations suffered the tragic loss of Dag Hammarskjold, its dedicated Secretary-General, and other members of his staff who accompanied him on his last journey to this troubled land. I have elsewhere paid tribute to his great personal qualities, to his unique contribution to the development of the United Nations in its formative years, and to his vision of the United Nations as a dynamic force for peace. In my view, too, the responsibili-

* August 24, 1962.

ties of the Organization in these changing times call for a dynamic rather than a static approach.

Since the late Secretary-General signed, on August 17, 1961, the introduction to his last report on the work of the Organization, the Congo crisis has continued to weigh heavily on the United Nations. The rounding up of mercenaries in Katanga and the serious incidents which followed in September 1961 culminated in the tragic death of the Secretary-General. The cease-fire signed in October was not long or ever fully honored by the Katangese, and the Security Council spelled out in November its authorization to the Secretary-General to use force in order to complete the removal of the mercenaries.

At the end of that month, Katangese outrages against United Nations personnel, civilian and military, and an overt attempt by roadblocks to immobilize the onuc force in Elisabethville brought about a situation there so explosive that even the uneasy peace that had prevailed since September could no longer be preserved. Hostilities broke out in December 1961 through failure of the Katangese to fulfil a promise to remove a strong roadblock. Later that month, after hostilities had come to an end by mutual agreement, a meeting was arranged between Prime Minister Adoula and Mr. Tshombe at Kitona, in an effort to reconcile their differences. Agreement was, in fact, reached, but Mr. Tshombe held it to be, so far as he was concerned, conditional on acceptance by the Katangese Legislature, and it was honored only in its less important aspects.

During the first months of 1962 the United Nations continued its effort to bring about a peaceful and mutually acceptable end to the Katangese secession. Prime Minister Adoula and Mr. Tshombe were brought together again for talks, this time in Leopoldville, and although large

areas of agreement seemed to be reached, the talks collapsed in June of this year. It has become increasingly clear
that the Katangese provincial authorities and the forces
supporting them have felt that time is on their side and
must accordingly be gained at all costs; they make gestures
of reconciliation leading to no practical results, whenever
the pressure builds up, while at the same time seeking to
further the aims of secession.

The core of the Congo problem is that of the secession
of Katanga; the problem of the Katanga secession is primarily a problem of finance; the problem of finance, in
turn, is the problem of the major mining companies. This
is not an oversimplification of the facts. The end of the
secession of Katanga would not mean a solution to all the
problems of the young Congolese Republic. Far from that.
But as long as this secession is not ended, neither can the
Congo move forward on the way to recovery, nor can the
United Nations effectively fulfil its mandate of effective
and massive technical assistance to the Republic.

The present situation in the Congo, which is particularly crucial—as I stated in the appeal sent to all member
states on July 31, 1962—in view of the lives, effort and
money already expended and currently being expended by
the United Nations and the financial crisis into which this
unprecedented drain on its resources has brought the
Organization, must improve before long. Even as this is
being written, a new effort toward reconciliation is being
made with, it appears, new promise. Progress in the Congo
is as essential for the good name of the Organization as for
the Organization's continued usefulness in similar circumstances that may arise in the future.

## II

Throughout the past year the financial difficulties confronting the Organization became increasingly serious as a result of the continuing need to incur large expenditures for onuc and unef while a number of member states failed to pay their assessments for the maintenance of these peace-keeping forces.

In an effort to ease the cash problem and maintain the Organization's solvency pending a long-term solution for its financial requirements, the General Assembly at its sixteenth session adopted two exceptional measures. The first of these was the request to the International Court of Justice for an advisory opinion on the question of whether the expenditures for maintaining onuc and unef constitute "expenses of the Organization" within the meaning of Article 17, paragraph 2, of the United Nations Charter and therefore represent binding, legal obligations on member states to pay their assessments for these operations. The second measure was the authorization granted to the Secretary-General to issue during 1962 and 1963 up to $200 million of United Nations bonds bearing interest at 2 per cent per annum, with the principal repayable over a 25-year period.

On July 20, 1962, the International Court of Justice by a nine-to-five majority gave an affirmative answer to the question posed to it by the General Assembly. As of August 1, 1962, 46 governments, including four non-member states, had announced their intention to purchase United Nations bonds having a total value of more than $72 million. Actual bond sales had been made at that date to 18 Governments in the amount of $27,308,257.

If, as a result of the Court's opinion, members in arrears in the payment of their onuc and unef assessments make payments of the amounts due, and substantial pledges and purchases of United Nations bonds are forthcoming from other members who have not yet been able to announce their intention to purchase United Nations bonds, the long-range financial prospects for the Organization would be more encouraging than has been the case since the beginning of the large peace-keeping operations several years ago.

For the immediate future, however, the financial difficulties confronting the Organization must be expected to continue, since no provision has been made for assessing members for the costs of ONUC and UNEF beyond June, 30, 1962, and some delay must be realistically anticipated before the members in arrears pay their full assessments. Nonetheless I sincerely hope and believe that member governments, who are all agreed on the indispensable role of the Organization in the world of today, will take appropriate action to solve its financial problems, which may otherwise severely limit its usefulness for the future.

III

In the course of the year, positive action was taken toward international cooperation in the peaceful exploration and use of outer space. Earlier difficulties were overcome, and in March 1962 the enlarged Committee on the Peaceful Uses of Outer Space met under encouraging signs, and later on, in May and June, the Scientific and Technical and the Legal Subcommittees held their first sessions in Geneva.

The willingness of the two leading powers to cooperate in outer space exploration was expressed in a heartening exchange of messages between the President of the United

States and the Chairman of the Council of Ministers of the USSR, holding out prospects of a cooperative approach to the immense task of probing cosmic space and using the knowledge so gained for the benefit of all mankind.

The Scientific and Technical Subcommittee agreed upon a series of recommendations concerning the exchange of information, the encouragement of international programs and the organization of international equatorial sounding rocket facilities which offer a basis for practical and useful action.

In the Legal Subcommittee no agreement was reached on the proposals submitted, but the meeting nevertheless afforded the opportunity for a valuable exchange of views. However, the discussions were regarded by delegations as a useful exchange of views on a number of important legal questions. It is my firm hope that a cooperative approach between the leading powers may be evolved without delay in this field so as to ensure that the exploration of outer space will not be a source of discord and danger, but an area of understanding and increased confidence.

To provide a focal point for international cooperation in this field, a public registry of information furnished by states on orbital launchings has been established within the Secretariat, as well as an Outer Space Affairs Section, including scientific advisers, to assist the Committee in receiving and disseminating information voluntarily supplied by member states. Within the United Nations family, the World Meteorological Organization, the International Telecommunication Union and the United Nations Educational, Scientific and Cultural Organization are engaged in far-ranging studies on specific space problems, and the first reports prepared by the specialized agencies will be laid before the Assembly at its seventeenth session.

IV

While the progress in outer space has thus been some-what encouraging, the same cannot be said in regard to the important problem of disarmament. The 18-nation disar-mament committee had the advantage that for the first time eight non-aligned states were participating in it. I feel that their participation is a signficant event. For one thing, it is a recognition of the fact that disarmament is a subject in which all nations, big and small, are concerned, and not just the great military powers. Further, the non-aligned states have been an important element exercising a moderating and catalytic influence in helping to bridge the gap between extreme positions of either side. It is re-grettable that one of the members of the committee, a great power, did not take part in its work. In spite of their meeting for three months between March and June of this year, and again from the middle of July, and in spite of orderly and business-like discussions in depth of the com-plex problem of disarmament, which helped to clarify the approaches of the parties, little progress has been made. At the same time, it is encouraging that both sides have, for the first time, submitted detailed draft treaty plans and that, in spite of the lack of progress, the parties are deter-mined to continue their negotiation.

I feel that, in this field as elsewhere, certain steps have to be taken first. It is my conviction that to facilitate progress in the field of general disarmament, the first step has to be a cessation of nuclear testing. This question therefore de-serves priority, and I hope that the suggestions of the non-aligned countries, such as that contained in their joint memorandum and in other ideas they have put forward, will provide a practical basis for a solution of this prob-

lem. I also sincerely hope that the nuclear powers will
realize that the whole world is hoping and praying that an
agreed first step may be taken soon.

v

On August 15, 1962, an agreement was signed between
the representatives of the Governments of Indonesia and
the Netherlands in regard to West New Guinea (West
Irian). This agreement represented the culmination of
nearly five months of negotiations which were initially
held under the auspices of Ambassador Ellsworth Bunker,
who acted as my representative, and were transferred to
United Nations Headquarters when most of the points
under negotiation had been discussed and preliminary
agreement had been reached on them.

The agreement remains to be ratified by both Governments and also needs to be approved by the General Assembly as a priority item in its seventeenth session. I believe that there will be no difficulty in this regard. I also
feel that implementation of the agreement will not only
lead to an easing of tension in the area, but also to a
greater sense of trust and confidence between the two
countries, which are to resume diplomatic relations.

One of the unique features of this agreement is that for
the first time the United Nations will have temporary executive authority (established by and under the jurisdic-
tion of the Secretary-General) over a vast territory. At a
later stage, the United Nations will assist and participate
in arrangements by Indonesia for the act of self-determination by the people of the territory. It is also noteworthy
that the entire expenses that may be incurred under the

terms of the agreement are to be shared by the two Governments and will not impose a financial burden on the United Nations.

### VI

The Charter recalls the determination of the United Nations "to promote social progress and better standards of life in larger freedom." This should serve as a timely reminder to all of us to rededicate ourselves to the task of making the Charter of the United Nations a living hope for all humanity; to eradicate poverty as a prime cause of conflict; and to strive energetically and purposefully toward the general welfare of mankind as a basis for a just and enduring peace.

Never before in history have there been greater opportunities to meet this challenge. Never before has man held within his grasp the means with which to eliminate progressively want and disease and to build a lasting foundation for a world free from privation and fear. The technological and scientific achievements of the past decade stagger the imagination and stand out as a tribute to man's creative genius. No doubt we are on the threshold of even greater achievements. Yet, much of the creative power of man unfortunately continues to be applied in large measure to the deplorable purpose of increasing his destructive potential, thus accentuating existing differences and conflicts.

The dangers inherent in the continuation of the armaments race and nuclear tests are only too apparent. If this Organization is to make the principles enshrined in the preamble of the Charter a living reality, there must be no pause in the determined, sincere and continuing campaign to reduce world tensions and hostility. The people of the world who continue to live in such a tense and surcharged atmosphere, replete with the ever-present threat of total destruction, are entitled to look forward to the dawn of a new era in which every man, woman and child in every country can be expected to live above want and in dignity, at peace with themselves and with the rest of mankind.

The emergence in recent years of scores of territories from colonial rule to independence, and the clear prospect that the remaining colonial areas will shortly take their rightful places among the family of nations, lend urgency to demands upon the international community to provide them with material and technical assistance if these new nations are to achieve the monumental tasks of making their newly-won independence meaningful through as rapid development of their economic and social potential as possible.

While much has been accomplished in the past two decades to mobilize resources on an international as well as on a bilateral basis to assist in lifting the living standards of two-thirds of the human race living in poverty and want, it is abundantly clear that the rate of development has fallen far short of meeting the needs and hopes of emerging peoples, and the risk cannot be ignored that their disappointment may well overflow to the extent of endangering an orderly pace of development. I have said and would like to repeat that the present division of the world into rich and poor countries is, in my opinion, much more real and much more serious, and ultimately much more explosive, than the division of the world on ideological grounds.

In a timely decision the General Assembly designated the present decade as the United Nations Development Decade, a global effort to mobilize, in cooperation with its

specialized agencies, the accumulated experiences and resources of mankind in a full-scale and sustained attack on
poverty, disease, hunger and illiteracy. These evils are not
only affronts to human dignity; each intensifying the
other, they menace the stability of governments, aggravate
tensions, threaten international peace.

In launching the United Nations Development Decade,
the General Assembly has dramatized the importance and
urgency of the work to be accomplished for reversing the
trend toward wider differences in levels of living between
rich and poor countries. Whether or not the latter will be
able to achieve self-sustained growth over the next few
years primarily depends on their own efforts and on an
increase in international cooperation and assistance for
which the Organization is at present neither the only
instrument nor the most important channel. Member
states have made it clear, however, that they wish the Organization to play a central role and to be a focal point for
the formulation and evaluation of measures and policies
which may affect or influence the pace and direction of the
development process in national or regional contexts.

In addition to making recommendations to governments, the General Assembly and the Economic and Social
Council have taken steps to ensure increased action
through United Nations organs. Less conspicuous than the
thrashing out of the political issues with which the United
Nations is seized, but hardly less far-reaching in the long
term, are the intensification of the work on industrial development and the emphasis laid on projections, planning
and programming for balanced economic and social development. The resolve of the Economic and Social Council to convene a United Nations Conference on Trade and
Development is a major move toward stimulating thought
and practical action of worldwide scope in a crucial area.

The progress already made in the preparations for the United Nations Conference on the Application of Science and Technology for the Benefit of the Less Developed Areas is a further harbinger of the growing capacity of the United Nations system to inspire, and help in bringing about, the achievement of the objectives of the Development Decade.

With the bolder approach of the Council and of its Commission on International Commodity Trade to the preoccupying questions of commodity prices and trade expansion, the decision of the Council to establish a Committee on Housing, Building and Planning, the setting up in the Secretariat of an economic planning and projections centre and of a centre for industrial development evidence the determination of our governing bodies to assert the overall responsibilities of the Organization and to improve its ability to contribute effectively to progress toward the objectives of the Development Decade.

With the increased contribution that the regional commissions and their secretariats are making to the global effort by assuming spearhead functions on the strength of their knowledge and experience of local conditions, with the growing interplay of operational work and research activity, and with the closer cooperation among agencies of the United Nations family exemplified by such projects as the joint United Nations/FAO World Food Program, the Organization should be able to play, in the worldwide strategy for fostering economic and social development, a role not less important than that devolving upon it for peace-keeping operations. As in the case of peace-keeping operations, its response to the challenge is conditioned by the ability to mobilize the services of experienced and dedicated personnel, and by the sustained availability of adequate financial resources, including provision for a controlled expansion of the staff resources necessary for carrying out the tasks laid on the Secretariat in a growing body of unanimously-adopted resolutions.

In this mobilization for speedier progress in economic and social development, the major effort has to be made by the countries themselves. In addition, two facts merit special attention.

The first is that the United Nations and its related agencies can go forward in their greater responsibilities from positions of considerable strength. Not only do they command a wealth of knowledge and experience, as also the services of a number of dedicated and talented people. They also have the full confidence of the developing countries they wish to serve.

In this connection, the increased resources of the expanded program of technical assistance and its reorientation toward higher priority objectives and improved procedures are worthy of note. The Special Fund, for its part, is demonstrating dramatically the fundamental soundness of its approach and the rich potentialities of its assistance to large-scale, high-impact pre-investment projects. At the same time, the modest but steady growth of the operational and executive personnel program has revealed the suitability of this type of assistance for an increasing number of situations.

The United Nations family of organizations is thus both eager and technically and organizationally qualified to assume the larger responsibilities placed upon it by the United Nations and requested of it by the developing nations. This is the first fact to be recognized in facing the challenge of the United Nations Development Decade.

The second fact, highly relevant to the first, is at this moment not quite so encouraging. It arises from the reality that bringing about the indispensable rate of advance in the low-income countries is going to cost much money. Many if not most of the low-income countries are making serious, in some cases even heroic, efforts to extract from their own very limited available resources the substantial amounts they must invest in their development. At the same time, a greater measure of assistance is required of the wealthier countries. The sum total of their contributions must be increased progressively during the United Nations Development Decade, and a growing proportion of that assistance could with undoubted advantage to each and to all be channelled through the United Nations.

Will the required resources be forthcoming—for a coherent, constructive program that can lift the developing countries to the place of self-sustaining growth as partners in a dynamic world economy? The task is one for all people of all nations, and it is sufficient to unite the world. It will not be accomplished without vigorous leadership and without the enthusiastic participation of the thousands of millions of ordinary men and women in the advanced and the low-income countries alike and together. In this task, the United Nations can, given the means, play a unique and indispensable role.

VII

In recent years the membership of the Organization has increased by more than double its original number and has made considerable progress toward true universality. A cursory examination of the growing number of items inscribed in the agenda of recent sessions provides convincing evidence of the wide scope of the subjects, from urgent items affecting the welfare of the international community to minute details of "housekeeping." In these circumstances it is not surprising that the conduct of business in the General Assembly and of its main Committees has in recent years become increasingly complicated and, in some instances, excessively prolonged.

In his letter of April 26, 1962, the President of the General Assembly, during its sixteenth session, transmitted to me for circulation to all delegations of member states a memorandum containing certain suggestions concerning changes which might be made in the work of the General Assembly in the interest of greater speed and efficiency. In commending the President's timely suggestions to the consideration of the General Assembly, I wish to enlarge upon a few of the points dealing with the broader aspects of the work of the General Assembly, namely, the problems arising from resumed sessions and the creation of subsidiary organs having overlapping terms of reference.

The General Assembly of the United Nations was conceived as a body which, among other things, would provide leading statesmen of the member states with an opportunity to come into close contact with each other and to lend not only greater authority to the Assembly's work, but, what is even more important, to help shape the decisions of individual member governments on major issues. All too frequently this purpose has been defeated in the general debate for reasons set forth by the President.

As regards his remarks concerning the grouping of items dealing with different aspects of the same problem, it is useful to bear in mind that it is not only the substance of the debate to which consideration must be given by each delegation but also the conclusions and recommendations which may have to be formulated. Were similar questions to be considered collectively, as suggested, it might avoid in turn the duplication of discussion as also the proliferation of special and other committees with overlapping responsibilities.

This is true of the political as well as the economic field. To mention just one example, in the field of non-self-governing territories, some four committees and special committees are dealing with matters that might usefully be combined, thus relieving the concerned delegations of otherwise added burdens and at the same time reducing costs and staff requirements. It may perhaps be possible to concentrate all the work in this field under the special committee which was set up pursuant to resolution 1654 (XVI).

I wish particularly to commend the proposal that the date for the beginning of the regular session of the General Assembly be advanced to the first Tuesday in September, thus adding two weeks to the duration of the Assembly's session. Such an extension might contribute materially to avoiding resumed or special sessions by giving added time for the conclusion of the Assembly's business during the regular session.

If I have touched upon an aspect of the work of the General Assembly, which is master of its own procedures, I have done so for two reasons. One of them is the personal reason that I have some experience of the floor. Secondly, I feel that the General Assembly should indeed be the Parliament of mankind in these days of rapid change, with the ever-present threat of nuclear global war. The present procedures might have suited an Assembly with fewer members and confronted by less momentous issues. They do not suit the present, when the membership is already approaching 110, and the agenda items, too, exceed 100. A streamlining of procedures has thus become progressively more urgent and necessary, so that the voice of the Assembly may be heard with respect and, in time, all over the world.

## VIII

I have so far dealt with specific problems and issues which have been engaging my personal attention. Before closing I would like to deal with a more general problem—that of the so-called "crisis of confidence" in the United Nations. The same historic process which has liberated so many countries and regions in the world from colonialism and which has enabled the Organization to make steady progress toward universality of membership has also upset the original balance of forces within the United Nations. As a result there are suggestions that the principle of one vote per member will perhaps have to be reconsidered. I would like to state unequivocally my position on this proposal.

On this, as on any other proposal, I am bound by the Charter provisions as they stand. In the preamble itself the United Nations expresses its determination "to reaffirm faith . . . in the equal rights . . . of nations large and small." Article 2 (1) states more explicitly: "The Organization is based on the principle of the sovereign equality of all its members." At the same time, and as a natural corollary, there is a reciprocal responsibility on the part of all sovereign states to recognize and respect the sovereign rights of other states. I believe that if the United Nations is to survive as a dynamic force for peace and security, these provisions have to be honored in the letter and the spirit of the Charter.

I have heard it said that if the Charter provision on this subject is not revised, then there will be an increasing tendency to settle major issues outside the United Nations. This prospect does not discourage me for a variety of reasons. In the first place, I do not believe that it was ever the intention that all problems should be solved within the

United Nations, nor was the United Nations conceived as the sole means of conducting international diplomacy. Clearly it is a relatively novel method of diplomacy, continuously available in the service of peace in addition to the normal bilateral and multilateral channels.

To the extent that problems which pose a potential threat to the peace and security of the world may be solved by discussions among the powers mainly concerned, whether within or outside the United Nations, the peace of the world is made more secure and I welcome it. Oftentimes it may happen that when such a settlement has been negotiated outside of the United Nations, the terms of the agreement may be brought forward for formal ratification by a principal organ of the United Nations in order to give it added authority and solemnity. Lastly, I have observed that many problems which are, hopefully, taken out of the United Nations' context finally come back to the United Nations for debate, negotiation, compromise and ultimate settlement. This is particularly true of global issues in which the small powers are as much interested as the major powers.

For these reasons I believe that the "crisis of confidence," if indeed there is such a crisis, is a passing phase. I have faith that the United Nations will survive this crisis and emerge stronger than before as a force for peace.

In re-stating my faith in the United Nations I am moved by one more consideration, and that is the increasing tendency to involve the United Nations in the process of combatting want and poverty and disease and in helping the advancement of the developing countries. Earlier in this introduction I have dealt at length with the United Nations Development Decade. Here I would like to say only this: that the constructive work of the United Nations "for the promotion of the economic and social advancement of all peoples" is the solid basis on which the political effectiveness of the United Nations must rest. The steady and unobtrusive work of the United Nations and its family of agencies to further economic and social progress may not make headlines, but it is more lasting in its contribution to the prosperity, and the peace, of the world.

## INTRODUCTION TO THE ANNUAL REPORT 1962-1963*

### I

The year under review has been marked by a number of developments which on the whole may be said to have brightened the international outlook and strengthened the United Nations as a result. The Cuban crisis, which erupted rather suddenly in October 1962, provided the United Nations with the opportunity to help avert what appeared to be impending disaster. A large number of Member States not directly involved in the crisis consulted with me on the need for action to ward off a confrontation of the two major nuclear Powers which seemed inevitable and I was encouraged to take the initiative in making certain proposals which had the immediate effect of tending to ease the situation. As a result of the high sense of responsibility and statesmanship demonstrated by the leaders of the Powers directly concerned, a well as the assistance which the United Nations was able to give, the danger of a major conflagration was averted. The United Nations also provided, both through the Security Council and the Secretariat, an opportunity for dialogues amongst the interested parties. By the end of the month, the situation had ceased to present the aspects of an imminent crisis, and by

* August 20, 1963.

the end of the year had reached a point where it ceased to give rise to anxiety.

The turn of the year also marked a sudden change for the better in the Congo. As a result, the terms of the United Nations mandate in the Congo, as far as the military force is concerned, have now largely been fulfilled. External military interference in the Congo has ceased, the territorial integrity of the country has been secured, and law and order have generally been restored and are being maintained, although the situation in one or two areas still gives some cause for concern. There were, however, moments of anxiety in December 1962 and January 1963 when it appeared that major acts of sabotage—some already committed and many more threatened—by the secessionist regime in Katanga might disrupt the economic life, not only of Katanga, but also of the Republic of the Congo itself. Fortunately, good sense prevailed in the end and the most serious of the threatened acts of sabotage did not take place. In the subsequent months there has been a steady improvement in the Congo situation, which is reviewed in greater detail below.

The year also saw the successful conclusion of the operation of the United Nations Temporary Executive Authority in West New Guinea (West Irian) and the first occasion for the exercise by the United Nations of executive authority, however temporary, over a vast region. Thanks to the cooperation of the two governments primarily involved, the United Nations team was able on 1 May 1963 to hand over the administration of the territory to the Republic of Indonesia, as envisaged in the Agreement between the Governments of Indonesia and the Netherlands on 15 August 1962.

Towards the end of the year under review the United Nations has had to assume new responsibilities. The

Yemen operation is now in full swing and is discussed in greater detail below. At the request of the Governments of Malaya, Indonesia and the Philippines and with the concurrence of the United Kingdom, I have sent a team of United Nations officials to Sarawak and North Borneo to carry out certain tasks as envisaged by the three Governments. Both the Yemen operation and the Malaysia mission have their special difficulties and problems, but they are continued evidence of the usefulness of the world body in reducing tension and facilitating a peaceful solution of issues which might otherwise lead to strained relations among the interested Governments for a protracted period.

The year is closing on an optimistic note on account of the signing of the partial nuclear test ban treaty. This has given the whole world a feeling of hope and I trust that the year to come will justify the current mood of optimism.

There has been much constructive work in the various fields of activity which are briefly mentioned in the succeeding sections of this introduction, and described in the annual report. In the field of outer space there has been some progress, though no spectacular results have been achieved. Some progress has also been made in the process of decolonization, although a few chronic problems remain to be solved. The United Nations Conference on Science and Technology was a milestone in the Development Decade, and preparations are now under way for the United Nations Conference on Trade and Development. Both the Expanded Programme of Technical Assistance and the Special Fund are continuing and stepping up their fruitful activities. However, the financial problem posed mainly by the cost of certain peace-keeping operations remains unsolved; and although the proposals I have in mind for

winding up the military phase of the Congo operation
may, if accepted, reduce the impact of the problem to some
extent, the financial issue is a priority item, the solution of
which is the primary responsibility of member governments, if the Organization is to continue to be effective in
the cause of peace, and of constructive effort for "the promotion of the economic and social advancement of all
peoples."

II

The achievement of disarmament continues to be the
most important problem of our time. After many years of
persistent but fruitless effort, two events took place recently, in the context of the disarmament negotiations,
which I believe are of major significance—the signing in
Geneva on 20 June 1963 of the memorandum of understanding establishing a direct communications link
between Moscow and Washington, and the signing in Moscow on 5 August 1963 of the treaty banning nuclear weapons tests in the atmosphere, in outer space and under
water.

In the field of disarmament, as elsewhere, certain pre-
conditions have to be met before substantial progress can
be registered. The agreements recently concluded do constitute important first steps, and help to meet these pre-
conditions.

Many countries, and in particular the non-aligned countries, both in the General Assembly and in the Eighteen-
Nation Committee on Disarmament, insisted that in the
absence of a test ban treaty no real progress could be envisaged in other fields of disarmament, and that the cessation
of tests should therefore receive the highest priority. The

signature of the treaty is a recognition by the major nuclear Powers of the validity of this approach.

The test ban treaty, although limited to three environments and marginal to the central problem of disarmament, is an important objective in itself. It will directly serve the humanitarian aim of ending the danger of ever-increasing radio-active fallout resulting from nuclear explosions. But it will also help restrict the spread of nuclear weapons and impose limitations on the development of new weapons of mass destruction, and thus be a factor in slowing down the arms race. This treaty could also point the way to the conclusion of a comprehensive treaty including a ban on underground tests.

Equally if not more important are the political implications of the test ban treaty. If this treaty is followed by agreement on other measures aimed at lessening international tension and establishing confidence among States, it may be the beginning of a new era of better understanding between nations, and create a more favourable international climate that would facilitate progress towards general and complete disarmament and the goal of stable international peace and security, which remains the primary purpose of the United Nations. It would seem, therefore, all the more urgent that the partial test ban treaty now concluded by the main parties be made universal by the accession of all States.

I believe that the opportunity so eagerly awaited by mankind will not be missed because of considerations of national interest, and that the enduring cause of world peace will prevail over short-range political considerations. I am strengthened in this belief by the improved relations between the Soviet Union and the United States, which have come about in spite of the difficulties of these two great world Powers in reconciling new developments and requirements in the fields of defence with their diverse interests and those of their respective allies.

The process of negotiating disarmament measures through the long years of mistrust about the intentions of the "other side" has been a formidable and sometimes baffling task. The usefulness and timeliness of the work of the Eighteen-Nation Committee on Disarmament has been amply proved in the short span of its existence. The Committee provides an effective forum for harmonizing the responsibilities of the great Powers with the interests of other countries and thus of humanity as a whole. In conditions of reduced international tension and of improved political climate, the role of the Committee may become even more significant than heretofore.

It will require the collective effort and wisdom of all members of the international community to ensure that the momentum generated by the recent agreements is maintained until the goal of global security and freedom from fear of war is reached.

III

In the course of the year, the development of co-operation in outer space exploration and use continued in an encouraging manner, especially in the scientific and technical field.

The Scientific and Technical Sub-Committee of the Committee on the Peaceful Uses of Outer Space, at its second session held in Geneva in May 1963, agreed upon a series of new or revised recommendations concerning the exchange of information, encouragement of international programmes, education and training, potentially harmful effects of space experiments and the organization of international sounding rocket facilities. The meeting of the Sub-Committee provided once more the occasion for the scientists of the two leading space Powers to continue their private talks on co-operative space programmes.

The World Meteorological Organization, the International Telecommunication Union and the United Nations Educational, Scientific and Cultural Organization continued to participate actively in the field of peaceful exploration and use of outer space.

No agreement was reached on legal problems relating to outer space, but a valuable exchange of views took place in the Committee and its Legal Sub-Committee. The discussion revealed areas of agreement as well as disagreement, and also indicated that on some questions there were encouraging indications of *rapprochement*. It must be borne in mind that the principal legal problems relate to issues of military security, and that in some respects it is difficult to separate the legal questions of peaceful use from problems of disarmament. Yet the effort should continue to be made to formulate more concrete principles of law and procedures that will foster the peaceful use of outer space. This is a task that cannot be left to the slow processes of customary law, but needs to be pursued vigorously by United Nations bodies in view of the rapid development of space technology, and the accelerated rate of space launchings.

IV

During 1963, United Nations activities in the economic and social field have been conducted with constant reference to the United Nations Development Decade. The United Nations Conference on the Application of Science and Technology for the Benefit of the Less Developed Areas (UNCSAT) has already been described as a mile· stone in the Decade, and the forthcoming United Nations Conference on Trade and Development should be another of no less importance. The spirit of the Decade has enlivened the discussions in the Economic and Social Council and in its subsidiary organs; it has inspired many resolutions and it will no doubt stimulate the work required for their implementation; it has sharpened the sense of purpose within the United Nations family, and is spurring their efforts towards a greater concentration of resources on tasks of recognized priority; and it is fostering a closer co-operation among all the organizations and agencies concerned.

The milestones already passed or in sight in the drive to move forward are, however, not enough. We have embarked on a long journey, and on the road ahead we also need guideposts which could indicate to us how to match resources and requirements. When the times comes, in a year or so, to assess the progress made, to project current developments into the second half of the Decade, to identify and remedy shortcomings and imbalances, it would certainly be most useful if achievements and advances could be seen against a background of well-defined objectives, at least for those sectors and areas of activity in which intentions can be translated into programmes of action. The more projects undertaken, at the national level or though international co-operation in any given field, can be related to each other in a framework designed to produce a combined and cumulative effect over the period, the greater will be the chances of sustaining and justifying the hopes that the proclamation of the Decade has aroused.

The Expanded Programme of Technical Assistance, which was initiated at a time when the highly developed

nations were becoming more conscious of the vital importance of extending technical help to those which were less
fortunate, was a prelude to the Development Decade, in
which it is now playing a very leading part.

The improved financial situation of the Programme has
been one encouraging sign; for the period 1963-64, it has
become possible to plan for the first time on the basis of an
income of slightly over $100 million for the two years to-
gether. The increased resources have made it possible to
meet, fairly satisfactorily, the rapidly increasing demands
raising from the emergence of many independent countries in Africa, although these resources are not enough to
allow for badly needed expansion in other regions. However, there is still no assurance that contributions will continue to increase at the rate which is necessary for the
continued progress of a growing programme. Speaking
generally, there is no doubt that the efficiency of the programme has been steadily improving. It seems clear that
this is partly due to improved techniques on the part of the
participating organizations; it is also very largely due to
more careful selection of projects by Governments, which,
in turn, can be partly accounted for by the spreading practice of national economic planning.

The Special Fund, for its part, has continued to fulfil
the General Assembly's intention that it be "a constructive
advance in United Nations assistance to the less developed
countries." The pace of its operations accelerated during
the period under review. New priority development projects approved for its assistance extended both the scope
and the geographical distribution of the Fund's activity.
The total programme approved to date amounts to 327
major projects in 120 developing countries and territories.
Towards the programme's cost of $672 million, the Special

Fund is contributing 42 per cent, and the developing countries the remainder.

These accomplishments reflect not only sound criteria on the part of the Governments and wise management principles on the part of the Special Fund. They are also the result of effective contributions by the United Nations and its related organizations which serve as Executing Agencies for the Special Fund. There is, however, one major disappointment which must be voiced: Governmental pledges to enable the Fund to finance new projects in 1963 were some 25 per cent below the $100 million target. It is therefore to be hoped that all participating Governments will help the Fund to obtain the $100 million it urgently requires in 1964. The scale of this major programme in the United Nations Development Decade *must* be raised somewhat more closely to the needs of the low-income countries, more closely to their capacity to absorb its assistance and more closely to the ability of the Special Fund and the Executing Agencies to help meet those needs. The need for more multilateral development assistance is very real. The time for meeting that need is rapidly growing shorter, because the processes of development are inevitably protracted—training is a vast, long and difficult as well as essential task, social and economic transformations are not easily prepared nor speedily accomplished, and investment on the scale required to achieve the aims of the Development Decade will not be forthcoming unless pre-investment work is completed in time.

The sums required and which can be effectively used, both for pre-investment and investment, are not nearly so large as many imagine. The resources required from the industrialized countries are within their capacities to provide; there are perhaps only one or two among them which are as yet devoting even one-half of the proposed 1 per cent of their steadily increasing national income for development in the developing countries. However, many of the political leaders of the industrialized countries are aware of the growing danger to their prosperity and world peace represented by the widening gap between their affluent and dynamic economies and the nearly static situation in so many of the developing countries, where progress is slow and inadequate in relation to population increase.

V

The operations of the United Nations involving the use of military personnel are varied in character and objectives. The truce observation missions in the Middle East and Kashmir and the United Nations Emergency Force in the Middle East have continued to perform their essential peace-keeping duties without notable incidents. Three other more recent operations, the United Nations Operation in the Congo (ONUC), the United Nations Temporary Executive Authority in West Irian and the United Nations Yemen Observation Mission, have attracted considerable attention.

The United Nations commitment in the Congo has now lasted for more than three years. In that time it has proved an exceptionally heavy burden on the resources of the Organization and of its Members, and there have been times when it seemed that hopes of positive results were not very bright.

In 1963, however, the situation has improved very considerably and, as I mentioned earlier, the United Nations mandate in the Congo, especially in its military aspects, has been largely fulfilled. While good reasons have been put forward for the continuation of the United Nations military commitment in the Congo, I sincerely believe that the time has come when, for various reasons, it is necessary to envisage the early withdrawal and winding-up of the United Nations Force in the Congo. It can no doubt be argued that some useful tasks could still be performed by the Force, but I am of the opinion that the time has now come when the Congolese Government should assume full responsibility throughout the Congo for the maintenance of law and order. I believe that in the past three years the Government and people of the Congo have begun to develop the means by which they can assume this responsibility. The retraining of the police and the army is, of course, a vital factor in this development, and as this progresses, there will be a parallel increase in the ability of the Congolese authorities to maintain law and order throughout the Republic.

Originally, it was envisaged that the greater part of the assistance to be rendered to the Government of the Congo by the United Nations would be in the field of technical assistance, or what is now called civilian operations. Here, despite the great difficulties of the last three years, the United Nations has, with the help of the specialized agencies, played an indispensable role in the Congo in providing experts for the maintenance of the essential services of the country, while at the same time providing training facilities designed to make it possible for the Congolese themselves to assume these responsibilities quickly. It is extremely important that this part of the United Nations effort should not suddenly be allowed to lapse for financial reasons. If it proved necessary suddenly to pull out these essential experts and close down the programme of training in various fields, the Government and people of the Congo would suffer a severe setback, and much of the effort of the United Nations in the past three years would have gone to waste.

I therefore hope that Governments will continue to support the civilian operations in the Congo by contibutions to the Congo Fund, until such time as it can become a normal technical assistance program under the usual auspices.

As in many countries, the future in the Congo is unpredictable and many difficulties and problems certainly lie ahead. I believe that the United Nations operation in that country, allowing for all its shortcomings and despite the violent criticism which has been levelled against it at various times and from various quarters, has provided a bridge from the desperate situation which existed in July 1960 to a solid basis from which the Government and peoples of the Congo can now progress towards a prosperous and peaceful future. If this belief is justified, it will mean, quite apart from the benefits that accrue to the Congo, that a great and novel experiment in international co-operation has proved its worth in a very difficult situation. For that success, great credit is due to all concerned, and in particular to the Governments which have so generously provided assistance in many forms. Much is still required, but it is perhaps a measure of what has been achieved that we are now able to envisage a great reduction in the scope and cost of this operation.

VI

Owing to the loyal co-operation of the Governments of the Republic of Indonesia and of the Kingdom of the Netherlands, the United Nations operation in West New Guinea (West Irian) did not encounter any major difficulties and was successfully concluded on 1 May 1963 with the transfer of the administration of the territory from the United Nations Temporary Executive Authority

(UNTEA) to the Republic of Indonesia. The United Nations military observer team, the small international staff under the United Nations Administrator and the security force were guided solely by the provisions of the Agreement of 15 August 1962, which the General Assembly took note of in its resolution 1752 (XVII). After the cease-fire arrangements had been successfully implemented, the main responsibility of the international administration, from October 1962 on was to ensure that there was no disruption in the public services and economic life on account of the departure of the Netherlands administration, and also to prepare the population for the important political changes which were taking place. Whatever may have been usefully accomplished during this brief period of seven months, the United Nations Temporary Executive Authority owes its success to the unfailing assistance from the Government parties to the Agreement (which also shared the expenses of the operation), the devotion of all those from many different nationalities who served with UNTEA, and the calm and friendly attitude of the population. On 13 March 1963, I was in a position to announce the decision of the Republic of Indonesia and the Kingdom of the Netherlands to resume normal relations and to exchange diplomatic representatives. This was a happy outcome of the solution of the question of West New Guinea (West Irian). The United Nations stands ready to assist the Government of Indonesia in the implementation of the remaining part of the Agreement relating to the act of free choice by the inhabitants of the territory and to help the same Government in the economic development of West Irian through a voluntary fund open to contributions from Member States of the United Nations and the specialized agencies.

## VII

In the course of 1962, I received communications from Thailand and Cambodia concerning certain difficulties which had arisen between them. At the same time the two Governments expressed a desire to find a solution to their dispute through one of the procedures enumerated in Article 33 of the Charter concerning peaceful settlement of disputes by negotiation, and they requested me to appoint a personal representative for this purpose. On 19 October 1962, I informed the members of the Security Council of my affirmative response to the above request, and my appointment of a personal representative.

According to the terms of reference, my personal representative is at the disposal of the parties to assist in solving all problems that have arisen or may arise between them, and the Governments of Cambodia and Thailand have both agreed to share equally all the costs involved. The two Governments also requested me, at the end of 1962, to extend the term of my personal representative for a period of one year, beginning 1 January 1963.

From 26 October 1962, my personal representative has remained in the area in continuous contact with the Governments and high officials of both countries. A number of investigations have been made at the requests of one or the other party, and certain suggestions advanced for their consideration on appropriate steps that could lead to improved relations between them. As long as the two Governments consider that my personal representative can help them in dealing with a delicate and often tense situation, I am willing to continue to provide such services, whose value and efficiency will depend very much on the goodwill of the two Governments and their sincere desire to normalize their relations.

The United Nations Yemen Observation Mission was established, after the Security Council had adopted its resolution of 11 June 1963, to facilitate the implementation of the disengagement agreement by the parties concerned in Yemen. The operation is agreed upon and financed by the parties themselves, and its success will depend upon the good faith of the two parties in carrying out the agreement.

In the conditions prevailing in Yemen, the implementation of the disengagement agreement is not an easy matter for either side, and it is as yet too early to make a judgement on the effectiveness of the Mission in assisting in bringing about the actual disengagement. It is to be hoped, however, that the efforts of this Mission in very difficult conditions, combined with the efforts of the parties themselves, will bring about the disengagement and the restoration of peace in Yemen, which is the desire of all concerned.

It will be clear from the preceding sections on the Congo, West Irian and Yemen that many Member States have made available to the United Nations military personnel for various very constructive tasks of peace-keeping. I have accordingly designated as my military adviser a senior military officer who was formerly the military adviser for the Congo operation. He and the small but expert military staff working under him in my office have played a truly valuable role in the support and functioning of the operations I have just mentioned.

VIII

One of the major developments of recent years has been the attainment of independence by a large number of countries and peoples formerly under colonial rule, whose right to freedom and equality is written into the Charter. Without intending to minimize the efforts of the peoples themselves in securing their freedom and of the contribution of the respective administering Powers, it may be said that the Organization, through its various organs, has made an important contribution towards this welcome development. The significance of this historic and dynamic process to the international community and to the future course of world events can be gauged from the transformation of the United Nations itself, as a result of the increase in its membership from the original 51 to the present 111 Members. The widening of the membership has also brought the Organization nearer to its goal of universality.

In this connexion, it is relevant to recall the year 1960 when, at its fifteenth session, the General Assembly admitted 17 newly independent countries—16 of them from Africa—to membership in the United Nations, bringing the then total membership to 100. By that time there was overwhelming recognition of the need for bringing about, by peaceful means and in an orderly manner, the inevitable transformation of the remaining colonial areas from dependence to independence as speedily as possible. This, coupled with the belief of the Member States that the emancipation of all dependent peoples would remove one of the major obstacles to the maintenance of peace, led to the adoption by the General Assembly on 14 December 1960, by resolution 1514 (XV), of the Declaration on the granting of independence to colonial countries and peoples.

The importance of this question to the Organization is evident from the amount of attention devoted to it by the General Assembly. The progress of implementation of the Declaration was extensively discussed in general terms, and also in relation to individual territories, by the General

Assembly at its sixteenth and seventeenth sessions as well as by the Special Committee which the General Assembly established for that purpose. It is a matter for satisfaction that progress towards independence is being made in a number of the territories which the Special Committee has examined this year; and mention may be made in this connexion of Kenya, Northern Rhodesia, Nyasaland and Zanzibar.

With regard to Portuguese Territories and South West Africa, the Member States responsible for their administration have refused to co-operate with the United Nations or to implement its resolutions. In the case of Southern Rhodesia, the United Kingdom has continued to maintain its constitutional position concerning that territory, but has co-operated with the Special Committee in its study of this question and has discussed the matter with a Sub-Committee of the Special Committee in London.

The question of the territories under Portuguese administration has lately been the subject of discussion in the Security Council on the initiative of the African Member States. In its resolution of 31 July 1963, the Security Council has requested me to ensure the implementation of the provisions of that resolution, to furnish such assistance as I may deem necessary and to report to the Security Council by 31 October 1963. The resolutions of the General Assembly on South West Africa [1805 (XVII)] and Southern Rhodesia [1760 (VII)], had already entrusted to me certain functions in relation to these territories.

IX

The situation in the Republic of South Africa continued to be a source of increasing concern during the period under review. The question of the racial policies of the

Government of the Republic of South Africa has been before the United Nations, in one form or another, ever since 1946. Successive resolutions of the General Assembly and the Security Council, expressing their serious concern at the racial policies of the South African Government, which not only are not in conformity with its obligations and responsibilities under the Charter, but are also a source of international friction, have been ignored by the Government of the Republic of South Africa. The Security Council has again been seized of this matter recently, and the participation in the meetings of the Council of several Foreign Ministers of independent African States reflects the urgency and seriousness of the problem. I sincerely hope that, in response to the repeated recommendations and decisions of the United Nations organs, the Government of the Republic of South Africa will abandon its policies of *apartheid,* and also implement measures aimed at bringing about racial harmony based on equal rights and fundamental freedoms for all the people of South Africa.

X

In the course of the year under review, the financial situation of the Organization has remained serious, owing to the continued failure of a number of Member States to pay their assessed contributions to the costs of the United Nations Emergency Force and the United Nations Operation in the Congo. Thus, at 30 June 1963, arrears for UNEF totalled $27.3 million and for ONUC, $72 million; at the same date the United Nations was operating under a deficit of some $114 million.

The drain on available resources was increased by the

fact that for the period 1 July 1962 to 30 June 1963 the General Assembly authorized expenditures for UNEF and ONUC up to a certain maximum, without appropriating the amount involved. The proceeds of the bond issue during this period compensated in some measure but fell considerably short of covering total expenses during the 12 months involved, as well as the accumulated arrears in contributions dating back to 1957 in the case of UNEF and to 1960 in the case of ONUC.

In a report to the General Assembly at its special session in May-June 1963, at which it considered the financial position of the Organization, it was indicated that, if all existing factors continued to operate, the deficit might reach a total of $140 million at 31 December 1963, and that cash resources would have been reduced to a dangerously low level.

Certain actions taken by the General Assembly at its special session may be expected to alleviate the situation to some extent. Thus, for the period 1 July 1962 to 31 December 1963, an amount of $9.5 million was appropriated for UNEF and $33 million for ONUC, to be financed by a combination of assessed and voluntary contributions. By a resolution on arrears in assessed contributions for these two operations the door was opened to more flexible arrangements, within the letter and spirit of the Charter, for bringing payments up to date, including the possibility of payment by installment. The authorized period during which United Nations bonds might be sold was extended from 31 December 1962 to 31 December 1963. Moreover, as plans for the systematic reduction and eventual termination of the military component of ONUC proceed, the main financial burden giving rise to present difficulties will gradually be lifted.

These are bald figures which have to be faced; and while

it is to be hoped that the prospects for improvement referred to above will yield some favourable results, the fact remains that the Organization is likely, for some time to come, to operate under a serious financial deficit and a cash position causing constant concern.

I trust that Member States will not fail to bear in mind the vital nature of this problem, which if allowed to persist without adequate and timely measures for its solution, must inevitably impair the effectiveness of the Organization and jeopardize its very existence. To the same end, the further endeavours to evolve a satisfactory method of financing future peace-keeping operations involving heavy expenditure deserve the attention and support of all concerned.

## XI

Towards the end of May 1963 a historic meeting took place in Addis Ababa—the meeting of the heads of 32 independent African States. It was a matter of deep regret to me that, although I had been invited to be present at this meeting by the Head of State of the host Government, it was not possible for me, for personal reasons, to attend the conference. Besides adopting a number of important resolutions on various questions of general interest, as well as problems of special interest to Africa, the Conference also approved a Charter and decided to establish an "Organization of African Unity." I was deeply impressed by the statesmanship shown by the African leaders at this conference and the reasonable and moderate tone of the resolutions which they approved. In regard to the Organization of African Unity, it is of course well-known that regional organizations are not precluded under the Charter of the United Nations, provided that "their activities are consistent with the purposes and principles of the United Nations." The Charter of the Organization of African Unity specifically states that one of its purposes shall be "to promote international co-operation, having due regard to the Charter of the United Nations and the Universal Declaration of Human Rights." I was also impressed by the recognititon by the leaders of the independent African States of the basic fact of their interdependence not only amongst themselves but as members of the international community.

I said in the introduction to the annual report a year ago that the Organization was facing a so-called "crisis of confidence," which was due to the emergence of so many independent States of Asia and Africa and the consequent change in the original balance of forces within the United Nations. Today, a year later, I feel I can say, without being charged with undue optimism, that this "crisis" has largely disappeared. I see on the other hand increasing recognition of the usefulness of the United Nations not only among statesmen, but also among ordinary citizens. I believe that today there is a better awareness of the United Nations, both on the part of those who support it, and of those who criticize it—mainly because of an inadequate understanding of the limitations under which we work; and oftentimes the United Nations is taken to task merely because it mirrors the complex problems and the shortcomings of the world. However, the public pronouncements of leaders in every walk of life and the statements made recently by both spiritual and temporal heads show that much hope is placed in the United Nations as an instrument for the promotion of better understanding and an enduring peace.

One element in the strength of the United Nations is

the progress towards universality that the Organization has made so steadily during recent years. I believe that this progress should be maintained and encouraged, and should not be reversed, even when situations arise involving deep emotions and strong convictions. I also believe that there should be room in the United Nations for Member Governments with widely differing political, economic and social systems. It is only by providing and maintaining a common meeting-ground for all peace-loving States which accept, and are willing and able to carry out, the Charter obligations, that the Organization can fulfil one of the basic purposes of the Charter: "to be a centre for harmonizing the actions of nations."

Recent developments which have already been reviewed at some length in this introduction support an encouraging view of the future. These developments have been taken in certain quarters, perhaps with somewhat more optimism than is justified, as ushering in a new era. The General Assembly has already recommended several measures, which could now be followed up as a result of the improved political climate following the signature of the partial test ban treaty; and I referred to most of them in a statement I made on that occasion. There are no doubt other steps which have not, so far, been discussed by the General Assembly, which could also usefully be taken. In this regard, the next 12 months may prove to be an interesting and perhaps even a fruitful period.

There is much discussion nowadays on ways and means to improve the peace-keeping capacity of the United Nations and its effectiveness as a dynamic instrument for safeguarding international peace and security. I welcome such discussion because it reflects an appreciation of what the Organization has already been able to achieve, sometimes under great handicaps. It is, no doubt, true that very often the problems that are left at the door of the United Nations are the difficult ones. This is as it should be; and in view of this circumstance, the United Nations cannot be expected to find without exception a satisfactory solution to every problem. At the same time, looking ahead, it is reasonable to assume that, as the Organization succeeds in solving one difficult problem after another, and resolving differences between Member Governments, it is gaining in strength and effectiveness almost imperceptibly. It is my earnest hope that this process will provide us with an ever-widening field of useful service in the cause of peace.

# 10

# In the Cause of Peace Around the World

TO THE PEOPLE OF THE U.S.S.R.*

Today I am concluding my five-day visit to the Soviet Union, and my heart is filled with thankfulness for the people and the government of this great country under Chairman Khrushchev for having made this visit possible.

I am no stranger to this country, since I had visited it in 1955, though in a different capacity. In Moscow, in Yalta and in Kiev I saw very striking changes. Innumerable new buildings have arisen in seven years; streets are cleaner and the people look happier. There was even a festive air in some of the places I visited. As usual, warmth and friendliness were in evidence all around.

The leaders of the Soviet Union with whom I had the opportunity to exchange views on some of the major problems facing the world today, impress me with their desire for peace and their keenness to do away with the vestiges of the last war. But fear and suspicion which for so long have characterized international relations are still in evidence here as in the West.

* Broadcast by Radio Moscow, August 30, 1962.

Let me be candid. When the Soviet foreign policy did concern itself with what was happening in the rest of the world—for instance in the Congo—it did so out of fear and suspicion: fear of losing potential friends and suspicion of what it regarded as "imperialist."

And I beg to be excused for saying that the Russian people do not fully understand the true character of the Congo problem. This lack of understanding is probably due to the absence of presentation of the other side of the coin, and I am sure that if only they have the means of knowing all the facets of the problem they will certainly revise their opinion of the nature of the United Nations' involvement in the Congo and decide to shoulder their share of the heavy responsibilities now being undertaken by the world organization in seeking a peaceful solution of the Congo problem.

I am saying all this with a heavy heart, because diplomacy demands honeyed words. I am not a believer in honeyed words, since they will not help the great and courageous people of the Soviet Union to arrive at a balanced appraisal of the situation.

I am particularly grateful to the President of the Presidium of the Supreme Soviet of the USSR, Mr. Leonid Ilyich Brezhnev, for having graciously granted me an audience; to Chairman Khrushchev, who received me as a member of his family and who gave me an illuminating exposition of the Soviet approach to major problems; to Mr. Kosygin, First Deputy Premier; to Mr. Gromyko, Foreign Minister, and to other Soviet leaders for the opportunity provided to me for a most friendly and useful exchange of views.

I shall certainly cherish the happiest memories of my present visit to this great country for years to come, and I very sincerely wish the people of the Soviet Union peace and prosperity, and friendship with all peoples which they desire.

I also want to take this opportunity of offering my grateful thanks to the people and Government of the Ukrainian SSR for the very warm hospitality accorded to me during my brief stay in Kiev.

## ADDRESS AT THE UNIVERSITY OF SAO PAULO, BRAZIL*

I consider it a privilege to have been asked to give an address at this University and I am fully aware that the halls of this School of Law, the oldest institution of higher learning in Brazil, carry the traditions and the memories not only of many of this country's most distinguished lawyers and masters of jurisprudence but also of so many of its statesmen and humanists. I also realize that by being asked to give this address to the University of Sao Paulo I am in a way addressing myself not only to every University in this country but also in every country of Latin America. For between Brazil and the other nineteen sister republics there has long existed a comradeship of ideals and a sharing of human values that is in the best tradition of international cooperation.

In the last two days I have been in Rio de Janeiro and in Brasilia. It is not much for a country as vast and as varied as yours where even in the age of jet, weeks and months rather than days are needed to visit all of its distinctive regions and cities. Yet these two cities have given me a deep insight into one aspect of the Brazilian character—its preoccupation with aesthetic values. The graceful and enveloping beauty of Rio, the young impetuous handsomeness of Brasilia have also their functional and practical side; for they show us that man need not live in cities

* Delivered August 8, 1962.

weighed down by the ugliness which many think is inseparable from urban concentrations.

Now I come to Sao Paulo, which, I am told, epitomizes
another facet of Brazil's personality—the urge toward
orderly progress, the determination to bring the country
abreast with the second half of the Twentieth Century. I
know that in the thousands of factories of this metropolis
are to be found the most modern examples of today's technology and that Sao Paulo is not only the fastest growing
city in the world today, but also the heart of one of the
world's greatest concentrations of industrial power.

And yet I have been asked to speak at the University of
this city. It shows that in the urge for industrialization you
have not forgotten those enduring cultural values without
which no nation can aspire to make a valid contribution
for the progress of mankind.

I am aware that here in the University's Law School
have been laid long ago the juridical foundations for
Brazil's outstanding contributions to international harmony. I may mention, for instance, the juridical concept
of arbitration with which you solved your frontier disputes
with neighboring countries and which continues to be one
of the central doctrines of Brazil's foreign policy.

I know, of course, that not all of Brazil's realities of
today are to be found in the striking beauty of Rio de
Janeiro, the daring architecture of Brasilia or the rugged
power of Sao Paulo. I know that there are areas of backwardness, indeed of destitution, and that much of your
national and governmental effort today turns toward the
solving of basic economic and social problems in such areas
as the northeast. I know that you are faced not only there,
but sometimes in the very backyard of your most modern
and handsome cities, with poverty, disease and illiteracy—
all problems with which we are vitally concerned in the

United Nations. Indeed, it could, perhaps, be said that in Brazil is to be found a synthesis of the whole range of problems of development with which the United Nations and its family of specialized agencies are concerned. Therefore, this nation and this city are a proper setting for my discussing with you the United Nations Development Decade.

The rapid evolution of dependent areas toward independence, particularly in the last two decades, has added a sense of urgency to the task of bridging the gap between the fulfillment of political freedom and the attainment of higher standards of living. Much in the same way as the countries of the American continent gallantly fought for their independence at the end of the eighteenth and the beginning of the nineteenth centuries, we have witnessed in recent years the emergence of Asian and African countries from colonial rule.

While the underlying force in both cases, the aspiration of the people to freedom and liberty, was the same, the time and the circumstances were different. In the latter case, it is not possible to overlook the role played in our times by the international community as represented by the United Nations, and the support which emerging nations have found in the world organization for their legitimate political and economic aspirations.

In 1945, when the United Nations was founded, it had 51 members; by 1955 the membership had increased to 76, and by 1961 to 104. By the end of this year some six more countries may join. This is a remarkable increase which is nothing more than a reflection of the changes which have occurred in the world.

While everyone has rejoiced at seeing the newly independent countries take their rightful place among the sovereign nations of the world and participate as equals in their deliberations, some quarters have expressed misgivings at the emergence in the United Nations of an unexpected majority of nations often too new, too poor, too small or too inadequately prepared to have the required stability, experience and qualified personnel to play the role they are called upon to play in the United Nations under the present Charter provisions.

To look at the historical phenomenon of the sudden emergence of new nations in Asia and Africa through a narrow political perspective, as was done by many when the countries of the American continent gained their independence, can provide only a distorted understanding of what is happening in the world today. It is equally misleading to consider it from the point of view of the impact which the membership of these nations may have in the mechanical functioning of the United Nations organs.

The fundamental and deep causes of the chain of events leading to the emergence to nationhood of areas which were dependent for centuries, remain to be adequately investigated. This will no doubt exercise the minds of historians, political scientists, sociologists, economists and philosophers for some time to come.

But what is more important from the point of view of governments and those involved in shaping the present and planning for the future, is to realize the full extent of the impact which the emergence of the new countries, all of them joining the ranks of developing nations, will have in the world—not in terms of voting in the United Nations, but in terms of the liberation of forces which hitherto had little effect on world affairs. It is going to affect the cultural and philosophical outlook of mankind. It is going to alter considerably the economic picture of the world, in terms of production, trade, economic growth and patterns of development. It will pose—in fact, it is already posing—tremendous challenges while at the same time offering exciting possibilities.

The sudden emergence of a great number of new sovereign entities, conscious of the inequalities of distribution of wealth and power throughout the world, anxious to improve their lot internally, and eager to play an active role internationally, has already made itself felt. It has initiated a period of adjustment, which may involve possibly many difficulties but which may result, in the long run, in a better world equilibrium.

How long, difficult or even violent is the adjustment going to be? The United Nations will have, I believe, something to offer in this connection. Whereas in the past new national entities have had great difficulties in establishing contacts with the rest of the world, in making their voice heard, or in airing their grievances or solving their difficulties, the United Nations and other international organizations now provide unique opportunities for multilateral contacts that may help to guide the newly released energies into peaceful and constructive channels of political development, as well as social and economic improvement and planning.

It is also useful to recall that, at a time when the world is growing accustomed to almost daily feats of new achievements in science, when man's technological capacity to subjugate and transform his natural environment is growing at an ever faster pace, the evidence of two opposing developments stands out as a strange paradox. On the one hand, modern means of transportation and communication and the complex requirements of man's present-day economic organization have created close ties of interdependence among all peoples; on the other hand, the difference between rich and poor nations, between those enjoying the ever-increasing fruits of affluence brought about by technological advances and those whose state of want has become by contrast more acute, tends to widen.

In the light of these divergent movements toward closer international relationships and contrasting standards of well-being, the principles embodied in the United Nations Charter appear particularly relevant to the conditions of our times. For the Charter is not only a first step in the direction of an organized international community, it also represents an explicit commitment on the part of the Organization's members to promote higher standards of living and conditions of economic and social progress. Most significantly, member states have pledged themselves to take joint as well as separate action for the achievement of these purposes. There has thus been, from the outset, a clear understanding that the attempt to establish an international machinery for the solution of political conflicts required parallel efforts to eliminate gross economic inequalities among nations.

Efforts to assist in lifting the living standards of two-thirds of the human race living in poverty and want began, in a limited fashion, almost as soon as the United Nations and its related agencies started to function following World War II. These largely uncoordinated activities gained new momentum in 1949 when the United Nations Expanded Program of Technical Assistance was launched, and nine years later—in 1959—a vital gap was filled by the introduction of the pre-investment development projects of the UN Special Fund.

Much has been accomplished as a result of these programs and—involving far greater sums of money—by programs carried out on a bilateral basis. However, it is abundantly clear that the pace of development falls far short of meeting present needs together with the new hopes of emerging peoples, and their disappointment may well determine the political and social complexion of the future. The present division of the world into rich and poor countries is, in my opinion, much more real and much more serious, and ultimately much more explosive, than the division of the world on ideological grounds.

To meet the challenge, the United Nations, in cooperation with its specialized agencies, has designated the present decade as the United Nations Development Decade, a global effort to mobilize the accumulated experiences and resources of mankind in a sustained attack on the age-old problems of poverty, disease, hunger and illiteracy.

The methods to be employed are not new; they are rather an intensification and redirection of efforts already being made—a coordinated program to which all member governments have wholeheartedly subscribed and for which each individual United Nations agency has pledged its enthusiastic support.

The main economic goal of the Decade is to create conditions in which the national income of the developing countries will be increasing by 5 per cent by 1970, and will continue to expand at this annual rate thereafter. At the present rate of population increase of 2 to 2½ per cent yearly, the attainment of this objective should double personal living standards within 25 to 30 years.

This increase in the national wealth of the poorer countries does not perhaps seem very great in itself. It is, however, twice the present estimated growth rate, and can mean the difference between an economy which is moving forward and one which is standing still or losing ground. It can mean the difference between order and chaos, between hope and despair, for the millions of people whose annual earnings, for the most part, fall short of $100 a year.

But regardless of the scope and quantity of outside assistance, the key to economic and social advancement rests upon the initiative of the people themselves. Each country must determine its own specific objectives, conditions and development potential, embodied preferably in a comprehensive development plan.

Assistance cannot be doled out to a passive recipient. While grants and loans and advisory services may be made available to developing countries, inventiveness and enterprise and the willingness to work hard cannot be borrowed.

This is why the Development Decade is laying so much stress on the mobilization of human resources as a precondition to the achievement of our goals. The unutilized talents of the people constitute the present major waste and the chief future hope of the developing countries. High priority must therefore be given to education and training in the developing countries so as to create not merely new techniques and skills but a receptive state of mind and a capacity among the people concerned to absorb and assimilate new processes.

The UN, in its twofold role of providing both a forum and an operating agency in the economic field, will assume even larger responsibilities than heretofore in helping governments to ensure the soundness of their national development plans—the core of a program on a worldwide scale. There is growing awareness of the need for worldwide action to halt the adverse trend in primary commodity markets. In the field of international trade, Latin America, like Europe, is moving ever closer to the establishment of a free trade area, showing an awareness of the need for bold and imaginative measures to increase the interchange of industrial products and gradually develop a market abroad for Latin American goods. Emphasis on the mobilization of human resources must also include better utilization of the labor force through higher levels of productive employment; improving the quality of the labor force by vocational training and education; and enlisting popular support for the tasks of national development and the participation of broad social groups in them.

A major task of the Development Decade will be to meet the expanding food requirements, estimated at about 4 per cent annually, of an expanding population and, at the same time, to provide for better and more balanced nutrition. FAO is focusing attention on this problem through its "Freedom-from-Hunger" campaign. There is an unmet demand for intensifying the discovery and exploitation of natural resources; manufacturing output in developing countries must increase by no less than 130 per cent if the goal of a rate of growth of 5 per cent a year in aggregate income is to be met.

In Latin America, Asia and Africa, from 19 to 24 million dwellings should be constructed annually during the Decade to eliminate existing housing shortages, to house the increase in population and to meet current obsolescence; and world health authorities have recommended the adoption of ten-year public health programs to raise health standards, educate professionals and strengthen health services.

One of the features of our present-day world is the technological explosion which will ultimately affect us all. Man is conquering space, harnessing the atom, achieving instant intercontinental televised communication and traveling at the speed of sound. An attempt to transfer some of this knowledge and thus accelerate the pace of scientific and technological development in the less-privileged countries will be made next year, with the convening of a UN Conference on the Application of Science and Technology for the Benefit of the Less Developed Areas, of which one of your distinguished compatriots, Professor Carlos Chagas, is the Secretary-General.

The important role of industrialization in creating new employment opportunities and raising the levels of income and standards of consumption in developing countries has received increased recognition. In debates at the United Nations, Brazil has been one of the countries that has constantly and consistently pointed to the need for devoting increased attention to industrialization. Recent actions taken by the General Assembly and the Economic and Social Council have dealt with the need to increase the efforts of the Organization in the field of industrial development by devoting a larger part of the UN's resources toward this purpose. The appointment of a distinguished Latin American as the Commissioner for Industrial Development, and the setting up at the UN of a Center for Industrial Development, are designed to integrate the work carried out by various UN bodies in this field and to strengthen the promotion of industrial development, through a vigorous program of assistance to developing countries.

If it is true that we are in process of going through a great technological revolution, must we not raise our sights, in the area of economic development, to a level commensurate with these scientific advances? For the first time in history, resources are available to match our most imaginative schemes. The truth about the developed economies today is that they can have, in terms of kind and scale of resources, what they *decide* to have. Defense spending may consume $120 billion annually, but at the same time the developed economies have never had higher living standards, and they are confidently improving upon these standards by 2 to 3 per cent annually. And even after all that wealth is poured into armaments, there is still

spare labor, idle capacity, a surplus of food and vast stockpiles of metals.

I cite these figures to emphasize the fact that the degree
of sheer abundance—and not narrow scarcity—is the hall-
mark of the advanced economies of today.

The means are therefore no longer a limiting factor; the
will to use our many and varied instruments of change and
growth is the only limitation. It is well within the power
of modern man to eradicate the vast areas of poverty in a
world of plenty. The investment capital exists, and if applied and applied wisely, it will multiply; scientific advances and new techniques exist waiting only to be redirected to the neglected problems. The natural resources
and human potential are there, waiting only to be discovered and put to work.

The United Nations is playing and will continue to play
a large part in what might be termed the preliminaries to
investment, a phase not yet too expensive in terms of capital. The goal set by the General Assembly for all UN technical assistance activities is $150 million a year, and it is
my hope that this may be increased by at least $25 million
annually so as to reach a figure of $300 million by 1970.

In determining the programs it will assist, the United
Nations has the advantage of pursuing no political, military or commercial interests. Recipient countries are well
aware of this, and know also that any suggestion we may
make on the administration of a given program is made
solely from the standpoint of having the program succeed.
An additional advantage is that both rich and poor nations
are included in United Nations membership, and are generally in agreement that all should work together toward
the common goal of a rapidly expanding world economy.

Let me now turn briefly to your area of the world, to
Latin America.

The countries of Latin America, with a long and well established tradition of international cooperation, have participated in the creation of new forms of international cooperation in more than one way. I wish on this occasion to limit my comments to the efforts carried out jointly by the Latin America nations through their participation in the work of the United Nations Economic Commission for Latin America. The work of CEPAL,* as it is known on this Continent, provides a good illustration of the kind of pioneering activities which led to the formulation of a set of consistent principles and practical means of action for promoting the economic development of the region's countries and the improvement of the standard of living of its people.

I do not want to give the impression here that the task has been accomplished. Far from it; after years of seeding ideas, developing techniques and measuring the tasks to be accomplished both at the national and international level, we are perhaps only at the threshold of a full-scale attack on the problem of development. But I do wish to underscore the important efforts made at the international level and the achievements to which this effort led in the years preceding the current Development Decade.

Working in a region endowed with rich resources but where the accidents of history have retarded economic development, CEPAL has repeatedly underlined Latin America's need to speed up vigorously its internal economic growth process which was fast becoming an urgent social need as a result of the region's high rate of demographic growth. While at the beginning of the century the population of Latin America was about 60 million, it has now reached approximately 200 million people, outnumbering the combined population of Canada and the

* Spanish initials for ECLA.

United States. According to demographic projections it will probably surpass both Africa and the USSR within about fifteen years and Europe towards the end of the present century.

The problems generated by this steep rise in population were further aggravated by a continuous deterioration of the area's terms of trade with the industrial centers of the world. Thus, while the prices of an increasing number of key manufactured goods—such as machines and other equipment—that Latin America must import have risen, both the prices and the demand for some of its main traditional exports have declined in international markets. The resulting losses in export earnings led to a chronic deficiency in the so-called import capacity of the region, a crucial element for economic stability and development. This again accentuated the need to substitute certain types of imports by initiating or expanding domestic production.

It has always been stressed in deliberations of United Nations bodies that there is no one "magic formula" that can quickly, simultaneously and completely solve all the different yet interwoven economic and social problems of developing areas such as Latin America. In particular, it is said that the mere inflow of foreign capital, even if forthcoming to the extent necessary, could not by itself solve some of the very deep-rooted structural deficiencies that will prevail and are hampering and retarding economic progress. But, at the same time, there is a growing awareness that the fundamental economic probelms of the region can find a truly adequate solution, only if all Latin American countries face them together through well conceived, clearly articulated and properly executed economic development policies and programs, which would serve to mobilize their resources and effectively apply their vital forces.

In addition to its efforts to stimulate and assist economic planning, CEPAL, as an instrument of the Latin American Governments within the community of nations, has been the spearhead for regional action in the establishment of new multinational mechanisms to cope with a whole array of development problems—mainly those connected with trade and broader market requirements of modern industry—which escape the possibilities of solution through action by individual countries alone. Some weeks ago the Latin American Economic Development Institute came into being. Last month, after almost a decade of concerted effort on the part of the governments concerned, signature of the Central American Economic Integration Treaty was completed with the formal adherence of Costa Rica. Thus, all the countries of the Central American region will now be working together in attaining fuller utilization of their resources, through a program aimed at achieving a common market within a specified number of years, integrated industrial development in the area and coordination of the agricultural and other basic sectors of their economies.

With the creation of the Latin America Free Trade Association, the first step has been taken toward the possible establishment of a common market within the region. This multilateral trade grouping, to which nine countries have adhered, includes already most of Latin America's territory and population. Such an important step is also a further expression of the new awareness that economic development poses a number of common problems, the solution of which requires a concerted approach.

It is abundantly clear that a process of regional cooperation has been set in motion, the forces of which are just beginning to develop. Their future shape will hopefully open new opportunities for more effective cooperation in

economic and social development. This can be expected
not only from a regional standpoint—which could be as
unsatisfactory for the solution of larger problems projecting beyond the bounds of specific regions, as the national
approach is ineffective for regional problems—but from
the viewpoint of a true and balanced economic system for
the world as a whole.

Within the United Nations every member country can
exert its influence in promoting a more determined and
substantial international attack on the vexing problem of
persisting underdevelopment. Collective thinking directed
to the problems of tomorrow may do a great service to
national governments, which are all too often overwhelmed by the transaction of day-to-day business. The
United Nations, with its regional ramifications, seems to
me well designed to provide centers for reflection where
habits of cooperation and a new international discipline
based on free consent can take shape.

As things stand at the moment, it seems likely that the
great revolution of our time—the transformation of the
poorer two-thirds of the world—may eventually be carried
out largely through the help of United Nations agencies.
Fortunately, for years the United Nations has been prepared to administer aid effectively; the Economic and Social Council and the General Assembly can debate the subject as deliberative bodies, and the execution is in expert
hands working strictly on business lines without any intru-
sion of politics or "strings."

Since the dawn of history, the economic and social conditions of human life have been changing at an ever accelerating pace. The acceleration has now become so rapid
that there is more change within a single lifetime than in a
long span of the past embracing centuries. We are running
a race with time. This race cannot be won by govern-

mental actions alone. It can be won only with the active participation of millions of private individuals who can read the signs of our times. There is a huge task here for education—and education may not be equal to the task unless we are prepared to break with some of the ancient habits and traditions which are out of time with the needs of the second half of the Twentieth Century.

## ADDRESS AT BUCHAREST UNIVERSITY, RUMANIA*

I feel it a great honor to be received in this fashion and since my arrival in this beautiful city of Bucharest, I have been overwhelmed with hospitality and warmth everywhere. I have myself been in the education profession in my country for a number of years and I feel very much at home in the midst of this University's faculty members and students. If I had my choice I would at all times go back to the teaching profession. But as you are aware circumstances have forced me to be where I am. In any case one day, when I have decided that my task for the world organization is completed, I may, perhaps, go back to the teaching profession.

Well, ladies and gentlemen, the world is under the shadow of the hydrogen bomb. Only the United Nations organization, with the co-operation of its Member States, can avert such a catastrophe. It has been my constant endeavour to bring about better understanding among peoples and to generate ideas of peace and international understanding among the member states. One of the primary objectives of the United Nations Charter is to save succeeding generations from the scourge of war. It is the main function of the United Nations to avert war. Although in

* Delivered May 7, 1963.

the performance of its political functions the United Nations machinery is weak and inadequate, it has been able to avert wars and conflagrations in many parts of the world, since its inception in 1945. The results achieved have not been very impressive. However, if it were not for the United Nations, the world would be in a much unhappier position than we are in today.

There are two schools of thought regarding the functions of the United Nations. One maintains that the United Nations should be just a mere forum for discussions and debates. Another maintains that the United Nations must develop into a really effective instrument for international conciliation. The second feels strongly that the United Nations must be a really effective force for peace. Needless to say, I belong to the second school. I feel very strongly that if humanity is to achieve real peace, real economic progress and real freedom from colonialism, the United Nations must play a potent part. But the United Nations will be as strong or as weak as its member states wish it to be. If the member states wish it to be strong, it will be strong. If the member states wish it to be weak, it will remain weak. So, the first important step to reactivate this Organization is for the citizens of all the countries of the world to study its aims and objectives and to try to understand its various activities.

The primary objectives of the United Nations can be classified into three categories. The first category is the preservation of peace. In other words, this can be classified as political activity. The second is the promotion of the economic and social welfare of the peoples of the world. The third category is the elimination of colonialism from the face of the earth.

For the achievement of these three objectives, the founders of the United Nations instituted three Councils.

The first is the Security Council to deal with the political aspects, the second is the Economic and Social Council to deal with the economic and social aspects, the third is the Trusteeship Council formed to facilitate the emergence of Trust Territories into independent States.

The accomplishments of the United Nations in the political field have not been very impressive, it must be admitted. But in the course of the last 17 years the United Nations has been able to avert catastrophes in many parts of the world such as in Kashmir, in the Middle East, in the Congo and in Cuba.

In the economic and social field, however, the United Nations has achieved very substantial accomplishments. In the Tursteeship Council field also the United Nations has acted as a midwife to the birth of several new nations. So, if we are to assess the success of the United Nations, we should examine its accomplishments in all fields. In the whole United Nations family, that is United Nations Headquarters in New York and its sister agencies in Paris, Rome and Geneva, etc., there are about 18,000 men and women working in all these organizations. Out of these 18,000 men and women, only 1,500 are employed in the political activities. Sixteen thousand five hundred men and women are engaged in non-political activities of the world organization. From this it is obvious that the United Nations activities are much more concerned with the non-political activities. But the political activities focus much more attention in the public mind than the non-political, because politics are much more sensational than economic and social developments. I am very glad to hear what the Rector has just said about the desire of the people of Romania to make the whole Balkan area denuclearized. This desire, I believe, is not confined only to Romania. This is the general desire of a large majority of people in the world today. For the past several years we have been hearing many African states expressing their desire to make Africa denuclearized. Just before I left New York, I received a communication from five Latin American countries expressing their desire to make Latin America denuclearized. The denuclearization of several territories in the world today denotes some kind of territorial disarmament, a trend which should be welcomed by all peace-loving people, but for the purpose of practical application we are faced with some difficult problems. Fear and suspicion still dominate international relations. But with our constant endeavors to eliminate fear and suspicion I think we will be able to improve the psychological and political climate.

What should be realized by all of us is that the hydrogen bomb is much more terrible, much more wicked than the evil which it is intended to eliminate. What is necessary in this second half of the twentieth century is better international understanding, the philosophy of live and let live and the philosophy of peaceful co-existence. To give you one parallel from history, let me cite an example from Europe. Some hundreds of years ago there were bitter wars fought between the Christians and the Moslems. These wars were called the Crusades. At that time the Christians considered the Moslems to be heretics and decided to put all Moslems to the sword. In the same manner the Moslems considered the Christians to be heretics and were bent on exterminating all Christians. With this psychological climate, very bloody and terrible wars took place between these two religious adherents. Tens of thousands of people were killed. When tempers calmed down and reason prevailed, it was realized by both sides that both Christians and Moslems could co-exist peacefully. Since then there were no religious wars between the Christians and the Moslems and the followers of these two religions exist in amity and friendship. It can safely be said that in the twentieth century there is religious tolerance.

Unfortunately today there is no political tolerance, but there is an unmistakable trend towards achieving this. It is the path of wisdom to tolerate each other's political convictions and beliefs as we tolerate religious beliefs of each other. Only with this spirit of tolerance and the philosophy of live and let live and the concept of peaceful coexistence will humanity proceed towards the goal of peace.

Personally speaking, I am a firm believer in the concept of thesis, antithesis and synthesis, and I also believe that the world is moving towards a synthesis. For the understanding of this concept, it will be necessary to go into the background of our concepts of education.

In many parts of the world today there is too much stress on the development of the intellect. The objective of education in many parts of the world is to create doctors, scientists and engineers. While this process of intellectual development is going on, I feel that sufficient attention is not paid to the development of the mind and the spirit. Mental and spiritual development is equally important as intellectual development. In my part of the world, there has been a stress on the mental and spiritual development of man at the expense of his intellectual development. Our ancestors did not pay sufficient attention to the intellectual aspect of life. Now in the twentieth century, in several countries there has been a stress on the intellectual development at the expense of the moral and spiritual development. Pure intellectual development unaccompanied by a corresponding moral and spiritual development will lead mankind from one crisis to another. Moral qualities of friendship, humility, the desire to understand the other point of view, are as important as intellectual excellence. I am sure that it should be the aim of all educationalists in the middle of the twentieth century to try to develop in young men and women all three aspects: intellectual, moral and spiritual development. Only then would men and women be fully integrated and the world would be a happier place to live in.

Let me once again thank you for the extraordinary hospitality accorded to me and your manifestations of peace and international understanding.

Let me assure you again that so long as I am performing the functions of the Secretary-General of the United Nations, it shall be my constant endeavour to strengthen international peace and understanding and fulfil the aims and aspirations of the United Nations Charter.

## ADDRESS TO THE HUNGARIAN ACADEMY OF SCIENCE*

The devastation and the suffering of mankind during the Second World War led the Governments of the Allied countries to search for means which would guarantee a lasting peace and security among nations. This was the meaning and the "raison d'étre" of the United Nations and has ever since been its guiding principle. Peace, however, is not merely the absence of armed conflict between nations or between peoples, although this is no doubt its main prerequisite. As the Preamble to the Charter of the United Nations makes abundantly clear, peace is a dynamic and positive objective which has to be achieved by the establishment and effective compliance with fundamental human rights, by the faithful respect for treaties and other international commitments and by the promotion of social progress and better standards of living in larger freedom. In a world where human problems have

* Delivered in Budapest July 2, 1963.

outgrown the national boundaries of even the larger and more richly endowed countries, and where interdependence has become a necessity and not only a convenience, the realization of man's rights, the respect for international law and the promotion of economic and social well-being in freedom, require an attitude of tolerance and understanding both by people in their daily lives and by nations in the conduct of their internal and international relations.

The notion of man as an essentially social being, which can be traced in the ancient philosophies of both East and West and which found such lucid expression in the writings of Aristotle, may in our time, perhaps, have to be redefined. For sociability, in the sense of an inevitable relationship not only between individuals but between societies and nations, is an inescapable fact of our age. No more can the nations of the world remain isolated from one another as it would be absurd to conceive of individuals living without contact with other human beings.

Indeed, such a recognition is found in the words of the Preamble to the Charter, where it is stated that the peoples of the United Nations are determined to "employ international machinery for the promotion of the economic and social advancement of all peoples." National means and national resources, by themselves alone, are not sufficient to achieve the economic and social well-being of mankind and therefore an international machinery is required to stimulate, to channel and to coordinate the efforts and the flow of resources in all directions where human needs so demand.

It is no accident of history nor a fancy of our times that the United Nations and so many other international agencies have come into existence in such a brief span. The pressures brought to bear, amongst other factors, by the fast-growing expansion of the economies in the advanced countries and the acute problems faced by the developing countries in their effort to meet the increasing aspirations of their peoples for economic and social advancement have brought into sharp focus the necessity of expanding international relations and of creating an international machinery suited to dealing with these questions from a much wider point of view.

The proliferation of international bodies and meetings, both inter-governmental and private, should not be a cause for concern as such. Their number is a response to the demands which are already evident. What is a matter for reflection, however, is whether in fact the response provided by the international bodies is adequate and whether their structure, their activities and the support given to them are consonant with present-day requirements.

The subject is one, of course, which lends itself to endless debate and it is not my intention to attempt to give any hard and fast reply. But I am convinced that the growth of international action, both in scope and depth, is an irreversible trend and that the existing machinery will have to be strengthened and improved if it is to meet the challenge of the future. In this there can be no retreat or abdication, for the responsibility for peace and the well-being of man kind is now a collective obligation—perhaps a condition for survival in which each and all of us have a stake.

While the international activities in the political field have been as a rule widely reported, efforts made in the economic, social and cultural spheres have passed comparatively unrecognized. And yet it is as important to ease tensions arising out of poverty, ignorance or disease as it is to solve thorny political problems. For peace is not only a

collective obligation but also an indivisible responsibility—
indivisible in the sense that peace cannot be split into its
political, economic, social or cultural components in the
vain hope of solving one without tackling the others.

The concept of peace as an international and indivisible
responsibility constitutes one of the cornerstones of the
United Nations and its family of agencies. Their respective
activities are framed within the over-all objective which is
common to all: how to save mankind from the scourge of
war.

One avenue of action to which I would like to devote
some thought on this occasion is that of international cultural exchanges. It is an area to which I attach great importance and where all nations should be able to cooperate fruitfully.

The term "culture" is very hard to define, but people
are primarily cultured or uncultured with respect to certain qualities of the heart. Culture connotes some mental
and spiritual excellence, just as health means a certain
physical excellence. Health does not mean one thing for a
Hungarian and another for a Burman. Similarly, culture
should mean one and the same thing for all. The so-called
different cultures mean either the different stages in our
approximation to the ideal of civilization or else the different expressions of cultural forms in different circumstances. But, the ideals which constitute the essential elements of culture are universal.

Hungary is a country with great cultural traditions. Its
history is endowed with innumerable instances of creative
expressions in the fields of literature, music and visual arts.
Many Hungarian thinkers, writers, poets and artists have
been of international fame, and I am very happy to learn
that one of the primary objectives of the Hungarian Government is the revival of traditional art forms in all fields.

Since culture has no national boundaries and since all forms of cultural expressions are antidote to the evil of the human breast, it is highly desirable that the peoples and governments all over the world should pay increasing attention to the need for cultural exchanges.

All of you, I am sure, will remember the historic Asian-African Conference held in Bandung, Indonesia, in April 1955. I had the privilege of participating in its deliberations as a member of my country's delegation. Besides adopting resolutions on Economic Cooperation, Human Rights and Self-Determination, Problems of Dependent Peoples, and World Peace and Cooperation, the Conference adopted a significant resolution on Cultural Cooperation. The Conference was convinced that among the most powerful means of promoting understanding among nations is the development of cultural cooperation, and all participating Governments reiterated their dedication to work for closer cultural cooperation.

The resolution further stated that true to the age-old tradition of tolerance and universality, the Conference believed that Asian and African cultural cooperation should be developed in the larger context of world cooperation. Side by side with the development of Asian-African cultural cooperation, the countries of Asia and Africa also expressed their desire to develop cultural contacts with others, since this would enrich their own culture and would also help in the promotion of world peace and understanding. I have no doubt that the distinguished leaders of thought, leaders of education and leaders of cultural activities who are assembled here today will subscribe to these sentiments.

Cultural exchanges through the means provided by international bodies are a relatively new experience. The Institute for Intellectual Cooperation of the League of

Nations made some interesting contributions in this field, and on a regional basis there are examples as well which have paved the way for programs on a broader international scale. With the rapid development of science and technology and the increase and improvement of mass media of communications and transportation, other more daring and effective methods became imperative. The concept itself of cultural exchange was considerably amplified by recognizing the close relationship between international understanding and the interchange of knowledge, the meeting of persons at all levels and the exchanges of scientific and artistic production.

Bilateral and multilateral programmes of cultural exchange have increased dramatically in the last two or three decades and even at this fast rate of increase, they fall short of meeting the demands of our times.

There is ample room both for increased bilateral and multilateral programmes of cultural exchange. In this gigantic task of effecting a world-wide redistribution of mankind's knowledge and cultural expressions, all genuine efforts—whether governmental, inter-governmental, or private—are welcome and should be encouraged.

When dealing with the subject of cultural cooperation, one cannot fail to mention the Agreement between the Union of Soviet Socialist Republics and the United States of America signed in January 1958, which provides for cooperation in exchanges in the scientific, technical, educational and cultural fields. This Agreement has covered periods of two years each, and has been extended twice, in November 1959 and in March 1962.

While the implementation of the Agreement has run from time to time into certain difficulties, it has provided a most useful contact between the two countries. This is evidenced by the fact that it has been renewed on two occasions.

We see in this Agreement an encouraging indication of the importance which both leading countries of East and West attach to the task of getting to know each other better and thereby being able to assess more accurately each other's intentions and actions. But it may go further in removing barriers of misunderstanding and in easing the tensions between East and West.

Within the United Nations family, UNESCO (the United Nations Educational, Scientific and Cultural Organization) has played a leading role in the area of cultural exchange. Not only has it assisted governments in facilitating contacts and information and offered useful forums for discussion, but it has also pioneered in a vast range of activities. In a broader sense, however, cultural exchange has been also the concern of the United Nations and of all of the specialized agencies.

I am firmly of the belief that culture in general is the patrimony of all mankind, although it may acquire particular expressions deriving from the genius of any given nation. It nourishes itself from the accomplishments of the past, wherever they may have originated, and constitutes a common force which pushes succeeding generations towards further achievements. Culture transcends all boundaries and is truly the symbol and the instrument of international understanding.

This has a particular significance now that the world has been suddenly ushered into the nuclear age. For with it have come untold possibilities and hopes, as well as terrifying dangers. Finding ourselves threatened by the gravest risks, but at the same time on the threshold of exciting developments in the fight against the age-old ills of mankind, we have been put face to face with the sad realization that while scientific and technological advances have made prodigious strides, man's ability to live in harmony with his fellow men has lacked corresponding progress. Is it not the case, then, for science, technology, art and all other manifestations of culture to provide an avenue for bringing peoples closer together and for helping in the solution of national and international problems?

It should not be surprising, therefore, that we in the United Nations should seek to expand the area of cultural and scientific exchange and cooperation as a means of promoting peace and understanding between all nations. May I recall in this connection, the International Conferences on the Peaceful Uses of Atomic Energy held in 1955 and in 1958, the establishment of the International Atomic Energy Agency, the calling of the Conference on New Sources of Energy in 1961 and, very recently, in February of this year, the Conference on the Application of Science and Technology for the Benefit of the Less Developed Areas.

On 19 December 1961, the General Assembly approved a resolution designating the 1960's as the United Nations Development Decade and defined the purpose of the Decade as being "to accelerate progress towards self-sustained growth of the economy of the individual nations and their social advancement so as to attain in each under-developed country a substantial increase in the rate of growth." This accelerated progress, of which the resolution speaks, requires not only intensified national efforts but substantial international assistance. In the "Proposals for Action" which I submitted to the Economic and Social Council in the summer of 1962 as an outline of what the United Nations could do to achieve the objectives of the Development Decade were included within the targets of high priority, the promotion of education and technical training and the adaptation of scientific and technological knowledge to the needs of the developing countries.

The United Nations Conference on the Application of Science and Technology for the Benefit of the Less Developed Areas was planned to be one of the important guide-posts for the Development Decade. Nearly two thousand papers were submitted to its consideration. The Conference brought home the fact that given the will and the means to act, the potential was available to initiate an all out, world-wide attack on poverty, sickness and ignorance.

In addressing a message to the Conference on its opening session, I remarked that the scientists of the world and the leaders of the developing nations together hold one of the keys to a better future and that it was essential that they be enabled to meet, converse and help each other. To this I wish to add now that another key to this better future which we all seek is the recognition of the necessity of breaking through the barriers of mistrust and the willingness to open the door to an era where science and technology can be utilized, not to threaten destruction but to promote the happiness and well-being of mankind.

Many other ways and means are being utilized to further international cooperation through cultural exchanges. The number of opportunities available to students in the form of international fellowships has shown steady increase, both from public and private sources; concurrently, the number of students enrolled in educational institutions outside their home countries has seen gains from year to year. Technical assistance missions, originating from bilateral or multilateral programmes, are an accepted feature of contemporary international life and are also on the increase. Contacts between scientists, artists, teachers and other exponents of cultural activity from different countries are now more frequent and extensive than ever before. International travel shows an upward trend as well. The formidable advances in the transmission of news have made it possible to bring the world to practically every doorstep.

All of these are encouraging signs. But the total facilities combined are still far from meeting existing requirements and their rate of expansion is hardly adequate to cover the increasing demand. There are also barriers still interposed in the way of free cultural exchanges.

The United Nations and its family of agencies cannot relent in its endeavour to promote the conditions which it considers essential to ensure peace, such as exchanges in the whole spectrum of the cultural field. To do otherwise would be to betray its most sacred obligation. But it can succeed only to the extent to which the member states of the Organization provide it with adequate support to meet the objectives of the Charter.

# 11

## Crises, Problems and Agreements

### ON DISARMAMENT*

It is a genuine pleasure for me to be present with you today, if only for a few moments, to bring you my greetings and best wishes for your success. I only wish that it were possible for me to attend more of your meetings but I am sure that you appreciate the reasons which prevent my doing so. I have, of course, been following your work with close attention and with great interest.

I need hardly stress to the members of this Conference the great, even vital, importance to all nations and all people of your labors here, and I am sure you all approach your tasks with a sense of responsibility to the entire international community.

The procedures of this Conference represent a significant improvement over previous disarmament conferences. Thus, the establishment of the Co-Chairmanship is a noteworthy development which provides an effective means for continuing the bilateral negotiations of your Co-

* Statement to the 18-nation Disarmament Conference, Geneva, May 3, 1962.

Chairmen, who can thus provide substantive as well as procedural direction to your work.

Apart from this, the presence of the non-aligned states in your midst is not only a recognition of this wider responsibility, to which I referred earlier; it also enables them to exercise, on a permanent basis, their catalytic and moderating influences in helping to achieve agreement among you. No previous disarmament conference has been so well equipped as regards at least the constitutional side of its work.

It is, of course, a matter of the profoundest regret and concern to everyone that you have not been able, thus far, to reach agreement on a treaty for the effective cessation of nuclear weapons tests, but the world will find some hope in the fact that you are persisting undiscouraged in your efforts to reach such an agreement, and that the joint memorandum of the non-aligned states has been accepted by the nuclear powers as a basis, if not the exclusive one, for continuing your negotiations.

It is a matter of gratification that, in the field of disarmament, there have been submitted for your consideration two documents setting forth comprehensive programs for total world disarmament—the Soviet draft treaty on "General and Complete Disarmament under Strict International Control," and the United States "Outline of Basic Provisions of a Treaty on General and Complete Disarmament in a Peaceful World."

During the seven weeks you have been in session at this initial stage of your work, you have been able to survey a considerable area of the difficult terrain you must traverse. It is understandable that, in the short time available to you for dealing with a subject of such vast scope, it may not have been possible to have made a great deal of headway in achieving agreement on the substance of the problem.

What is important, however, is the evident seriousness, persistence and patience with which you have undertaken your complex task and the cordial atmosphere which has characterized your discussions. It is encouraging to know that the members of this Conference have all stated their intentions to pursue their consideration of the problem with determination and desire to find a solution.

All of you know, I am sure, the great interest which all the members of the United Nations have in your work. It is a matter of satisfaction that your consideration of the interrelated problems of general and complete disarmament and the maintenance of peace recognizes the central and indispensable role of the United Nations.

I am happy to have had this opportunity to offer you my sincere good wishes and earnest hopes for your success.

## ON ECONOMIC, SOCIAL AND HUMAN RIGHTS PROBLEMS*

I welcome the opportunity of making a brief statement by way of introduction to this item—the general review of the development and coordination of the work of the United Nations family—which forms a necessary complement to the one we have just debated. We have been concentrating on the international activites that should be extended and intensified in the United Nations Decade of Development in order to reach the goals set by the General Assembly; it behooves us now to examine what we have to build upon, and such housekeeping matters as the machinery at our disposal, the appropriateness of our procedures, and how our decentralized system of institutions has been organizing itself for its new and greatly enlarged tasks.

I shall first make a few remarks regarding the develop-

* Statement to the Economic and Social Council, Geneva, July 13, 1962.

ment of the activities of the United Nations family. On this subject, I can be very brief indeed, since the executive heads of many of the agencies will be addressing you shortly. Then I shall discuss, with the Development Decade very much in view, some aspects of coordination—in regard to which there are a number of positive results to report; and finally, I shall have something to say about a matter which concerns the United Nations itself, rather than its sister agencies, namely the question of the practices and procedures in regard to programing and budgeting for our economic and social activities. A careful review of this question seems to me to be essential if the United Nations is to be in a position to provide the services its members are asking of it.

The reports before the Council—I refer particularly to those of the specialized agencies, of the Administrative Committee on Coordination, as well as of the ad hoc working party set up to review the rather voluminous documentation under the present item—make it abundantly clear that proposals for action by the United Nations family in the Development Decade have a solid institutional basis. They show that the proposals are not just an enumeration of desirable objectives but things that are feasible in terms of international expertise and machinery. In fact, a remarkable range of international activities, covering almost every field of human endeavor, has been built up over the years in response to the constantly growing demands from governments.

This process, and the development of individual programs, have been reviewed and oriented by the intergovernmental organs of the United Nations and the agencies at every stage. The last such general scrutiny—the so-called "Program Appraisal"—was undertaken by a distinguished committee appointed by the Council whose report appeared in 1960. That report, entitled *Five-Year Perspective, 1960-1964,* has been a principal source of inspiration in the formulation of my own proposals. I should like at this point to underline one of the conclusions it drew, that the nations of the world have at their disposal the basic international machinery for carrying out effectively a far larger and broader program than has hitherto been attempted. That conclusion remains as valid today as when it was written.

I come now to questions of coordination. When I met the heads of all the agencies in the ACC two months ago, I was a newcomer to a vast subject with which many representatives on the Council are thoroughly familiar. It will not surprise you, Mr. President, that I was struck by the complexity of our interagency relationships and the number of matters that require constant attention, if the United Nations family is to work in a unified way. But what struck me still more forcibly was the firm foundation for cooperation and coordination that had been built up, and what I may call the reality of the United Nations family—the sense of devotion clearly felt by all my colleagues to the common goals embodied in the Charter and the agency constitutions. I left the session with the knowledge that, in the course of the past year, progress in coordination and concerted action had been made in a considerable number of fields. It was also clear to me that there was a closer mutual understanding and that there were fewer outstanding problems than when we had begun our discussions.

The progress to which I have referred is reflected in the ACC's report. Moreover, almost every section of that report bears directly on the urgent tasks confronting governments and the United Nations family of organizations, in the Development Decade. My proposals for the Decade underlined the crucial importance of development planning; the ACC has discussed aspects of this question, with reference particularly to the Development Planning Institutes which are to be linked to the regional economic commissions.

I also stressed the importance, among the first steps in the development process in many countries, particularly those with newly won independence, of extending education and training, and building up a sound and efficient public administration; here again, the ACC has provided a framework for a concerted approach by the United Nations organizations. It has also promoted such an approach in other sectors including industry, water resources, urbanization, housing and community facilities, as well as programs benefiting children and young people.

The ACC's report shows finally that, although we may still be quite far from the goal set by the Council, some progress has been made toward better coordination of assistance at the country level through the Resident Representatives, and with the cooperation of the secretariats of the regional economic commissions.

While the ACC provides an indispensable mechanism for dealing with matters of concern to all or several agencies, the direct consultations and cooperation that individual agencies maintain with one another are of no less importance. Indeed, some of the most significant recent developments from the point of view of coordination have been of this kind. Among such developments might be mentioned the establishment of the Joint UN/FAO World Food Program, the joint session of the UN Commission on International Commodity Trade and the FAO Committee on Commodity Problems; numerous arrangements in the field of education—for example, an FAO/ILO/UNESCO agreement on  cooperation in the field of

agricultural education; the growth of closer working relationships between the International Development Association and the United Nations and other agencies. I might
also mention that we are, I believe, on the road to closer
and more fruitful collaboration among the agencies concerned—and particularly the United Nations, the ILO and
the Bank—in the promotion of industrial development.

I need hardly say that problems of coordination arise
within, and not only among, our different international
organizations. We have such problems within the UN organization itself—problems common to all large organizations, but also problems due to the geographical dispersal
of our activities and our intergovernmental organs. I believe the United Nations record would not suffer by comparison with that of most national administrations, but it
is the constant preoccupation of my colleagues and myself
to obviate, if we can, such internal problems of coordination, or to solve them if they arise. A useful contribution
to the same end is being made by the Economic Policy
Board which I have recently reconstituted in connection
particularly with the program for the Development Decade.

With such a short experience of the economic and social
work of the United Nations family, and being well aware
of the findings that have been submitted to you by the ad
hoc committee, I hesitate to formulate at this stage specific
conclusions or recommendations regarding interagency
coordination. Let me just put to you two quite general
observations, one on the negative, the other on the positive
aspect of the matter.

Last year the Secretary-General's introductory statement
noted that the task of coordination among the United Nations family was becoming in certain respects more exact-
ing and difficult because of such factors as the increase in

the scope and complexity of the tasks now being undertaken; the process of decentralization and the expansion of
activities in the regions; and the growth of bodies within
and outside the UN, at Headquarters and at regional
levels, each of which was in one way or another concerned
with a wide range of subjects. An ever-greater effort of
coordination is being made, but the process is becoming
increasingly costly in terms of time and money. One immediate reason for this is the growth in the number and
scope of reports being called for. Even a report that con-
fines itself to enumerating and describing the activities of
the UN family in a particular field is likely to involve a
good deal of interagency consultation and clearance, in
addition to the job of compilation and writing. One that
attempts to go further by defining more closely the concepts and aims of different organizations, or by proposing
new approaches and arrangements, inevitably requires a
long process of interagency discussion and represents a
major undertaking. While a good deal of such work is absolutely necessary, from the Secretariat's as well as the
Council's point of view, I would plead that we should not
be asked to do too much at a time. It would be helpful
indeed if the Council would scrutinize its standing requests for studies and reports relating to coordination, as
well as all new proposals for additional documentation of
this kind, with a view to eliminating whatever is not really
essential. May I also make a plea for greater flexibility in
the fixing of deadlines for the completion of Secretariat
studies and reports, and whenever possible for meetings?
This by itself would enable all organizations to make a
more effective response, with the means at their disposal,
to the requests made of them.

My second—and positive—observation relates to the
potent influence toward unity that can be exercised by the

Development Decade itself. Within each government and in the Economic and Social Council the existing and potential contributions of the United Nations and the various agencies are being looked at and appraised as a whole. This is a dynamic process which should lead to a more fully concerted approach and closer cooperation among our various organizations than has so far been realized. From the point of view of the secretariats, too, inter-agency cooperation and coordination will assuredly be strengthened as we seek to broaden and quicken our understanding of the magnitude of the challenge which confronts us, and to concentrate our energies upon the tasks of highest priority which each of our organizations is best fitted to perform. I believe that we have in the Development Decade all we need in the way of such a unifying conception and a look forward with confidence to ever-closer cooperation within the UN family in the years ahead.

However, the extent and effectiveness of the contribution each organization can make to this common enterprise will naturally be dependent upon the resources at its disposal. Enough has been said earlier this week about the need for a substantial increase in the funds available for technical and pre-investment assistance; what I must emphasize now is the no less pressing need of the United Nations itself to match the expanding workload created by decisions of the Council and the General Assembly by an adequate expansion in the regular budget. Owing principally to the difficult financial position of the Organization, a conscious effort was made during recent years to limit requests for additional credits in the regular budget. As a consequence, the considerable growth of the UN's own programs during this period has not been matched by a comparable strengthening of the means for carrying them out. I refer particularly to the staff establishment, to the provision for consultants, and to credits for travel necessitated by the desired contacts between the regional commissions and Headquarters, and with the specialized agencies. Such limited increases as have been requested under these headings in the UN budget were in the main to strengthen resources in the economic and social area. They were, however, by no means adequate to meet the full impact of the expansion which has taken place in the programs in this field.

One result of this state of affairs has been that the absorptive capacity of the United Nations staff has been strained beyond reasonable limits. In certain units, the workload has more than tripled while their establishment has barely been increased. Such a situation cannot continue without a serious breakdown of the standards of performance. Indeed, it has become a matter of urgency that the situation should be rectified.

Another consequence has been a lack of balance between the various activities, as their growth has been conditioned more by attitudes prevailing in certain specialized organs, and even by the hazards of the language used in reports and resolutions, rather than by any over-all judgment on priorities and the appropriate relationship between various activities. One notable example in this respect —and by no means the only one—is public administration, where the strength of the Secretariat has remained markedly below the needs, as expressed in the demands of the governments.

Furthermore, there has ceased to exist within the Department of Economic and Social Affairs, whether at Headquarters or in the regions, the minimum elbow room which is needed to face situations of crisis and emergency, such as have developed from time to time in recent years, or to take up new projects of great scope such as the Development Decade itself, without having to cancel or postpone other activities of high priority.

To help meet this situation, a policy of "controlled expansion" in the economic and social fields, based on a careful review of needs, priorities and resources, seems to me to be essential. If such a policy were to be adopted and adhered to, it would require a number of steps, some of which I can take under my own responsibility, while others would require action by the General Assembly and the Council.

In the first place, controlled expansion would mean an attempt at establishing certain yearly targets for the total budget in the economic and social field. This would seem to be completely consonant with the spirit of the General Assembly's resolution on the Developement Decade. In determining such targets, which should be flexible while being related to each of the major sectors of activity, the General Assembly would certainly need the guidance of the Council.

Secondly, there should be an acceptance of certain disciplines in the process of decision-making in relation to the program of work. In particular, it would seem important that the priorities and targets established by the Council, together with the Council's views on the incidence and rate of expansion, should be brought to the attention of all the Council's committees and commissions, and constitute the framework for the decisions to be taken by them.

Thirdly, there is need for some improved procedures to ensure that new requests are made with due regard to existing criteria and available resources. Most of the specialized agencies have developed such a mechanism for the simultaneous elaboration of their program of work and determination of annual resources. It is not certain that the United Nations, with its multiple centers of initiative, could adopt the same procedure. I feel, however, that the question of procedures for improving the present situation should be studied as soon as possible, in the first instance by the Economic and Social Council.

These issues are by no means new; they figured quite prominently several years ago in the discussions of the Council and in the reports of the Advisory Committee on Administrative and Budgetary Questions. I have raised them again today because of their critical importance for the development of the economic and social activities of the Organization, and because I feel sure that the Council will wish to consider, in the context of this general review, the instutitional and procedural changes that may be necessary if the United Nations itself is to make the maximum contribution to the Decade of Development.

### TO THE PEOPLE OF FINLAND*

I want to take advantage of this occasion to say how much I have looked forward to the opportunity of visiting Finland and how much I have enjoyed my visit here. Your country is, in many respects, so much like mine. Both countries practise the policy of nonalignment, not only as a matter of self-interest because we have powerful neighbors, but because the policy suits the genius of our people. Incidentally, it has enabled both Finland and Burma to make a significant contribution toward world peace in the United Nations and elsewhere.

The foreign policy of Finland was so well described by your President when he visited the United Nations last October and addressed the General Assembly. He said:

* Delivered at a Banquet in Helsinki, July 18, 1962.

"We in Finland are, to a large extent, a nation of coopera-
tors." He then went on to say: ". . . and we know that true
cooperation is best advanced by strengthening independent individuality. We believe in the possibility of har-
monizaton through conciliation of dissimilar interests for
the benefit of all."

I believe that the reference to harmonization through
conciliation of dissimilar interests is really the key to the
role that the United Nations can and should play. The
Charter states that one of the purposes of the United Nations is "to be a center for harmonizing the actions of nations."

In this country, which produced the great composer
Sibelius, I may perhaps indulge in a musical simile. Surely
we would not need a harmonizing influence if there were
no dissimilar instruments. You may play a quartet without
a conductor, but not a symphony.

I cannot help thinking that in the United Nations we
have all classes of musical instruments. We have the economically advanced countries, whose aid is always sus-
pected to come with strings. We have the great military
powers who represent the brass, and occasionally we have
forceful speakers who beat the big drums. Then we have
the wind instruments which are capable of playing high
and low and also of blowing hot and cold at the same time.
Thus we have an orchestra made up of dissimilar instruments, with the responsibility of harmonization falling on
the United Nations. Surely this is the rightful role of the
United Nations, and surely it is unreasonable and unrealistic to expect the United Nations to be the instrument of
the national policy of any one country, however enlightened that policy may be and however much it may be
conceived in the global interest!

Before closing, I would like to express my sincere thanks

to Finland for the consistent support it has given to the world organization. To quote your President again, he said these simple words, "Finland believes in this organization." That belief has been turned into action by the constructive role that Finland has played in major issues, and by the fact that on so many occasions the United Nations has recognized the complete disinterestedness and objectivity of Finland. In this role, your Ambassador, Mr. Enckell,* has played a great part and I feel that I should take this opportunity to pay public tribute to him.

Finland was one of the earliest to pledge a contribution, along with the other Scandinavian countries, to the United Nations bond issue, and the second United Nations bond was issued to Finland on 8 March, the first day of sale. These acts speak louder than words, and for them, I am truly grateful.

### TO THE PEOPLE OF NORWAY†

I certainly feel it a distinct honor that Norway was one of the first countries which extended to me an invitation, and as you are no doubt aware, I was to make the visit much earlier if not for the session of the General Assembly.

I want to take this opportunity to pay a tribute to the Government and people of Norway for their consistent support of the United Nations ideals. The first distinguished Secretary-General of the United Nations, who is here with us today, came from this country; and at every session of the General Assembly, Norway's contribution to

* Ralph Enckell, Permanent Representative of Finland to the United Nations.

† Delivered at a Dinner in Oslo, July 10, 1962.

the discussion of various problems has been very significant.

To cite a few instances, at the sixteenth session of the General Assembly, the Norwegian delegation was one which took the lead, following my statement on the financial position and prospects of the United Nations, in co-sponsoring a draft resolution which was subsequently approved and which authorized me to issue United Nations bonds up to the amount of $200 million.

Once I had taken steps to implement my mandate, as a result of the resolution adopted by the sixteenth session, the Norwegian Government was the first to purchase UN bonds in the amount of $1,800,000.

The Norwegian delegation was also a co-sponsor in the Fifth Committee of the draft resolution relating to the expenses for the maintenance of the United Nations Emergency Force, whereby the Assembly decided to apportion the amount appropriated among all members in accordance with the regular scale of assessments subject to certain provisions. Norway was also among those proposing the dedication of the United Nations Library as a memorial to the late Dag Hammarskjold.

These are only some of the instances to illustrate Norway's active and positive contribution to the successful operation of United Nations activities.

Your country has also made a great contribution to the economic advancement of less developed countries both through the United Nations agencies and on a bilateral basis. Norway has been one of the strong supporters of the Expanded Program of Technical Assistance and the Special Fund. In the circumstances of the world today, we have to turn again and again to those willing donors who recognize the importance of the United Nations work in the economic and social field. Perhaps we will have many more occasions to turn to Norway for such contributions, and we hope that your generosity toward such worthy causes will never flag.

It seems to me that the most serious source of world tension today is the division of the world into rich nations and poor nations. Since the end of World War II rich nations are getting richer while the poor nations are getting poorer. This ever-widening gulf is ultimately, in my view, more explosive than the division of the world on ideological grounds.

There are millions of people in the world who do not have enough to eat and enough to cover themselves with, and whose children cannot go even to the primary schools. It seems comic to talk to them about the virtues of democratic principles and the dignity of man. How to arrest the widening gulf between the rich and the poor is the problem of this decade and of several more decades to come. If the skills and resources of the advanced countries of the world are to be successfully adapted to the needs and problems and conditions of the developing countries, then it will not only mean the arresting of the widening gulf, but it will also mean the dawn of a new era of peace and amity among peoples.

## ON ALGERIAN INDEPENDENCE*

We are gathered together to raise the flag of the Republic of Algeria among the flags of the member states of the United Nations.

This symbolic act concludes an important chapter of modern history.

* Statement on the occasion of the raising of the Algerian flag at the United Nations, October 9, 1962.

The admission of Algeria to the United Nations is the end of a long and painful drama. It is a drama in which all of us have had a part. As a representative of Burma some years ago, I had the honor of sponsoring one of the resolutions of the General Assembly urging the independence of Algeria. I also had the privilege of serving as Chariman of the Asian-African Standing Committee on Algeria for over four years. The representatives of many countries played a significant part in this development, especially those of Algeria's sister Arab republics of the Maghreb and the Middle East. To be sure, there were differences of view among the members of the United Nations. Today, these differences are reconciled in the fact that henceforth Algeria is free and independent.

This fact was made possible first of all by the people of Algeria themselves. They fought for their independence. They gave their lives to this cause. They have now achieved it.

Algerian independence was also made possible by the courage and patriotic dedication of the leaders of the Algerian people. We are proud today to see among us one of the great leaders of Algeria's national struggle, the head of the Algerian Government, Mr. Ben Bella. We salute him for the courageous and gallant people which he represents and for what he is in himself. But we also salute in him all the heroes of Algerian independence who fought beside him, and especially those who fell in the struggle.

The final achievement of Algerian independence was also made possible by the courage and realism of France. For France, the question of Algerian independence was a profoundly divisive political issue. Today, France is one of the chief sponsors of the admission of Algeria to the United Nations. The Government and the people of France, and the President of the French Republic, General de Gaulle, whose statesmanship, vision and courage contributed so significantly to this happy development, deserve our heartiest congratulations.

Finally, may I say that I am proud that it falls to my lot as Secretary-General of the United Nations to officiate at this flag-raising ceremony. For the United Nations also has an important share in the attainment of Algerian independence, not only because the question of Algeria was one of the important political problems before successive General Assemblies, but also, and perhaps more importantly, because the very existence of the United Nations as an association of free and independent nations, bound together by the purposes and principles of the Charter, creates a framework of international order in which every free and independent nation has its own inalienable place, not as a privilege but as a right. The existence of this framework of international order pledged to secure the freedom and independence of every nation, large and small, exerted, and continues to exert, a profound moral pressure in the direction of widening still further the boundaries of human freedom. The entry of the free and independent Democratic and Popular Republic of Algeria confirms the fact that the United Nations is indeed an effective force in the liberation of all nations from all forms of alien rule. It adds strength to the reality of the United Nations as an organization of the world community, in which every nation can find a tangible expression of its independence and in which every nation can develop friendly relations with all the other nations of the world on a basis of dignity and self-respect.

A new chapter now opens in the history of the United Nations. I have every confidence that it will be a chapter marked by mutual respect and statesmanlike magnanimity among all those who, only a short time ago, were on opposing sides, but who today share as friends the joy of welcoming Algeria as a full and equal member of the United Nations.

## ON THE CUBAN CRISIS*

Today the United Nations faces a moment of grave responsibility. What is at stake is not just the interests of the parties directly involved, nor just the interests of all member states, but the very fate of mankind. If today the United Nations should prove itself ineffective, it may have proved itself so for all time.

In the circumstances, not only as Acting Secretary-General of the United Nations but as a human being, I would be failing in my duty if I did not express my profound hope and conviction that moderation, self-restraint and good sense will prevail over all other considerations. In this situation, where the very existence of mankind is in the balance, I derive some consolation from the fact that there is some common ground in the resolutions introduced in the Council. Irrespective of the fate of those resolutions, that common ground remains. It calls for urgent negotiations between the parties directly involved, though, as I said earlier, the rest of the world is also an interested party. In this context I cannot help expressing the view that some of the measures proposed or taken, which the Council is called upon to approve, are very unusual, and I might say even extraordinary, except in wartime.

At the request of the permanent representatives of a large number of member governments, who have discussed the matter amongst themselves and with me, I have sent,

* Statement before the Security Council, New York, October 24, 1962.

through the permanent representatives of the two Governments, the following identically worded message to the President of the United States of America and the Chairman of the Council of Ministers of the USSR:

I have been asked by the permanent representatives of a large number of member governments of the United Nations to address an urgent appeal to you in the present critical situation. These Representatives feel that in the interest of international peace and security all concerned should refrain from any action which may aggravate the situation and bring with it the risk of war. In their view it is important that time should be given to enable the parties concerned to get together with a view to resolving the present crisis peacefully and normalizing the situation in the Caribbean. This involves on the one hand the voluntary suspension of all arms shipments to Cuba, and also the voluntary suspension of the quarantine measures involving the searching of ships bound for Cuba. I believe that such voluntary suspension for a period of two to three weeks will greatly ease the situation and give time to the parties concerned to meet and discuss with a view to finding a peaceful solution of the problem. In this context I shall gladly make myself available to all parties for whatever services I may be able to perform. I urgently appeal to Your Excellency to give immediate consideration to this message. I have sent an identical message to the President of the United States of America.

I should also like to take this occasion to address an urgent appeal to the President and the Prime Minister of the Revolutionary Government of Cuba. Yesterday Ambassador Garcia-Inchaustegui of Cuba recalled the words of his President, words which were uttered from the rostrum of the General Assembly just over two weeks ago, and I quote:

Were the United States able to give us proof, by word and deed, that it would not carry out aggression against our country, then, we declare solemnly before you here and now, our weapons would be unnecessary and our army redundant.

Here again I feel that on the basis of discussion, some common ground may be found through which a way may be traced out of the present impasse. I believe it would also contribute greatly to the same end if the construction and development of major military facilities and installations in Cuba could be suspended during the period of negotiations.

Mr. President, I now make a most solemn appeal to the parties concerned to enter into negotiations immediately, even this night, if possible, irrespective of any other procedures which may be available or which could be invoked.

I realize that if my appeal is heeded, the first subject to be discussed will be the modalities, and that all parties concerned will have to agree to comply with those responsibilities which fall on them before any agreement as a whole could become effective. I hope, however, that the need for such discussion will not deter the parties concerned from undertaking these discussions. In my view it would be short-sighted for the parties concerned to seek assurances on the end result before the negotiations have even begun.

I have stated in my message to both the President of the United States of America and the Chairman of the Council of Ministers of the USSR that I shall gladly make myself available to all parties for whatever services I may be able to perform. I repeat that pledge now.

During the seventeen years that have passed since the end of World War II, there has never been a more dangerous or closer confrontation of the major powers. At a time when the danger to world peace was less immediate, or so it appears by comparison, my distinguished predecessor said:

The principles of the Charter are, by far, greater than the Organization in which they are embodied, and the aims which they are to safeguard are holier than the policies of any single nation or people. The discretion and impartiality . . . imposed on the Secretary-General by the character of his immediate task may not degenerate into a policy of expediency . . . A Secretary-General cannot serve on any other assumption than that—within the necessary limits of human frailty and honest differences of opinion—all Member Nations honour their pledge to observe all articles of the Charter . . .

It is after considerable deliberation that I have decided to send the two messages to which I have referred earlier, and likewise I have decided to make this brief intervention tonight before the Security Council including the appeal to the President and Prime Minister of Cuba.

I hope that at this moment, not only in the Council Chamber but in the world outside, good sense and understanding will be placed above the anger of the moment or the pride of nations. The path of negotiation and compromise is the only course by which the peace of the world can be secured at this critical moment.

### ON HUMAN RIGHTS DAY 1962*

Today marks the fourteenth anniversary of the proclamation by the United Nations of the Universal Declaration of Human Rights. This great and inspiring instrument was born of an increased sense of responsibility by the international community for the promotion and protection of man's basic rights and freedoms. The world has come to a clear realization of the fact that freedom, justice and world peace can only be assured through the international promotion and protection of these rights and freedoms. This truth was enunciated on the occasion

* Message marking Human Rights Day, December 10, 1962.

of the celebration of the tenth anniversary of the adoption of the Declaration by a great lady whose recent passing we now mourn. I refer to the late Mrs. Franklin D. Roosevelt who served as Chairman of the Commission on Human Rights during its first five years and who was one of the principal architects of the Declaration. She said that:

.... basically we could not have peace, or an atmosphere in which peace could grow, unless we recognized the rights of individual human beings. . . . their importance, their dignity. . . . and agreed that that was the basic thing that had to be accepted throughout the world.

The adoption of the Universal Declaration of Human Rights was the first step in meeting the moral challenge of our time. This was, however, only a beginning; much remains to be done, many problems and difficulties to be faced and overcome. The ultimate goal must be to translate into the realities of everyday life the norms set forth in this Declaration. The achievement of this goal will justify all our effort, all our resourcefulness and all our faith.


### TO CHILDREN AND YOUNG PEOPLE*

It is not often that someone who does my kind of work gets the chance to sit and talk to millions of children in many countries. But that is my good fortune today.

We have come to the end of another year, and I must tell you that it has really been rather a difficult and dangerous one. There is a lot of distrust and bad feeling between some important countries. There are places which have serious troubles, like the Congo in Africa, where the

* Television message for Christmas Day, 1962.

peace and unity of the country is not yet settled. There was serious fighting between China and India; and in October things were so tense over Cuba that many people thought a war would break out. But that war was stopped, by the wisdom and common sense of the leaders concerned. And there was something else around to prevent disaster: the United Nations.

Now, many of you, I am sure, know quite well what the United Nations is: more than one hundred countries meet together and they speak for nearly all the people in the world.

The United Nations has become quite worried at the way the world is divided between the poor countries and the rich ones; between those countries where there is enough to eat, where the children go to school, where there are enough doctors and nurses—and the other countries where these things are missing or insufficient.

The very fact that you have a television set or a radio makes it likely that you are on the fortunate side of this great gap between the haves and the have-nots. Very probably you go to school, you live in a house with running water and electricity—and maybe you don't have too much time to think of the millions of other children without all these very important advantages. The United Nations has been thinking about them for a long time now, and what is more, has been doing quite a lot to help them.

I think you know what the initials UNICEF stand for: United Nations Children's Fund. UNICEF is the only one of the United Nations' services to the world which gives all its time to helping children. For 16 years UNICEF has been working to bring the children of the poorer countries food and medicine, and has been helping train doctors and nurses to care for children. It is now also helping in training teachers for children so that they will grow up to be useful citizens of their country.

Now the United Nations has drawn up a great plan. Most of you will be quite grown up when it is finished. This is a plan to improve life for two-thirds of the people in the world, and it is called the United Nations Development Decade.

Those of us who work in the United Nations, and for it, are doing all we can to make this great plan a reality. If it succeeds, then you have a good chance of living your grown-up lives in a world which is steadier, happier and more peaceful than this one of 1962.

Good luck and happiness to you all.


## TO THE UN STAFF*

I am very happy to be with you on this occasion and to have this opportunity to say a few words to you. I know that it is many years since the Secretariat had occasion to celebrate Staff Day on such a big scale as is planned for this year. I hope that in the years to come Staff Day may be an annual function. I believe that it is a good idea for us to get together like this once a year, and to rededicate ourselves to the high principles of the Charter as well as the great traditions of the Organization.

Today I would like to begin by thanking all my colleagues in the Secretariat for the wonderful support and cooperation they have given me from the time that I took charge as Acting Secretary-General. On that occasion I referred to the many problems facing the Organization and said: "If I am to discharge these responsibilities, surmount

* Address delivered in the General Assembly Hall, New York, on U.N. Staff Day, September 14, 1962.

these difficulties, and resolve these problems, I shall need, in the first instance, the wholehearted support, friendly understanding, and unstinting cooperation of all my colleagues."

I want to take this opportunity to acknowledge publicly my deep debt of gratitude to all my colleagues for the excellent team spirit they have shown. During the ten months that I have been in charge, the work of the Organization has become no easier. The Congo continues to be a drain on our reservoir of experienced men and women. We have undertaken new responsibilities, for example, in West New Guinea. I know that many of my colleagues have had to work long hours and bear heavy burdens, and they have done so cheerfully. For all this I am truly grateful.

Friends, as you are all aware, the United Nations is supposed to be undergoing a "crisis." I have referred at some length to this problem in my Introduction to the Annual Report, which many of you might have had a chance to read. If we are to survive this "crisis" I shall need the continued understanding and esprit de corps of all staff members. We have to show the world that we, coming as we do from different countries with different ideologies and traditions, are united in the service of the United Nations.

Working as we do here, we have a great opportunity to learn that in this complex world of today there is no point in thinking in terms of black and white. It is no longer true to say that there are two sides to every question: there are many sides. We thus have a unique opportunity to cut through cliches and to see how right-minded persons can have widely divergent views on the merits of specific proposals for solving the problems of our complex existence. We have to learn to understand each other and to develop a spirit of "one world." We have to develop such a spirit because, thanks to the technological revolution, especially in the field of transport and communication, we have indeed only "one world" today. I would therefore hope that my colleagues in the Secretariat would look upon their service in the United Nations as an opportunity for not only propagating the spirit of "one world," but for setting an example of "one worldliness" to the rest of the world. In this way the Secretariat can help the Organization to survive the so-called "crisis," and to emerge stronger than before in its ability to serve the cause of peace.

There is, however, one crisis which is real—and that is the financial crisis. I have recently had occasion to meet with the Staff Committee representatives and I have listened to their problems and grievances with sympathy. I wish I could do more to redress those grievances, but there is the problem of matching resources with needs. In view of the present financial situation of the United Nations I feel that in some cases the redress of even the most genuine grievances may have to wait. I would appeal to you to be patient meanwhile.

One other problem which I know has been agitating you all is the question of "geographical distribution." Here again I would like to say this—that I believe that this problem should be solved if the United Nations is to be more effective in the future. At the same time, I would assure you that in doing so I would certainly not allow the legitimate interests of the existing career staff to be adversely affected. We all know that the Secretariat is effective only to the extent that it commands the confidence of all member states. Such confidence requires that no member state should nurse a grievance that it is not adquately represented in the Secretariat for lack of effort on the part of the Secretary-General. However, I do not believe that this problem can be solved overnight, but only over a period of time as vacancies arise and new posts are created. I would also need to have the willing cooperation of the under-represented countries themselves if we are to solve this problem speedily and to our mutual satisfaction.

Before closing I would like to wish all of you the best of everything and hope that the festive program that has been planned for today will be an enjoyable one. I myself look forward very much to participating in these festivities.

### ON APARTHEID IN SOUTH AFRICA*

I welcome you to the first meeting of the Special Committee on the policies of apartheid of the Government of the Republic of South Africa, established by General Assembly resolution 1761 (XVII).

The General Assembly has asked this Committee to keep the racial policies of the Government of South Africa under review when the Assembly is not in session, and to report either to the General Assembly or to the Security Council, or to both, as may be appropriate from time to time.

It may be recalled that the question of racial policies of the Government of South Africa has been before the United Nations, in one form or another, since 1946. The General Assembly has adopted altogether 28 resolutions on the subject. The Security Council also adopted a resolution on 1 April 1960 after the serious incident at Sharpeville.

In these circumstances, the General Assembly and the Security Council expressed their serious concern that the

---

* Statement to the opening meeting of a Special Committee to deal with this problem, April 2, 1963.

racial policies of the South African Government were not only not in conformity with its obligations and responsibilities under the Charter of the United Nations, but that they were also a source of international friction and a danger to the maintenance of international peace and security.

The lack of response on the part of the Government of South Africa to the repeated recommendations and decisions of the United Nations organs has given rise to increasing concern among Member States, a concern which I share.

I wish to add, on this occasion, that the attitudes of the South African Government and its leaders, as disclosed in recent statements concerning the role of the United Nations, is also a matter of serious concern to us.

Finally, I wish to express the hope that your deliberations will be constructive and fruitful. The Secretariat will provide all the assistance it can to facilitate the discharge of your responsibilties.

## ON THE NUCLEAR TEST BAN TREATY*

On this happy occasion, I should like, first of all, to thank the Governments of the Soviet Union, the United States and the United Kingdom for having invited me to be present here at this historic ceremony. I regard this gracious gesture more than anything else as an expression by the three Governments of their deep faith and confidence in the United Nations and all that it stands for.

In the situation that confronts humanity today, with the accelerating arms race and with no significant abatement

*Statement at ceremony of signing of the Nuclear Test Ban Treaty, Moscow, August 5, 1963.

in mutual suspicions and mistrust, any agreement between the major powers is a significant event. What makes this present occasion a truly historic one is the fact that today for the first time we are witnessing an important and, I have no doubt, significant breakthrough in the protracted and often seemingly frustrating negotiations that have been conducted in the field of disarmament over the years.

This agreement has been made possible by the statesmanship and courage displayed by the leaders of the three powers and equally by the untiring and devoted efforts of their able negotiators, to all of whom I extend my sincere and heartfelt felicitations. It is my earnest hope that, in the same spirit of accommodation and understanding that has characterized the recent negotiations, every effort will be made to reach agreement on the discontinuance of all test explosions of nuclear weapons for all time. This is clearly envisaged by the preamble to the present Treaty itself, and is devoutly hoped and prayed for by peoples the world over.

The agreement signed today will not eliminate the risk of war: only general and complete disarmament and the establishment of adequate and effective international machinery for maintaining peace will achieve this. This same thought has no doubt prompted the signatories of the Treaty to proclaim in its preamble that their  principal aim is the speediest possible achievement of an agreement on general and complete disarmament under strict international control in accordance with the objectives of the United Nations. However, as the three-power communiqué so rightly puts it, the present agreement constitutes an important first step toward the reduction of international tension and the strengthening of peace.

Although the test-ban issue has virtually monopolized the agenda of successive sessions of the General Assembly of the United Nations, other equally important measures aimed at the relaxation of tension have been repeatedly brought up for discussion. I should like to refer briefly to some of them, but the order in which I deal with these measures will not, I hope, be construed in any way as an indication of priorities or their relative importance.

Firstly, there is the question of the wider dissemination of nuclear weapons. Repeatedly, the General Assembly has referred to the danger of the proliferation of nuclear weapons and has called upon all Governments to make every effort to achieve a permanent international agreement, subject to inspection and control, on the prevention of the wider dissemination of these weapons of mass destruction. It is significant that while the resolutions of the General Assembly place a special responsibility on the nuclear powers to refrain from relinquishing control of such weapons to others not possessing them, they recognize at the same time that the countries not possessing nuclear weapons have a great interest and an important part to play, which they could do by refraining from manufacturing or otherwise acquiring such weapons and, further, by refusing to receive such weapons in their territories.

The problem of the means of delivering nuclear weapons is an equally important one. There have been proposals for limiting the production of delivery systems and for the destruction of all but an agreed limited number in the early stages of an agreed programme of general disarmament. It is my hope that this important issue will receive further consideration by all the concerned parties with a view to reaching a satisfactory solution.

The problem of surprise attack has also figured in the past in debates at the United Nations. Proposals made during recent weeks could lead to the early renewal of the surprise attack talks which have been adjourned since December 1958.

I would also hope that the proposal, initiated in the fall of 1961, for convening a special conference for signing a convention on the prohibition of the use of nuclear and thermo-nuclear weapons for war purposes, will now receive wider support.

Finally, I should like to mention the problem of denuclearized zones in different geographical areas in the world. Various proposals bearing on this have been made from time to time. Obviously, the initiative must come from the countries in the regions as has been the case in respect of Africa and Latin America. But it is equally clear that the proposals must have the support and the backing of the nuclear powers themselves. I should like to express my earnest hope that such support will be forthcoming.

I have touched upon only some of the more important measures that are directed at further relaxation of existing tensions. I am happy to note that there are indications that the three Governments who participated in the recent talks will continue to negotiate in a determined effort to find further ways and means for the maintenance of international peace and security. I should like to close by wishing them all success in their endeavors.


### THE GUILTY GENERATION*

Let me begin by congratulating the American Association for the United Nations on its fortieth anniversary, going back over the last four decades to the early days of the League of Nations itself. When the United Nations

* Address delivered at a Dinner of the American Association for the United Nations, New York, November 11, 1963.

completed its eighteenth anniversary this year many people remarked that the United Nations had withstood better the trials and tribulations of our times which are infinitely more complex than those which led to the downfall of the League. Some of you may recall that on Friday, 4 October, the Emperor of Ethiopia appeared before the General Assembly at its Eighteenth Session and he said and I quote:

Twenty-seven years ago, as Emperor of Ethiopia, I mounted the rostrum in Geneva, Switzerland, to address to the League of Nations an appeal for relief from the destruction which had been unleashed against my defenceless nation by the Fascist invader. I spoke then both to and for the conscience of the world. My words went unheeded, but history testifies to the accuracy of the warning that I gave in 1936 . . . When I spoke at Geneva in 1936 there was no precedent for a Head of State addressing the League of Nations. I am neither the first nor shall I be the last Head of State to address the United Nations, but only I have addressed both the League and this Organization in this capacity. The problems which confront us today are, equally, unprecedented.

Tonight I would like to go back, not only over the last forty years of history but over the last forty centuries for which fairly reliable historical accounts are available. During all these forty centuries, while man has yearned for peace, his history has, in fact, been marked by conflicts. History is so often a chronicle of "old unhappy far-off things, of battles long ago." The great epics we have in Sanskrit, like the Mahabaratha, or in Greek, like the Iliad, are also chronicles of conflicts. We remember Alexander as Alexander the Great, but not Aristotle. Cyrus and Darius also earned the epithet of greatness, but not Firdausi or Hafiz. We remember Caesar better than Cicero. We remember, too, Genghis Khan and Tamerlane and Charlemagne. The reason is that they were all great warriors and conquerors.

In attempting to explain this phenomenon many psychologists have come to the conclusion that man is by nature a pugnacious animal. Our daily life is marked by struggle and conflict, and this conflict and struggle for existence are a reflection of man's inner conflict. Even the theorists of evolution have shown that the human species is the end product of a ruthless struggle for existence involving the survival of the fittest.

Before men were organized as nations they were organized as tribes and before they were organized as tribes they were organized as villages. Villagers fought against their neighbouring villagers and to this day primitive society is marked by inter-village raids. Gradually, villages with a common origin identified themselves with each other as tribes, and the conflicts became inter-tribal.

Then came the great religious conflicts of the early Christian era and the Middle Ages, the conflict between Jew and Gentile, between the Christians and the Pagans. The latter culminated in the Crusades which dragged over three centuries. Two centuries later, when the Reformation divided Christianity itself, religious conflicts within Christianity reached a new high level of bitterness and inhumanity. We all know that religious conflict and intolerance did not die with the Middle Ages. In our own lifetime we have seen the treatment of the Jews by Hitler and his gang, culminating in the horrors of the concentration camps, and the incredible savagery of Auschwitz and Buchenwald.

There are, of course, several other instances of conflicts arising mainly out of religious zeal in many areas of the world. History records numerous examples of wars waged by religious zealots, whether they be Christians or Jews, Moslems or Hindus, Buddhists or Confucianists.

In Asia, we witnessed in the sixteenth century, and thereafter, the conquest of the greater part of the Indian sub-continent by the Moslems. In due course the Moslem dominion extended over other parts of South and South East Asia—notably the territory now known as Indonesia. Four centuries later, after two hundred years of British rule, we also saw the final sequel to this chapter of history —the partition of the Indian sub-continent.

In their search for the wealth of the Indies the great navigators and seafarers of Europe discovered instead the Americas, both North and South, and the islands of the Caribbean. In the centuries that followed, Spain and Portugal established vast empires in South and Central America and the Caribbean, while the English and the French vied for control over the vast territories and great wealth of North America.

More than one route to the Orient was eventually discovered and in due course the Moslem empires in South and South East Asia gave place to European colonialism. The British, French, Dutch, Portuguese and Spanish all established their territorial claims on the Asian continent, and often fought each other to expand and maintain their empires. The nineteenth century saw the big scramble for Africa where, in addition to the above-mentioned imperial powers, countries like Belgium, which had missed the race in Asia and elsewhere, acquire vast colonies. Since the unification of Germany took place only in the second half of the nineteenth century, that country was rather late in the race; and it was primarily its struggle for "lebensraum" in Europe that led to two world wars which, in the language of the Charter, have "twice in our lifetime brought untold sorrow to mankind."

At the end of the First World War there was a totally new development which has led to a wholly different situation, especially in Europe and more recently in Asia. Towards the end of World War I we saw the great Russian revolution take place. At first, the development of communism was confined more or less to the Soviet Union and some of its immediate neighbours. The end of the Second World War saw the spread of communism to other eastern European countries. The Second World War also left a divided Germany in its wake—a legacy which has proved a continuing source of conflict.

The most important development of communism after the Second World War, however, was the triumph of communism on mainland China. Although China has for long been the most populous country in the world, it had never been able to play a really effective role in world politics because of its own internal divisions and weaknesses. Today the influence of Peking on world affairs is unmistakable and if I may say so, I wonder if it would be wise, or even possible, indefinitely to ignore China, especially when dealing with problems affecting the peace and security of the world.

It will generally be agreed that, in recent years the main source of conflict is ideological. In the economic field it may be described as the conflict between capitalism and communism. It has also been depicted—and here there is room for argument—as the conflict between democracy and totalitarianism. It is this ideological conflict which has been christened the cold war, and which has plagued international relations in the period following the Second World War.

I do not believe that some day the whole world will turn out to be either capitalist or communist. I am not aware of a single compelling factor which would inevitably turn the United States into a communist society nor do I see any prospect of Russia some day turning capitalist. Many perceptive economic analysts have noted that neither capitalism nor communism has remained unadulterated over the years and both systems have shown a capacity for adapting themselves to changed circumstances. Furthermore, there are many countries in the world today, especially developing countries, which have found it necessary to follow a course which represents a compromise between the two systems, which may be called a mixed economy or a socialistic pattern of society. In such cases they have taken over elements from both systems and assimilated them in an effort to retain the value of private initiative without sacrificing social and economic justice.

At the present time, we have also to deal with another source of conflict which is also a direct consequence of World War II. One of the basic aims of the Charter of the United Nations was to promote the development of non-self-governing territories to the status of nationhood. The decade following World War II saw most of the countries of Asia gain their independence from colonial rule, so that today there are only a few vestiges of colonialism still left in Asia. It is only in the last five years that we have seen a most remarkable progress in Africa in the same direction. The conflict in Africa today is mainly centred around those colonial territories where enough progress is not being made towards self-government. How long it will take to complete the process of decolonization in Africa is anybody's guess. I hope that, for the good of the world, the process is not delayed unduly. As I have said on another occasion it is the experience of history that when freedom is delayed too long, extreme forces rise to the surface and dominate the scene, and in the long run pose a threat to the orderly development and peaceful progress of the countries involved.

There is one more source of conflict to which I may refer at this stage. In the nineteenth century millions of human beings whose skin was not white accepted, somewhat philosophically, the "white man's burden." Today there is no such acceptance of this outmoded doctrine. In this country itself we have witnessed during recent years a remarkable assertion of the rights of all citizens, irrespective of their colour, to take part fully in the political life, and to share equally in the economic and social progress, of the country. There are many other countries, no doubt, where there may be a problem of minorities who feel that their legitimate rights are not fully recognized. In all these countries the struggle continues, and I am sure it will continue until the legitimate grievances of the minorities are redressed and they have the assurance of fair treatment. There is, however, only one country which has officially continued to differentiate between man and man on the basis of the colour of his skin and of his racial origin, and this discrimination has been enshrined as a cardinal principle of State policy. The prospect is far from rosy and I cannot regard with equanimity the future in this part of the world.

The post-war world has witnessed yet another revolt— the revolt of the have-nots. Just as black- and brown-skinned humanity accepted over the centuries the "white man's burden" they were also willing to accept poverty as a fact of life. The last fifteen years have been marked by a categorical rejection of this concept. While the ideological conflict has resulted in a division of the world into East and West, the gap between rich and poor countries has led to a kind of North-South division of the world. The rapid growth of population and the lack of economic and technological progress in the developing countries have led to a situation where inevitably the gap between the rich and poor countries has steadily continued to widen. I regard this as a most dangerous situation.

Economic aid alone is no solution to this problem because such aid, although very desirable, is no substitute for fair and stable prices and expanding markets which the developing countries need in order to get themselves over the hump of industrialization. Many economists have pointed out that the financial assistance given in the form of economic aid in the last decade, large as it has been, had hardly made up for the loss sustained by the developing countries on account of falling commodity prices. This explains the increasing interest of the developing countries in the work of the United Nations in the economic field. They look to the world Organization for global plans and a world machinery for expanding world trade and extending the right kind of aid. They also look for assistance to enable them to make up rapidly for the stagnation and shortages that have in many cases marked the long era of colonial rule, and to build bridges over the gulfs inevitably created in the dissolution of colonialism.

If my brief reading of human history as represented in the above analysis is correct, we have in the world of today three or four causes of conflict and tension, which are either legacies of past conflicts, or which closely parallel those that have characterized ancient history and the history of the Middle Ages. First and most dangerous of all, we have the ideological conflict between East and West. Then we have the North-South conflict between the rich and poor, the have and have-not countries. We also have the struggle against colonialism and the struggle for equality, especially for racial equality. Religious conflicts have not entirely disappeared and can still be a source of friction here and there. The most serious of these, as I have stated above, is, of course, the ideological conflict in its various manifestations.

A solution to these problems and these conflicts cannot be expected overnight. It has to be sought with patience and diligence at the conference table and elsewhere, using the force of argument instead of the argument of force. This is the main task of the United Nations which under the Charter is designed "to be a centre for harmonizing the actions of nations in the attainment of . . . common ends."

We may ask at this point what are these common ends. Surely the most important of these common ends is the survival of humanity itself! In an eloquent message on the occasion of United Nations Day 1963 the President of India, who is also renowned as a philosopher, stated:

Humanity is not a mere organization, but a living organism united from within by those spiritual values which are inseparable from man's dignity and freedom. . . . There is one God, hidden in all things, all pervading, the inner soul of all things. We tear asunder this invisible bond and break the body of humanity if we use violence against one another.

Whatever our divisions and differences, we have this common interest in survival; and in the world of the hydrogen bomb there is no alternative to the peaceful solution of our differences. In modern war, there is only one victor, and his name is Death.

Similarly, we have a common stake in human progress and prosperity. I have had occasion to observe elsewhere that the technological progress of man has been so rapid that, properly applied, it can produce enough of the world's goods to go around for all, so that all may live free from want and hunger. The goal of the Charter of the United Nations, "to promote social progress and better standards of life in larger freedom" is within reach of us, provided we have the will to share our abundance. It is no longer necessary to think in terms of narrow national interest, and in fact it is short-sighted to pursue an instinctively insular approach to international economic problems. Prosperity like peace is indivisible, while poverty has to be stamped out like the plague that it is.

In regard to ideological, religious and racial conflicts, the Charter calls on us "to practise tolerance and live together in peace with one another as good neighbors." Almost a month from today we will be celebrating the fifteenth anniversary of the Universal Declaration of Human Rights, which I called the other day the Magna Carta of mankind. In the United Nations we have been trying hard to appeal to the conscience of man to fight racial discrimination and religious intolerance.

Even this very session of the General Assembly has adopted a declaration on the subject of racial discrimination and is engaged in a similar effort on the subject of religious intolerance. If I may say so, too much importance cannot be given to these activities because they go back to a fundamental fact. Intolerance, the inability or unwillingness to see the other man's point of view, and the refusal to live and let live—these are the basic causes of misunderstandings between human beings as much as between nations. As the UNESCO Charter reminds us, it is in the minds of men that the defences of peace have to be constructed, since it is in the minds of men that wars begin.

Forty-five years ago today, the First World War came to an end with the signing of the Armistice. The League of Nations was then established, to ensure that mankind would not suffer the calamity of another blood-bath. The political philosophy of the League as embodied in the Covenant is expressed in the basic idea that "international anarchy" is the root cause of war. The founders of the

League believed that the world needed a system fulfilling the same function for competing and conflicting ambitions beyond national frontiers, as governments provided for similar situations within national frontiers. This involved the establishments of a legal framework to settle disputes between nations, either by a judicial or arbitral process, and the prevention of a resort to violence in breach of the law by the employment of overwhelming collective force. The League system, to be effective, needed the power to compel compliance with the law. Without this power it could not persuade; but given the power the use of force could have become unnecessary and persuasion would have proved practicable. Unfortunately, the League had neither the will nor the means to organize such overwhelming collective force. It was also handicapped by the absence of the United States and developed into essentially a European club, although a few non-European States were also admitted as members. Thus the League failed to prevent the steady erosion of international morality that we saw in the 1930's, and which culminated in the Second World War. The terrible weapons developed during and since that war have given us the conviction that, if we are not able to prevent a third world war, we shall go down in history—if history should survive—as the guilty generation, the generation which did nothing to prevent the annihilation of mankind itself.

I hope I have said enough tonight to make you feel that the enlightened and courageous support of the international idea that you have given for the last forty years has been worth while. Today there is no alternative to international action for the solution of global problems and conflicts, just as there is no alternative to the methods of peaceful persuasion and conciliation. On the other hand, it is demonstrable that all human beings have a common stake in progress and prosperity, as they have in peace and survival. I hope that on this occasion you will rededicate yourselves to the ideal of international cooperation, so that we may truly be able to say to our children and our grandchildren that we in our generation did our best "to save succeeding generations from the scourge of war."

# 12

## In Memoriam

### ON JOHN F. KENNEDY*

Today we are gathered in this Assembly of 111 member governments to pay solemn tribute to the memory of a martyr. I feel bound to participate on this occasion, not only on my own behalf, but also on behalf of the entire Secretariat.

On 20 September 1963 John F. Kennedy, President of the United States of America, addressed the General Assembly of the United Nations. He said, *inter alia*, and I quote:

We meet today in an atmosphere of rising hope, and at a moment of comparative calm. My presence here today is not a sign of crisis but of confidence . . . I have come to salute the United Nations and to show the support of the American people for your daily deliberations.

Exactly nine weeks later, President Kennedy fell a victim to an assassin's bullet and all of us at the United Nations felt that we had lost a friend—not only a friend of the

* Statement to the General Assembly, gathered in Memorial Meeting, November 26, 1963.

Organization, not alone a friend of peace, but a friend of man.

I recall with equal vividness a time, some two years and two months ago, when the United Nations was plunged in gloom because of the sudden death of its Secretary-General. At that time President Kennedy made a special appearance before the General Assembly of the United Nations, and in the course of his address he said, and I quote:

So let us here resolve that Dag Hammarskjold did not live— or die—in vain. Let us call a truce to terror. Let us invoke the blessings of peace. And, as we build an international capacity to keep peace, let us join in dismantling the national capacity to wage war.

Although we all know that "man is born under sentence of death, with but an indefinite reprieve," death is a tragedy whenever it comes. It is human to feel sorrow at the passing away of anyone dear to us, even when death comes as a merciful release from chronic suffering and pain. But when a young and dynamic leader of a great country, with his brilliant promise only half fulfilled, is felled in the prime of life by an utterly incomprehensible and senseless act, the loss is not only a loss to the bereaved family, whose head he was, nor even the country over whose destinies he presided with rare ability and distinction as Head of State. It is a loss suffered by the entire world, by all humanity, for the late President embodied a rare and quite remarkable combination of intellect and courage, of vigour and compassion, of devotion to the arts and sciences—all focussed on serving his basic concern for the well-being of mankind.

It is a strange irony that President Kennedy, like President Lincoln—and I note that some have already begun to speak of Kennedy as a "younger Lincoln"—both being dedicated to the paths of peace and reconciliation—should have come to a violent end at the hands of assassins. I have the feeling that President Kennedy was sincerely seeking to carry forward to fulfilment the monumental task which began in this country a hundred years ago.

Throughout his public career, President Kennedy sought to reduce tension, to uphold the law and to discourage violence whether in word or deed. On a recent occasion he observed, and I quote:

And if we cannot end now our differences, at least we can help make the world safe for diversity. For, in the final analysis, our most basic common link is that we all inhabit this small planet. We all breathe the same air. We all cherish our children's future. And we are all mortal.

President Kennedy was mortal, like the rest of us. Not so his place in history, where he will live as a great leader who sought peace at home and abroad, and gave his life as a true martyr, in the service of his country, and of all mankind.

Let us all, here and now, draw inspiration from his example, and let us resolve that he "did not live—or die—in vain. Let us call a truce to terror. Let us invoke the blessings of peace."